The Mystical Experience in Abraham Abulafia

SUNY Series in Judaica: *Hermeneutics, Mysticism, and Religion*
Michael Fishbane, Robert Goldenberg, and Arthur Green, Editors

The Mystical Experience in Abraham Abulafia

Moshe Idel

Translated from the Hebrew
by Jonathan Chipman

State University of New York Press

The Mogen David logo for the SUNY
Judaica series was used with permission
of the National United Jewish Appeal.

Published by
State University of New York Press, Albany

Printed in the United States of America

For information, address the State University of New York Press,
90 State Street, Suite 700, Albany, NY 12207
Library of Congress Cataloging-in-Publication Data
Idel, Moshe, 1947-
The mystical experience in Abraham Abulafia.
(SUNY series in Judaica)
Bibliography: p. 23
Includes index.
1. Abulafia, Abraham ben Samuel, 1240-ca. 1292
2. Cabala—History. 3. Ecstasy (Judaism) I. Title.
II. Series.
BM526.I34 1987 296.7'1 87-1869
ISBN O-88706-552-X
ISBN O-88706-553-8 (pbk.)

CONTENTS

Foreword

Shlomo Pines

As is understood by the thirteenth century mystic Abraham Abulafia, Kabbalah is not primarily a form of gnosis or theosophy. In effect, his view has nothing in common with the Sephirotic Kabbalah, whose object is the penetration of the structure of Divine being and the processes occurring therein. With the help of his profound erudition, Moshe Idel has devoted patient and exhaustive study to the analysis of the extant material from the voluminous Abulafian corpus. He concludes that the mystical technique, experiences and doctrines of this author are focused upon the human being and his upward progress along the path leading to prophetic-mystical ecstasy.

This description leaves the reader with a clear sense of the disparity among the elements composing the corpus in question. Idel begins by discussing the senses of sight and hearing of the mystic in a state of ecstasy and the techniques enabling him to reach this state. He observes that the processes spoken of here which have parallels in Yoga (i.e., in its breathing exercises) and in Greek hesychasm: namely, the peculiar importance given to the pronunciation of Divine Names. All of these have no bearing upon the theoretical basis of Abulafia's thought, a structure which, at least in terms of its terminology, betrays philosophical influence.

There is no doubt that it was a powerful mystical impulse which led Abulafia as commentator of the *Guide of the Perplexed* to declare in the same work that a certain technique, consisting of the permutation of Hebrew letters composing certain words, is far superior to the cognitive path recommended by the philosophers as a means of apprehending and cleaving to the Active Intellect (i.e., the supreme goal of the Aristotelians). The cognition spoken about by Abulafia is one which is easily obscured by the imagination.

Essentially, both Maimonides and, even more emphatically, Abulafia, understand the imagination as opposed to the intellect. On the other hand, Abulafia's attitude to the imagination, like that of Maimonides, entails a certain unacknowledged ambivalence. It is inconceivable that Abulafia thought, in contradistinction to Maimonides, that the imagination played no role whatsoever in the visual and aural experience of the prophets, an experience which he understood as one of mystical ecstasy. While Maimonides states that all the prophets are philosophers, and Avicenna, in the last work written before his death, articulates his belief that the prophets are mystics, Abulafia inverts Avicenna's statement: all the true mystics are, in his opinion, prophets. From this, the inevitable conclusion is that he himself was a prophet.

Acknowledgments

The present volume is part of a larger project intending to present the major views of the ecstatic Kabbalah, which will include three other studies, to be published by State University of New York Press. The second one will be a collection of essays entitled *Studies in Ecstatic Kabbalah* to be published in 1988. The third volume will be called *Language, Torah and Hermeneutics*, and the final volume, *Abraham Abulafia, a Spiritual Biography.*

Most of the material to be analyzed in these volumes is related to the work done for my Ph.D. thesis and to research performed in the decade following. Thanks are due to many individuals and institutions who generously assisted me: to Professor Shlomo Pines, who was the *Doktorvater*, whose immense erudition and profound wisdom served as a source of inspiration; to my colleagues and friends, Professors Yehudah Liebes, Shalom Rosenberg and Isadore Twersky, and to my wife Shoshanah for her constant and indispensable help.

The late Professors Ephrayim Gottlieb, Gershom Scholem and Hayyim Wirszubski introduced me to the field of Kabbalah and their encouragement and discussions helped me in many ways.

Thanks are due also to Mr. Jonathan Chipman, who has kindly undertaken the difficult task of translating the complex and complicated material included in this volume.

I am grateful to the following institutions: The Institute of Hebrew Microfilms at the National and University Library in Jerusalem whose directors, Professors M. Beit Arieh, I. Ta-Shema and B. Richler, and staff enabled me to peruse its large collection of microfilmed manuscripts; to the National and University Libraries in Jerusalem, to the Wiedener and Andover Libraries in Cambridge, Massachusetts, and to the Library of the Jewish Theological Seminary of America in New York. Thanks are due to all the libraries that permitted me the use of manuscript materials in their possession.

Last but not least, the Memorial Foundation for Jewish Culture in New York generously assisted me during the years of collecting and studying the pertinent material. Research funds from the Institute for Jewish Studies and the Faculty of Humanities at the Hebrew University, Jerusalem, helped me to prepare this work for publication.

Journal Abbreviations

AJSreview	*Association of Jewish Studies review*
HTR	*Harvard Theological Review*
HUCA	*Hebrew Union College Annual*
JJS	*Journal of Jewish Studies*
JQR	*Jewish Quarterly Review*
MGWJ	*Monatschrift für die Geschichte und Wissenschaft des Judentums*
PAAJR	*Proceedings of the American Academy for Jewish Research*
REJ	*Revue des Études Juives*

Introduction

1. The Question of Abulafia's Status

In describing *Ḥayyê ha-ʿOlam ha-Ba*, one of the principal works of R. Abraham Abulafia, the noted mystic R. Hayyim Joseph David Azulai (1724-1807), better known as the *Ḥid"a*), wrote:[1]

> This is a book written by R. Abraham Abulafia, concerning the circle of the seventy-two letter [Divine] Name, which I saw on the manuscript parchment. And know that the *Rashba* [R. Solomon ibn Adret] in his *Responsa*, sec. 548,[2] and Rabbi *Yašar* [R. Joseph Solomon del Medigo of Candia], in *Sefer Maẕref le-Ḥŏḵmah*,[3] expressed contempt toward him as one of the worthless people, or worse. However, I say that in truth I see him as a great rabbi, among the masters of secrets, and his name is great in Israel, and none may alter his words, for he is close to that book mentioned, and his right hand shall save him.

These remarks of the *Ḥid"a* aptly summarize the problem involved in Abulafia's thought and his role in the development of the Kabbalah. To begin with, despite his greatness as a mystic, being "among the masters of secrets," he was fiercely attacked by the major halakhic figure of his generation, R. Solomon ben Abraham ibn Adret, and was placed under the ban. It follows from this that R. Azulai's words, "as one of the worthless people, or worse," were a deliberate understatement, intended to safeguard the honor of both Abulafia and his critics. The fact that *Ḥayyê ha-ʿOlam ha-Ba* remained in manuscript form until the eighteenth century would suggest that the effect of *Răshba's* ban had not worn off even then, or for that matter until our own day. Nevertheless, it seems to me that, between the final years of the thirteenth century, when Abulafia was excommunicated by his opponent in Barcelona, and the seventeenth century, a striking change occurred in the status of the banned Kabbalist. A figure such as R. Azulai (*Ḥid"a*), who was expert in all dimensions of Jewish culture and who at the same time represented post-Sabbatian Kabbalistic thought in the East, did not hesitate to praise the man and to describe his system in glowing terms: "his name is great in Israel, and none may alter his words." Such a drastic change—from excommunication to a position in the foremost ranks of Jewish mystics—is indicative of the unprecedented phenomenon in the development of Jewish mysticism.

The present study describes a central question in the vast *corpus* of R. Abraham Abulafia. The exploration of this question—the nature of the mystical experience and related matters— will clarify the importance of this Kabbalist within the framework of medieval Jewish mysticism, and assist our understanding of the ambivalent attitudes toward Abulafia in different periods. Who was Abraham Abulafia, and what was his uniqueness as a Kabbalist?

2. Abulafia's Life

Unlike many other Kabbalists who preceded him or were his contemporaries, Abulafia provided extensive details regarding his life. These are quite numerous, and have not yet been discussed in a detailed biography of Abulafia; this subject will be discussed elsewhere. In this context I shall present only the basic information concerning Abulafia's life, based exclusively upon the testimony contained in his own writings.[4]

Abraham was born in the Hebrew year 5000 (1240 C.E.) in Saragossa in the province of Aragon to his father, Samuel; the family moved to Tudela, where Abulafia continued to study with his father until the death of the latter, when Abraham was a young man of eighteen years. Two years later, Abulafia left Spain and travelled to the land of Israel in search of the mythical River Sambatyon. However, the battle between the Mamelukes and the Tatars in Ein-Harod brought an abortive end to Abulafia's Palestinian travels in the city of Acre. He returned to Europe via Greece, where he was married, and after a few years he went on to Italy. There, in Capua, he studied philosophy and especially the *Guide of the Perplexed* with R. Hillel of Verona, and after some time returned to Catalonia. In 1270 he had a vision, in which he was commanded to meet with the pope. During that same period, and possibly in the same place, he began to study the Kabbalah, which he had earlier opposed, his studies being concentrated primarily on the commentaries of *Sefer Yezirah*. From Catalonia he travelled to Castile, where he taught the *Guide* to R. Joseph Gikatilla and R. Moses b. Simeon of Burgos, two of the leading Castillian Kabbalists during the 1270's and 1280's. After leaving Castile, he spent the next several years—apparently the entire second half of the 1270's—wandering about, possibly going as far as France.

At the end of the decade, he again taught the *Guide* in the Greek cities of Thebes and Patros, and in 1279 returned to the Italian city of Capua, where he continued to teach the work of Maimonides. Because of his peculiar method of studying the *Guide*, based on combinations of letters and similar linguistic techniques, as well as his messianic statements about his intention to meet with the pope, he was persecuted by his fellow Jews. At the end of the Hebrew year 5040 (i.e., Fall 1280), he attempted to meet with Pope Nicholas III, who rejected these overtures. While the pope was still in his vacation palace in Soriano, near Rome, Abulafia made a daring attempt defying the pope's threats to burn him at the stake, and arrived at the castle. However, soon after his arrival the pope suddenly died, thus saving Abulafia from a certain death.

After a brief period of imprisonment in Rome by the "Little Brothers"—the Minorites—Abulafia left the Apennine Peninsula, arriving in Sicily in the year 1281, where he continued his literary and messianic activities. He succeeded in establishing not only a circle of students and admirers who "moved at his command," but apparently also opponents. His prophetic and messianic pretensions evidently caused the leaders of the island to turn to R. Solomon ben Abraham ibn Adret (ca. 1235-ca. 1310, known as *Rashba*) for instructions on how to deal with this personality; and ibn Adret, who was both an halakhic sage and a Kabbalist, began an all-out war against Abulafia. Even if his letters against the ecstatic Kabbalist did not always find a sympathetic ear among Abulafia's many disciples in Sicily, there is no doubt that Abulafia's status was nevertheless severely damaged, and he was forced to go into exile on the island of Comtino near Sicily, at least for a brief period. The polemic between Abulafia and ibn Adret continued throughout the second half of the 1280s and concluded, insofar as we can tell, with Abulafia's death towards the end of the year 1291. In any event, there is no indication of any activity of Abulafia following that date.

3. Abulafia's Writings

Abulafia was an extremely prolific Kabbalist author, doubtless among the most fertile of the thirteenth century. He left behind him an extensive literary heritage, much of which has survived, although certain important items have been lost.[5] During a relatively short period of time, during the twenty years between 1271 and 1291, Abulafia composed nearly fifty works, long and short, which may be divided into several principle literary types:

Handbooks for Mystical Experience

The most significant and fully developed genre is that of handbooks for the acquisition of prophecy (i.e., ecstasy) and cleaving to God (*devequt*)—i.e., what is in contemporary language called mystical experience. These books detail various techniques, some elements of which will be described below. The most important of these works are *Ḥayyê ha-ʿOlam ha-Ba*, referred to above; *Ôr ha-Seḵel, Imrê Šefer, Ôẕar ʿEden Ganuz*, and *Sefer ha-Ḥešeq*. The former three enjoyed extensive circulation, at least insofar as is indicated by the large number of surviving manuscripts, and there can be no doubt that these enhanced Abulafia's prestige among Kabbalists.

Interpretation of Classical Jewish Texts

Abulafia composed a commentary on the Torah, entitled *Sefer ha-Mafteḥot*, almost all of which is extant. He likewise interpreted *Sefer Yeẕirah* and Maimonides' *Guide* a number of times each, as well as the "prophetic books" which he himself composed.

Prophetic Works

Beginning in 1279, Abulafia composed a series of "prophetic" books, the vast majority of which have been lost. Their nature is, however, apparent from the single work of this genre which has survived, *Sefer ha-Ôt*, as well as from the extant interpretations which the author gives to his other works of this kind. One may assume, on the basis of these two documents, that these books contained Abulafia's mystical and messianic visions, which he enjoyed during a very fruitful spiritual period. Several of the subjects of these visions, such as "the man" and "the circle," will be discussed in detail below.

Occasional Works

There are also occasional works, such as epistles and poems, which constitute only a small part of his corpus; albeit, the epistles' contribution to our understanding of Abulafia's thought and his spiritual development is particularly significant.

All told, some thirty works or fragments of works written by Abulafia have survived, preserved in some one hundred manuscripts. Only a very small proportion of his total *oeuvre* has been printed, and even this small number has had the misfortune to have been printed with many mistakes. It follows from this that in almost every case one needs to refer to the manuscripts—an unusual phenomenon if one is speaking about a key figure for the understanding of Kabbalah as a mystic phenomenon. The refusal of the Kabbalists and printers to publish Abulafia's literary works creates great difficulties in clarifying his system and, as the reader will find below, the bulk of the material considered here comes from manuscripts scattered over different continents, awaiting a wider audience. This is the reason for our constant reliance upon manuscripts.

However, an understanding of Abulafia's mystical path cannot suffice with these written testimonies alone. There is considerable material extant from the period preceding him, such as the writings of the Ashkenazic Hasidim or those of R. Baruch Togarmi, from which Abulafia learned basic fundamental areas of his thought. Until now, the topics in these works relevant to Abulafia's thought have not received detailed treatment, a fact which presents difficulties for the understanding of Abulafian thought. No less important are those works which were influenced by Abulafia's writings, such as the anonymous *Sefer ha-Z̲eruf* and *Ner Elohim;* the works of R. Isaac of Acre, first and foremost the *Ôz̲ar Ḥayyim; Šaʿarê Z̲edeq*, attributed to R. Shem Tov Ibn Gaon; and R. Judah Albotini's *Sullam ha-ʿAliyah.*

Thus, analysis of Abulafia's mysticism demands reference to an entire Kabbalistic school, spreading over many years and requires careful study of the writings of many different Kabbalists. However, the difficulties entailed and the time demanded to master this extensive background are well justified, as only study of this type can enable us to understand the complex development and spread of ecstatic Kabbalah of the Abulafian type through various regions—Italy, Greece, Palestine[6]—and assist us in comprehending properly that most important contemporary mystical phenomenon: Hasidism.[7] The present work will clarify only a few of these questions, and others will be dealt with elsewhere, while such major questions as the contribution of ecstatic Kabbalah to the shaping of Hasidic mysticism will still require extensive clarification.

4. Survey of Research

Scholars had already addressed themselves to Abraham Abulafia's Kabbalah by the middle of the nineteenth century, when Moritz Landauer described the work of this Kabbalist first based upon the manuscripts available in the Munich Library.[8] Unfortunately, Landauer's distinction as the pioneering scholar of Kabbalistic manuscripts did not assist him when he came to describe the spiritual configuration of Abulafia's Kabbalah. Because he was convinced that Abulafia was the author of *Sefer ha-Zohar,* he arrived at a totally misguided picture of his thought, in those few cases where he attempted to do so. In the second half of the nineteenth century, we find general remarks concerning the life and works of Abulafia—but not an analysis of his system—in the major works of Heinrich Graetz,[9] Moritz Steinschneider,[10] and Adolph Jellinek.[11] The latter in particular devoted several studies to Abulafia's thought, some of which he published. His most important contribution was in the separation of *Sefer ha-Zohar* from the sphere of the ecstatic Kabbalah and its attribution to R. Moses de Leon.[12] Research was henceforth free to address itself to the clarification of Abulafia's system on the basis of authentic documents.

At the end of the nineteenth and beginning of the twentieth century, writers in Kabbalah reiterated the theories of their predecessors, including Landauer's erroneous view that Abulafia was the author of *Sefer ha-Zohar.*[13] Significant progress in this respect was not made during that generation until the beginnings of Scholem's research. In a series of studies of ecstatic Kabbalah,[14] as well as an entire chapter devoted to Abulafia in his comprehensive work, *Major Trends in Jewish Mysticism,*[15] Scholem expanded, corrected, and improved upon the bio-bibliographical descriptions of his predecessors. But Scholem's major contribution was in the primary analysis of Abulafia's Kabbalistic thought and the determination of his place as one of the important creators of Kabbalistic literature. However, despite Scholem's major accomplishments in removing scholarly errors and the reconstruction of Abulafia's ecstatic mystical system itself, Abulafia's Kabbalah was not included in a long series of phenomenologically oriented works, many of which were presented at the discussions of scholars of religion at Ascona.[16] Thus, for example, ecstatic Kabbalah is completely absent from Scholem's discussions concerning *devequt,* the significance of the Torah in

Kabbalah, and the problem of mysticism and religious authority. In all of these areas, the ecstatic Kabbalah could have contributed substantially to expanding the understanding of the Kabbalistic phenomenon.

Since Scholem's studies, only a few and to a large extent tangential, other studies have been written concerning Abulafia,[17] nearly all of them inspired by Scholem.[18] The present study represents the first in-depth study of a central subject in ecstatic Kabbalah—that of the religious experience. The material presented here is essentially an expansion and reworking of one section of a more extensive work devoted to Abulafia's thought, presented as a doctoral dissertation at the Hebrew University under the guidance of Professor Shlomo Pines. Since its original presentation in 1976, I have published a number of articles concerning matters which I did not discuss at length in the dissertation, and the data presented in those studies enriched my own perception of Kabbalah in general and of ecstatic Kabbalah in particular. Several chapters from the dissertation have been reworked from a broader perspective, derived from ten years of additional study. The present expansion also includes significant new material, based on the study of hundreds of manuscripts. Some of this material has been identified for the first time as belonging to the school of ecstatic Kabbalah and was previously unknown in the research literature. My method of dealing with Abulafia's thought has been to gather the relevant material from the scores of manuscripts and to present it, with the intention of enabling the reader to have unmediated connection with the texts, but also to interpret them, both by presenting them within a specific context, as well as by deciphering the allusions and sources of the author. The success or failure of this approach may only be judged by the overall picture thereby created, which will hopefully contain fewer internal contradictions and will clarify to the reader matters which are discussed in Abulafia's writings in scattered places and in fragmentary form.

5. Abulafian and Theosophic Kabbalah

I would like to conclude this introduction by describing several characteristics of Abulafian Kabbalah in comparison with that of the theosophical-theurgic school—that is to say, that Kabbalah which concentrated upon discussions concerning the nature of the Sefirot (theosophy) and the theurgical significance of the *mizwot*, i.e., the ability of the Kabbalist to alter the Sefirotic system, which had been hurt by the sin of Adam.[19]

Abulafia describes this system with two basic terms: *prophetic Kabbalah* and *the Kabbalah of Names*. The former term (which I have generally translated as ecstatic Kabbalah in the body of this work) refers to the goal of this mystical path: namely, the attainment of 'prophecy' or 'ecstasy,' i. e., manifestations of revelation and union with the Divine *(devequt)*, designated by the classical term *prophecy (nevu'ah)* in the absence of any other more suitable, comprehensive term. The second term, *the Kabbalah of Names*, refers to the esoteric traditions concerning the nature of the Divine Names and their use in order to attain ecstasy. The two terms are not new in principle and were at most adjusted to the needs of Abulafia's particular system.

This Kabbalah is distinguished from the other Kabbalistic systems of its time both by the essential purpose of ecstatic Kabbalah, as well as by the techniques for its attainment. In the extensive Kabbalistic literature composed during the last third of the thirteenth century in Catalonia and Castile, a central place is given to discussions concerning the nature of the divine system, including both its deepest and most remote level—the *Ên Sof* (the Infinite)—and its revealed aspect—the ten Sefirot. An additional characteristic of this literature is the stress upon the role of the *mizwot*, whose performance in the Kabbalistic manner, with the intention of actualizing the effect of these acts upon the Divine world, is a basic element of Spanish Kabbalah, and specifically of *Sefer ha-Zohar*. This complex doctrine of Divinity, developed above and beyond that which existed in a Kabbalah at the beginning of the thirteenth century, was alien to the spirit of Abulafia, who sees in it a danger of heresy. He accuses certain Kabbalists—apparently referring to Ibn Adret, among others—of being even worse than Christians: while the latter believe in a triune God, the Sefirotic Kabbalists believe in a system of ten distinct divine forces!

Abulafia advocates a theology similar to that of Maimonides in lieu of the Kabbalistic theosophy; he stresses primarily the understanding of God as Intellect/Intelligible/Act of Intellection, a definition allowing, as we shall see below, for the union of the actualized human intellect and the divine Intellect. The position of the *mizwot* is also different in Abulafian Kabbalah from that in classical Spanish Kabbalah.[19] While the Kabbalists of Castile and Catalonia stress the mystical path which travels via the performance of the *mizwot*, Abulafia teaches a completely different way, consisting primarily of the pronunciation of Divine Names and a complex technique involving such components as breathing, singing and movements of the head, which have nothing whatsoever to so with the traditional commandments of Judaism.

Another significant and striking difference between ecstatic Kabbalah and the theosophical-theurgic is manifested in their respective exegetical approaches. While that of Abraham Abulafia is filled with uses of numerology and plays on letters—*gemaṭria, noṭariqon,* and letter-combinations (*ẕerufê otiot*)—as may be seen from his commentaries, the main bulk of Spanish Kabbalistic exegesis is essentially symbolic, and only in passing do they make use of the methods favored by Abulafia. In using these methods, this ecstatic Kabbalist followed in the footsteps of the Ashkenazic Hasidim, as he also did in his mystical techniques based upon letter-combinations and pronunciations.[20]

Another difference between these two branches of Kabbalah is to be found in their relationship towards the community or the public. Abulafia, more than any other Kabbalist who preceded him, stressed the need for isolation in order to achieve prophetic ecstasy. This elevation of the ideal of separation or withdrawal from society in order to attain religious perfection developed simultaneous with the emphasis in theurgic Kabbalah upon the communal religious service within a community of mystics, as expressed in *Sefer ha-Zohar*. This school turned towards the *ḥavurah,* the mystical confraternity, the combined force of whose members is able to repair the Divine world, and through that world the entire cosmos.

Finally, an interesting difference which does not pertain directly to the different Kabbalistic systems, but to the biographies of their leading figures: namely, that the vast majority of the works of the ecstatic Kabbalah were written by itinerant Kabbalists. This was the case with Abulafia; this was also, apparently, the fate of *Šaʿarê Ẕedeq,* by his own testimony, and of R. Isaac of Acre. By contrast, through the 1280's we do not know of any Kabbalists who contributed to the formation of the theosophical-theurgic Kabbalah whose lives were uprooted. At most, one hears of a move from Catalonia to Provence and back again, or visits to the various cities of Castile, but not of migration from one continent to another. Many of the Spanish Kabbalists—such as Nahmanides, ibn Adret, and R. Todros Abulafia —resided permanently in the major cities and constituted the religious establishment. On the other hand, the ecstatic Kabbalists found difficulty in striking roots in any one place, but tended to wander about without being subject to any system of authority for any extended period of time. If we add to this the tension that grew up between Abulafia, the spokesman of the ecstatic Kabbalah, and R. Solomon ibn Adret, who was among the major representatives of the theosophical-theurgic Kabbalah, we may conclude by saying that we have two mystical schools whose ideational and experiential structure differ from one another in the most radical conceivable manner.

Abulafia was considered by the Christian Kabbalist Johannes Reuchlin[21] as a pillar of Christian Kabbalah,[22] as well as one of the two pillars of Jewish Kabbalah. Christian Kabbalah is based to a considerable extent upon the thought of Abulafia, whose writings were translated into Latin and Italian.[23]

Notes to Introduction

1. *Šem ha-Gedolim, Ma'areḵet Sefarim,* VIII, sec. 76.

2. I intend to devote a lengthy discussion elsewhere to the details of the polemic between Abulafia and Ibn Adret, one of the main records of which is found in this responsum of the latter.

3. See Chap. 12, fol. 31b. In practice, *Yašar* of Candia copied the attack of R. Judah Hayyat, found in the introduction to his Commentary to *Maᶜareḵet ha-Elohut* (Mantua, 1558), fol. 3b of the introduction. It is astonishing that a person as expert in Kabbalistic literature as R. Azulai saw fit to mention *Yašar*'s copy of this attack rather than the original, cited here explicitly at the end of Chap. 11.

4. The most important sources for Abulafia's life were published by Jellinek, *Bet ha-Midraš, III, pp. xl–xlii, and Idel, "Abraham Abulafia and the Pope." See also idem.,* "Maimonides and the Kabbalah," on Abulafia as teacher of the *Guide of the Perplexed* (in press).

5. For a full listing of Abulafia's original works—both those that have been preserved and those that were destroyed—and the material ascribed to him or belonging to his circle, see Idel, *Abraham Abulafia,* pp. 3–85.

6. On this subject see Idel, "Ecstatic Kabbalah and the Land of Israel," in *Studies,* essay *VI.*

7. See Idel, "Perceptions of Kabbalah."

8. M. Landauer, *Literaturblatt des Orients,* vol. 6 (1845), pp. 380–383, 417–422, 471–475, 488–492, 507–510, 525–528, 556–558, 570–574, 588–592, 747–750.

9. Heinrich Graetz, *History of the Jews* (Philadelphia, 1956), IV: 4–40; *idem.,* "Abraham Abulafia, der Pseudomessias," *MGWJ* 36 (1887), pp. 557–558.

10. For the places of publication of his edition of *Sefer ha-Ôt* and the epistles, and for *We-zot li-Yihudah and Ševaᶜ* Netivôt ha-Torah, see the list of abbreviations, p. 234.

11. See, for example, *Hebräische Bibliographie* 4 (1861), pp. 71–79, and his numerous footnotes to the descriptions of the manuscripts in the Munich Library.

12. See A. Jellinek, *Moses ben Schem-Tob de Leon und sein Verhältniss zum Sohar* (Leipzig, 1851).

13. See David Neumark, *Geschichte der jüdischen Philosophie des Mittelalters* (Berlin, 1907), 1: 183,225; Shimeon Bernfeld, *Daᶜat Elohim* (Warsaw, 1931), pp.142–146; Azriel Günzig, "Rabbi Abraham Abulafia" (Heb.), *ha-Eškol* 5 (1964), pp. 85–112; S. Karppe, *Études sur les origines et la nature du Zohar* (Paris, 1901), pp. 294–306.

14. See Scholem, *Šaᶜarê Ẓedek*, pp. 127–139; *idem.*, *Kabbalistic Manuscripts*, pp. 225–230; *idem.*, "Chapters from *Sefer Sullam ha-ᶜAliyah* by R. Judah Albotini," (Heb.), *Qiryat Sefer* 22 (1945–46), pp. 334–342.

15. Pp. 119–155. See also his lectures on Abulafia and the texts he published from manuscripts in his *Abraham Abulafia.*

16. One of the reasons for the absence of any reference to Abulafia's writings in these studies is the fact that his approach is significantly different from that of the Kabbalistic mainstream with which Scholem dealt in the above-mentioned studies, including that on *devequt.*

17. See Abraham Berger, "The Messianic Self-Consciousness of Abraham Abulafia," in *Essays on Jewish Life and Thought Presented in Honor of S. Baron* (New York, 1959), pp. 55–61: Pearl Epstein, *Kabbalah, the Way of the Jewish Mystic* (Rome, 1984), pp. 109–120. See also the extensive references to Abulafia in the writings of Aryeh Kaplan, who made considerable use of material from the ecstatic Kabbalah in order to present an original Jewish mystical path to the modern reader.

18. See, for example, the remarks of David Bakan, *Sigmund Freud and the Jewish Mystical Tradition* (New York, 1965), pp. 75–82.

19. On the difference between these two tendencies in Kabbalah, see Idel, *Abraham Abulafia*, pp. 434-449; *idem.*, *Kabbalah: New Perspectives*, Introduction, pp. IX—XVIII.

20. On the difference between the Abulafian hermeneutics and that of the theosophical-theurgical school, see Idel, *Abraham Abulafia*, pp. 239–240; *idem.*, "Infinities of Torah in Kabbalah," pp. 151-152; *idem.*, *Kabbalah: New Perspectives*, pp. 200-210.

21. Gershom Scholem, *Die Erforschung der Kabbala von Reuchlin bis zur Gegenwart*, (Pforrheims, 1969), pp. 11–12.

22. Chayyim Wirszubski, *A Christian Kabbalist reads the Torah* [Heb.], (Jerusalem, 1978), pp. 22, 38.

23. See *idem.*, "*Liber Redemptionis*—An Early Version of Rabbi Abraham

Abulafia's Kabbalistic Commentary on the *Guide of the Perplexed* in Latin Translation by Flavius Mithridates" (Heb.), *Proceedings of the Israel Academy of Sciences and Humanities* 3 (1969), pp. 135–149; M. Idel, "Aegideo da Viterbo and the Writings of Abraham Abulafia," (Heb.) *Italia 2 (1981)*, pp. 48-50.

Chapter One

Techniques for Attaining Ecstasy

Abraham Abulafia's system differs from that of other medieval Jewish thinkers in presenting a detailed, systematic path enabling the seeker to attain to mystical experience. In this system various concepts used to describe reality by Arab and Jewish philosophers are transformed into subjects of personal experience by means of a suitable technique. This technique paves the way towards the zenith of mysticism: the total unity between man's intellect and the supreme Being, whether this is understood as God or as the Active Intellect. While other medieval thinkers as well saw this experience as their soul's desire, which they strove to attain with all their strength, we nevertheless do not find in philosophical works of this period any detailed, specific instructions as to the means of realizing such contact. The discussions by R. Abraham ibn Ezra and Maimonides and by their disciples concerning the nature of 'prophecy,' in which they saw the hallmark of this ideal experience are not to be read as concrete instructions, rooted in a specific path towards the realization of the desired goal. They rather describe a phenomenon from the distant past, namely, Biblical prophecy, without claiming—although not explicitly denying—that similar experiences are possible within their own generation.

In my opinion, the path propounded by Abulafia in his books is an adaptation of the Jewish mystical traditions which he had learned from the Ashkenazic world of Franco-Germany to the spiritual needs of Jews educated within the philosophical schools of Spain and Italy, which primarily thought in Maimonidean concepts. To these were added elements originating in mystical techniques outside of Judaism—Greek-Orthodox hesychasm, Indian Yoga and possibly also Sufism. The last mentioned is, however, primarily visible in the writings of his students, rather than in Abulafia's own writings. We shall therefore begin by describing the elements of technique as they appear in the writings of Abulafia and his disciples. As recitation of the Divine Names was the main technique developed by this school, we shall begin our discussion with this topic.

1. The Ecstatic Character of the Recitation of the Divine Names

The recitation of the Name or Names of God as a means of attaining ecstasy is a widely-known mystical practice, playing a significant role in techniques known from India, Tibet and Japan, in Islam and in Orthodox Christianity. We shall not discuss these techniques in detail here; some will be mentioned again at the end of this chapter for purposes of comparison with the material found in Abulafia. Before discussing Abulafia's system, however, we shall examine the Jewish precedents for use of the Divine Names in order to achieve changes in human consciousness. In late antiquity, in *Hekalot Rabbati* we read:

> When a man wishes to ascend to the Merkavah, he calls to Suryah,the Prince of the Presence, and adjures him one hundred and twelve times with the Name *ṭwṭrsy'y h'*, which is read *ṭwṭrsy'y zwrṭq ṭwṭrky'l ṭwfgr 'srwyly'y zbwdy'l wzhrry'l tnd'l šqhwzy' dhybwryn w'dyrryrwn Ha-Shem Elohei Yisra'el.* He may neither add nor subtract from these one hundred and twelve times—for were he to add or subtract he might lose his life—but he shall recite the names with his mouth, and the fingers of his hands shall count one hundred twelve times—and immediately he ascends to and rules the Merkavah.[1]

A similar passage appears in another treatise belonging to this literature:

> His mouth utters names and the fingers of his hands count one hundred eleven times; so shall whoever makes use of this aspect [i,e., technique], let his mouth utter names and the fingers of his hands count one hundred eleven times, and he must not subtract from these names, for if he adds or subtracts, he may lose his life.[2]

Both these passages would seem to imply that this refers to an established custom connected with the "descent to the Merkavah." Similar methods were used during the Gaonic period; in one of his responsa, R. Hai Gaon (939-1038) writes:

> And likewise [regarding] a dream question: there were several elders and pious men who [lived] with us who knew them [the Names] and fasted for several days, neither eating meat nor drinking wine, [staying] in a pure place and praying and reciting great and well-known verses and [their] letters by number, and they went to sleep and saw wondrous dreams similar to a prophetic vision.[3]

In another responsa, R. Hai Gaon testifies that:

> Many scholars thought that, when one who is distinguished by many qualities described in the books seeks to behold the Merkavah and the palaces of the angels on high, he must fast a number of days and place his head between his knees and whisper many hymns and songs whose texts are known from tradition. Then he will perceive within himself and in the chambers [of his heart] as if he saw the seven palaces with his own eyes, and as though he had entered one palace after another and seen what is there.[4]

The former passage from R. Hai Gaon refers to "great and well-known verses and letters by number"; G. Vajda contends that the sense of the phrase *letters by number* refers to groups of letters which equal one another in their numerical value (i.e., gematria).[5] In my opinion, this refers to the use of the Divine Name of seventy-two letters: the "great and well-known verses" are probably the three verses, Exodus 14:19-21, each one of which contains seventy-two letters in the Hebrew original, i.e., "letters in number." The second quotation also seems to me to be connected with the use of Divine Names. In *Sefer ha-ᶜAruḵ* of R. Nathan b. Jeḥiel of Rome (1035–ca. 1110), we again read in the name of R. Hai Gaon, that "*Pardes* is that which is expounded in *Heḵalot Rabbati* and *Heḵalot Zutraṭi;* i.e., that they would perform certain actions, and pray in purity, and use the crown and see the *Heḵalot* and the bands of angels in their position, and see how there was one chamber after another, and one within another."[6] G. Scholem has suggested that the expression "use the crown" signifies the use of the Divine Name.[7] A younger contemporary of R. Hai Gaon, Rabbenu Ḥananel, many of whose ideas were borrowed from the works of R. Hai, likewise writes about the sages who entered *Pardes,* stating that they "prayed and cleansed themselves of all impurity, and fasted and bathed themselves and became pure, and they used the names and gazed at the *Hekalot*."[8] In Rashi's opinion, the ascent to heaven signifying the entry into *Pardes* was performed "by means of a name."[9]

Similar testimony appears among the Ashkenazic Hasidim; *Sefer ha-Ḥayyim*, attributed to R. Abraham ibn Ezra, presents an interesting description reflecting the widespread use of Names:

> A vision *(mareh)* occurs when a man is awake and reflects upon the wonders of God, or when he does not reflect upon them, but pronounces the Holy Names or those of the angels, in order that he be shown [whatever] he wishes or be informed of a hidden matter—and the Holy Spirit then reveals itself to him, and he knows that he is a worm and that his flesh is like a garment, and he trembles and shakes from the power of the Holy Spirit, and is unable to stand it. Then that man stands up like one who is faint, and does not know where he is standing, nor does he see or hear or feel his body, but his soul sees and hears—and this is called vision and sight, and this is the matter of most prophecy.[10]

The disputant of the anonymous author of *Sefer ha-Ḥayyim*, R. Moses Taku (ca. 1235), describes a similar technique in a surviving fragment of his book, *Ketav Tammim:*

> And two of those who were lacking in knowledge [among] the schismatics [thought] to make themselves prophets, and they were accustomed to recite Holy Names, and at times performed *kawwanot* during this recitation, and the soul was astounded, and the body fell down and was exhausted. But for such as these there is no barrier to the soul, and the soul becomes the principle thing [in their constitution] and sees afar; [but] after one hour, when the power of that Name which had been mentioned departs, he returns to what he was, with a confused mind.[11]

The last two passages corroborate one another: during the procedures of reciting the Names, the body trembles violently, freeing the soul from its dependence upon the senses and creating a new form of consciousness. The process is in both cases compared to prophecy; one should note that prophecy is also mentioned, in a similar context, in R. Hai Gaon's previously quoted words: "similar to a prophetic vision."

R. Eleazar of Worms (ca. 1165–ca. 1230, the *Roqeaḥ*), a contemporary of the above-mentioned anonymous author of *Sefer ha-Ḥayyim*, also knew the technique of recitation of the Names of

God—a usage likely to bring about results similar to those mentioned in the works of R. Hai Gaon or in *Sefer ha-Ḥayyim*. These are his comments in *Sefer ha-Ḥokmah:*[12]

> *Abg ytz*[13]—these the six letters, each and every letter [standing for] a [Divine] name in its own right[14]: *A - Adiriron; B - Bihariron ; G - Gihariron; Y - Yagbihayah; T - Talmiyah; Z - Zatnitayah.* By rights, one oughtn't to write everything or to vocalize them, lest those lacking in knowledge and those taken [sic—should be 'stricken'] in understanding and of negligible wisdom use them. However, Abraham our father passed on the name of impurity to the children of the concubines, in order that they not know the future by means of idolatry.[15] Thus, some future things and spirits were revealed to us by means of the [Divine] attributes, through the pronunciation of the depths of the Names, in order to know the spirit of wisdom—thus far the *Sefer Yirqaḥ.*[16]

R. Eleazar of Worms' statements reflect an awareness of the antiquity of involvement in Divine Names and their recitation as a means of acquiring knowledge of the future or various wisdoms; the patriarch Abraham already knew these secrets and attempted to conceal them from the children of the concubines, and they were subsequently passed down from generation to generation until the Jewish medieval mystics. The expression, "pronunciation of the depths of the names," is particularly interesting in light of the fact that Abulafia—who explicitly admits to Eleazar's influence—was to see his own Kabbalah, that of Names, as the deepest path within the Jewish esoteric tradition. All of these quotations share the fact that they were formulated outside of the framework of the great speculative systems of the age—the Aristotelian and the Neoplatonic. Indeed, they reflect those types of approaches which Mircea Eliade, the scholar of comparative religions, would designate as "shamanistic."

Upon the emergence of philosophy, the use of Divine Names became transformed into a means for realizing forms of consciousness which transcend the ordinary frame of mind. R. Isaac ibn Latif (ca. 1210–ca. 1280) writes in *Ginzê ha-Melek:*[17]

> The attainment of [knowledge of] the existence of God is the highest form, including three kinds of comprehension *(hasagah),*[18] which are: conceptual comprehension, prophetic comprehension, and that comprehension which is hidden until the coming of the Righteous one, who shall teach [it]. The first kind is the comprehension of the existence of a first cause for all [things], by means of conclusive

> proofs: this is speculative philosophical comprehension, grasped through knowledge of those things which exist apart from the First Cause. The second kind is comprehension that the First Cause acts by a simple will, designated as spiritual speech, and this is [known as] prophetic comprehension, grasped by means of the Divine influx emanated upon the prophets by knowledge of the secret of His glorious names, through the comprehension of each one of them and of their wholeness; this level is one to which the master of conceptual speculation has no entry. The third kind is comprehension of this knowledge by means of the Name which is completely and utterly hidden [and] described as within, and this is the essence and the highest of comprehensions, and it is this one which is reserved in the future for those who fear God and contemplate His name [Malachi 3:16].

The first kind of understanding mentioned here is that of natural theology based upon philosophy, which is the province of "scholars of speculation." The second is a combination of the approach of R. Solomon ibn Gabirol (ca. 1020–ca. 1057; known in Latin as "Avicebrol"), which asserts the identity of will and speech,[19] and speculation upon the Divine Names. At the time, the explicit connection between prophecy and contemplation of the Divine Names was an unusual one and, in my opinion, is indicative of the penetration into Ibn Latif's thought of a view from one of Abulafia's sources. The third kind of comprehension mentioned above involves the hidden Name of God; this is an allusion to the Name *ʾhwy*, which was considered the hidden Name of God both by the circle of *Sefer ha-ʿIyyun* and by Abulafia.[20] The similarity to Abulafia is particularly great, as both Abulafia and Ibn Latif believed that knowledge of the hidden Name of God will be realized in the times of Messiah. In *Ôẕar ʿEden Ganuz*, Abulafia writes:[21]

> What we have seen in some of the books of those sages[22] concerning the division of the names is that one who has knowledge of their essence will have a great and wondrous superiority in Torah and wisdom and prophecy above all his contemporaries. These are the things which God has chosen above all else in the world of the soul; therefore, He has given them to the soul *in potentia*, and when they go from *potentia* to *actu*, the soul acts on another soul, so that the souls are renewed, and this knowledge shall save many souls from Sheol.

Three different approaches to the Divine Names appear in this passage: that true knowledge of the Names is liable to make one wise; that they are capable of bringing an individual to the level of prophecy, i.e., to a mystical experience; and that they contain hidden powers to change reality by "renewal" of souls. All three of the approaches combined here—the informative, the magical, and the ecstatic—were present within the circle of Kabbalists whom Abulafia knew. R. Moses b. Simeon of Burgos, described by Abulafia as one of his students, writes:

> It is truly known that those prophets who concentrated intensely in deed and in thought, more so than other people of their species, and whose pure thoughts cleaved to the Rock of the World with purity and great cleanliness—that the supernal Divine will intended to show miracles and wonders through them, to sanctify His great Name, and that they received an influx of the supernal inner emanation by virtue of the Divine names, to perform miraculous actions in physical things, working changes in nature.[23]

These words of R. Moses of Burgos indicate that a technique for receiving prophetic flow by means of Divine Names was known in Spain in the second half of the thirteenth century. As we shall see below in the chapter on prophecy and music, Abulafia's approach to music was likewise known to the circle of R. Moses of Burgos.

Before we continue to analyze Abulafia's technique, I should like to mention one feature common to all the passages quoted above: namely, that they refer to the Divine Names as distinct linguistic units, which the one 'prophesying' must repeat several times. In these passages, the Name is not broken down into a multitude of units, which constantly change by means of different combinations and vocalizations. This technique of breaking-down or atomizing the Name is the most distinctive characteristic of Abulafia's technique; the Holy Name contains within itself 'scientific' readings of the structure of the world and its activities, thereby possessing both an 'informative' character and magical powers. It is reasonable to assume that both qualities are associated with the peculiar structure of the Name.[24] However, in Abulafia's view this structure must be destroyed in order to exploit the 'prophetic' potential of these Names and to create a series of new structures by means of letter-combinations. In the course of the changes taking place in the structure of the Name, the structure of human consciousness likewise changes. As Abulafia indicated in a number of places,[25] the Divine Name is inscribed upon man's soul, making it reasonable to assume that the process of letter-combination worked upon the Name is understood as occurring simultaneously in the human soul: "In the thoughts of your mind combine and be purified."[26] We shall now see how the Divine Names are used as a means of attaining mystical experience or, as Abulafia writes,[27] "in the name my intellect found a ladder to ascend to the heights of vision."

Just as the letters themselves generally appear on three levels—writing, speech and thought[28]—so do the Names of God; one must 'recite' the Names first in writing, then verbally, and finally mentally. The act of writing the combination of the letters of the Divine Names is mentioned in several places in the writings of Abulafia and his followers, only two of which we shall cite here: "Take the pen and the parchment and the ink, and write and combine Names"[29] and, in *Ŝaʿarê Z̲edeq,*[30] "when midnight passed [over] me and the quill is in my hand and the paper on my knees."

The second level, that of verbal articulation, is more complex, including several components which must be analyzed separately: 1) the seeker of mystical experience must sing the letters and their vocalization (this point will be discussed separately in the chapter on music and prophecy); 2) he must maintain a fixed rhythm of breathing; 3) his head must be moved in accordance with the vocalization of the letter pronounced; 4) he must contemplate the internal structure of the human being. These last three procedures will be discussed below at greater length.

The third level involves the mental combination of the Divine Names: "Know that mental [letter-]combination performed in the heart brings forth a word, [the latter] being [the result of the letter-]combination, entirely mental and born from the sphere of the intellect,"[31] A brief description of the movement from one level to another appears in *Ôz̲ar ʿEden Ganuz:*[32]

> One must take the letters *ʾmš yhw,* first as instructed in the written form which is an external thing, to combine them, and afterwards one takes them from the book with their combinations, and transfers them to one's tongue and mouth, and pronounces them until one knows them by heart. Afterwards, he shall take them from his mouth [already] combined, and transfer them to his heart, and set his mind to understand what is shown him in every language that he knows, until nothing is left of them.

An explicit process of interiorization is presented here: the letters of the Divine Name undergo a process of 'purification' by which they are transformed from tangible letters, existing outside of the intellect, into intellective letters, existing in the heart. This process is one of construction of the intellect, beginning with sensibilia and ending in intelligibilia. Thus, through the combination of the letters on all three levels, one may arrive at the highest level of consciousness: prophecy, or mystical experience. Several passages will be cited below indicating that this technique allows a 'prophet' to achieve unique spiritual attainments. The Castilian Kabbalist R. Isaac b. Solomon ibn Abi Sahula, a contemporary of Abulafia, writes: "It is known that when he received this verse ('I am that I am' [Ex. 3:14]), Moses our teacher, of blessed memory, attained the very essence of wisdom and the highest level in the renewal of miracles and wonders, by the combination of its letters."[33] The process of attaining wisdom is described in impressive terms in Abulafia's *Ḥayyê ha-Nefeš*:

> And begin by combining this name, namely, *YHWH*, at the beginning alone, and examine all its combinations and move it and turn it about like a wheel returning around, front and back, like a scroll, and do not let it rest, but when you see its matter strengthened because of the great motion, because of the fear of confusion of your imagination and the rolling about of your thoughts, and when you let it rest, return to it and ask [it] until there shall come to your hand a word of wisdom from it, do not abandon it. Afterwards go on to the second one from it, *Adonay*, and ask of it its foundation [*yesodo*] and it will reveal to you its secret [*sodo*]. And then you will apprehend its matter in the truth of its language. Then join and combine the two of them [*YHWH* and *Adonay*], and study them and ask them, and they will reveal to you the secrets of wisdom, and afterwards combine this which is, namely, *El Šadday*, which is tantamount to the Name [*El Šadday* = 345 = *ha-Šem*], and it will also come in your portion. Afterwards combine *Elohim*, and it will also grant you wisdom, and then combine the four of them, and find the miracles of the Perfect One [i.e., God], which are miracles of wisdom.[34]

From this passage, as well as from the one cited above from *Ôẕar ʿEden Ganuz*, we learn that one must combine the letters of a given Name, and then combine them in turn with the combinations of the letters of another Name. This activity is referred to by Abulafia by the term *Maʿaseh Merkavah*, i,e., the act of combining [*harkavah*] the letters of one Name in another, which brings about the receiving of metaphysical knowledge, i.e., the standard meaning of *Maʿaseh Merkavah* in Abulafian Kabbalah. In *Sefer ha-Ôt*, p. 75, we read:

> One who concentrates upon the Ineffable Name which is combined in twelve ways—six of them inverted—which causes the grandeur of Israel, shall rejoice in it, and the joy and happiness and gladness will combine in the heart of each one who seeks the Name, in the Name *Yhʾwhdyhnwh Eloha El Ŝadday YHWH Ẕewaot*.

The first and second of these Names are combinations of one Name within another: *YHWH - ADNY - YHWH - YHWH.*[35]

2. Combinations of Letters of the Divine Names

The two Divine Names most frequently used by Abulafia in letter-combination are the Name of seventy-two letters, whose combinations are mostly described in *Ḥayyê ha-ʿOlam ha-Ba,* and the Tetragrammaton (the Name of Four Letters or the "Ineffable Name"), details of whose combinations are discussed in *Ôr ha-Seḵel.* We shall begin our discussion with the latter.

The method of combination expounded in *Ôr ha-Seḵel* is exemplified by the use of the letter *Aleph,* which is combined in turn with each of the letters of the Tetragrammaton, so that one arrives at four combinations, as follows: *ʾyʾhʾwʾh.* Each of these units is in turn vocalized by every possible permutation of the five vowels, *ḥolam, qamaz, ḥiriq, ẕere, qubuẕ,* in the sequence of both *ʾy* and *yʿ* and so on. One thereby derives four tables, each containing fifty vocalized combinations. The following is an example of one of these tables: [36]

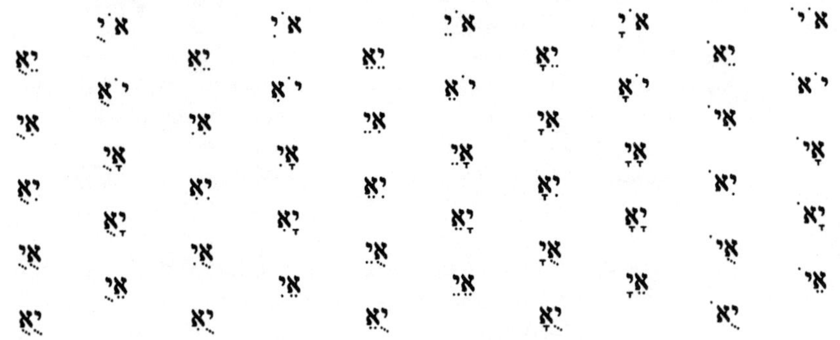

This table, as we have mentioned, is one of four in which the letter *aleph* is combined with the four letters of the Divine Names. But, as Abulafia states in the book, it is not only by chance that he 'chose' this form of combination as an example; in his view, the letter *Aleph* constitutes part of the hidden Divine Name, *ʾhwy.*[37] However, this explanation seems a kind of exegesis of material which he already found in his earlier sources. In one of the works of R. Eleazar of Worms (ca. 1165–ca. 1230), we find a combination-technique quite similar to that of Abulafia; in this technique, the letter *Aleph* is also combined with each of the four letters of the Tetragrammaton, each unit being vocalized by two vowels. We shall cite one example:[38]

אֶיְ	אֶיֳ	אֶיֵ	אֶיִ	אֶיַ	אֶיֶ
אַיְ	אַיֳ	אַיֵ	אַיִ	אַיַ	אַיֶ
אִיְ	אִיֳ	אִיֵ	אִיִ	אִיַ	אִיֶ
אֵיְ	אֵיֳ	אֵיֵ	אֵיִ	אֵיַ	אֵיֶ
אֳיְ	אֳיֳ	אֳיֵ	אֳיִ	אֳיַ	אֳיֶ
אְיְ	אְיֳ	אְיֵ	אְיִ	אְיַ	אְיֶ

The main difference between Abulafia's table and R. Eleazar's lies in the total number of vowels used: rather than five vowels,[39] as in Abulafia, in R. Eleazar there are six, by means of the addition of the *šewa*. The total number of combinations thereby increases geometrically. In my opinion, Abulafia adapted an Ashkenazic system of combination to the Sephardic system of vocalization, based upon five major vowels; the *šewa*, counted as a vowel by the Ashkenazim, disappeared, thereby decreasing the total number of vocalized combinations. Abulafia, for whom this system of combination was exemplified by the use of the letter *Aleph* and the other letters of the Ineffable Name, saw this as an allusion to his view that the Name *ʾhwy* is the Hidden Name of God.

Whereas the system described above is based upon a square, each of whose sides contains a different combination of the letters of the Divine Name, the system found in *Ḥayyê ha-ʿOlam ha-Ba* is based upon the circle. The Name of seventy-two letters is recited while contemplating circles, each of which contains nine letters out of the 216 letters of the Name; one thereby arrives at a system of twenty-four circles, containing *in toto* all in all the Name of seventy-two letters. It seems to me that the source of this system can also be identified; in the longer commentary to Exodus by R. Abraham ibn Ezra (1089–1164), the author describes the mathematical qualities of the letters constituting the Ineffable Name, and thereafter writes that "all of the numbers are nine from one direction, and ten from the other direction. If one writes the nine in a circle, and doubles over the end with every number, one will find the units on the left side, and the tens, which are like units, on the right side."[40] It seems unlikely to assume that Abulafia based his system in *Ḥayyê ha-ʿOlam ha-Ba* upon circles of nine letters by mere chance, without any relation to the above quotation from Ibn Ezra's commentary.[41] As was the case in the adaptation of R. Eleazar of Worms' system of combination to the Sephardic system of grammar, here Abulafia incorporated the idea of the nine-letter number into a circle with the seventy-two letter Name. It is worth mentioning that the nine letters within a circle reappear in Abulafia's *Sefer ha-Hafṭarah,*[42] where they appear within the circle of the letters of the forty-two letter Name, while preserving the number nine. We should also note that the use of concentric circles in order to combine the letters of various Divine Names likewise appears in other works of Abulafia, such as *Imrê Šefer*[43] and *Gan Naʿul.*[44] It is also interesting to note that circles including Divine Names appear in Islam as well, as one learns from a study by G. Anawati,[45] although I have not yet found significant points of contact between the use of the circle in Abulafia and in the Arabic sources.

Techniques for Recitation of the Names

As we have seen above, the procedure for reciting the Name contained a number of elements, each of which will now be enumerated separately.

A. Breathing

Any technique in which the pronunciation of letters occupies a central place must attach importance to proper principles of breathing. Discussions of breathing appear in Yoga, in Sufism and in Hesychasm, albeit with different emphases.[46] Abulafia's writings contain brief statements about and allusions to a technique of breathing to be practiced by one who pronounces the Ineffable Name. We shall attempt here to analyze the fragmentary material which has come down to us. The most significant of these passages appears in *Mafteaḥ ha-Šemot,*[47] where it states:

> One must take each one of the letters [of the Tetragrammaton] and wave it with the movements of his long breath (!) so that one does not breathe between two letters, but rather one long breath, for however long he can stand it, and afterwards rest for the length of one breath. He shall do the same with each and every letter, until

> there will be two breaths in each letter: one for pausing when he enunciates the vowel of each letter, and one for resting between each letter. It is known to all that every single breath of one's nostrils is composed of taking in of the air from outside, that is, *mi-ba''r le-ga''w* [from outside to inside], whose secrets allude to the attribute of *Gevurah* and its nature, by which a man is known as *gibbor* [mighty]—that is, the word *ga''w ba''r* [a rearrangement of the consonants of the word *gibbor*]—for his strength by which he conquers his Urge.[48] As in the secret of *abg ytz̠ qrʿ sṭn* with *ygl pzq šqw z̠yt*,[49] composed of the emission of breath from within to outside, and this second composition is from *g''w* to *b''r*.

This passage combines together two significant elements: the technical description of breathing, and the theoretical discussion of the meaning of breathing. The technical aspect includes three different elements, comprising one unit: 1) the intake of air, namely, breathing; 2) the emission of air while pronouncing the letter and its vowel; 3) the pause between one breath and the next. In his epistle *Ševaʿ Netivot ha-Torah*, p. 7, Abulafia refers to "the secret of the Name and the vocalization of some of its letters, their knowledge, and the resting breath, the interrupting [breath] and the extending [breath]." Comparison of the three terms used in *Sefer Mafteaḥ ha-Šemot* indicates that the resting breath is parallel to the phrase, "he shall rest for the length of one breath"; the extending breath parallels the intake of air before pronouncing a letter, "so that he not breathe between two letters, but takes one long breath, as much as he is able to stand in length"; while the interrupting breath is parallel to the emission of air which accompanies the pronunciation of the letter, "one for pausing, as at the time of pronouncing the vowel of that letter." Abulafia refers to three breaths elsewhere as well,[50] but only for purposes of *gemaṭria*, without any technical interpretation likely to assist in the understanding of his approach.

The division of the breathing process into three stages is not new; it already appears in Yoga, in which the process of breathing is divided into *puraka*, the intake of breath; *recaka*, the emission of breath; and *kumbhaka*, the retention of air.[51] True, there is no exact parallel between the retention of breath in Yoga, whose aim is to use up the oxygen present in the air one breathes by means of slight physical effort, to the state of rest mentioned by Abulafia, which follows the emission of breath. It may be that the word 'halt,' which refers to the holding of the air in order to pronounce the letter of the Divine Name, is a parallel to the halt practiced in Yoga, but we cannot state this with any certainty.[52] In both systems, one arrives at an extremely slow pace of breathing, which is a goal in and of itself in

Yoga, and in practice also in Abulafia. Without stating so directly, he emphasizes the need for a long period of emission, on the one hand, and the maximum exploitation of the air held in the lungs, on the other: "that he should not breath between two letters except for one long breath, for so long as he is able to stand." Indeed, in *Peᶜulat ha-Yeẕirah,* he states that "one should pronounce one letter of the Name with a great voice, in one breath, until he exhausts his breath from breathing out."[53] In *Ôr ha-Seḵel,* he similarly states:

> When he begins to pronounce one letter with a given vocalization, one should remember that it alludes to the secret of the unity, so do not extend it more than the length of one breath and do not interrupt it during that breath at all until you complete its expression. And extend that [particular] breath in accordance with the strength of the length of one breath, as much as you are able to extend it.[54]

As we have seen, one ought to extend both the breath and its emission. The same is not true, however, for the pause between breaths; *Mafteaḥ ha-Šemot* speaks of the pause as equalling the length of one breath, while in *Ôr ha-Seḵel* there is a slight variation:[55]

> Do not separate between one breath and the breath of the letter, but cling to it, whether one long breath or a short one. . . . But between the letter of the Name and the *Aleph,* in the direct ones, or between the *Aleph* and the letter of the Name, in the inverted ones,[56] you may take two breaths—no more—without pronouncing anything. At the end of each column, you may take five breaths, and no more, but you may also breathe less than five breaths.

Ḥayyê ha-ᶜOlam ha-Ba gives a different version, which allows for the possibility that one may take three breaths between the pronunciation of each letter.[57]

Another rule entailed in the art of pronouncing the Names refers to the prohibition against pronouncing the letters while breathing in: "and it is possible that the speaker [i.e., the person who recites] may breathe, and will not speak with his lips between the emission of air and its intake, but he is not allowed to speak with his mouth and take in the breath together,[58] but that the speech and the emission of air may occur together."[59]

Turning to the theoretical significance of breathing, we find that the process of intake and emission of air is alluded to in the afore-cited passage from *Mafteaḥ ha-Šemot* by the words *mi-ba"r le-ga"w,* which symbolize the attribute of *Gevurah* within man—that is, his ability to overcome his evil Urge. For this reason, man pronounces the Name of forty-two letters[60] incorporating the expression *qeraᶜ saṭan* ["cut off Satan"] which corresponds, in my opinion, to "conquering his Urge." The ability to overcome corporeality, tantamount to the Evil Urge and to Satan, by means of breathing is likewise alluded to in another formulation from *Ḥayyê ha-ᶜOlam ha-Ba:*

> And you may yet again, if you wish, breathe three breaths which are one. . . . And immediately the Satan will die, for they were enemies to the perceptions which are in the blood of man, and the blood is the animal [attribute]. But the secret of the one breath is *Šadday*—[i.e.,] *Šin Dalet Yod*—and that is the second seal . . . which killed the demons with the seal of the Messiah, which kills the evil blood, and also kills the evil attribute, so it immediately dies by the hand by the strength of those three breaths.[61]

The function of the three breaths which are one is that, as they constitute one unit connected with the pronunciation of one letter, they may destroy or murder the Satan and the imagination, i.e., the adverse perceptions inherent in the blood of man, in the evil blood, etc. On the other hand, the breath is the means of strengthening the spiritual element in man: the "precious hand," *Šadday*, the seal of Messiah.[62] Elsewhere in the same work, Abulafia writes about:

> . . . eighteen breaths, which will add to you years of life, which are the life [in gematria: 18] of the soul, from the two creatures in which there is the life of the soul. And there are in you two nostrils in which they are mingled, and understand this, for they are the nostrils of the soul, whose secret is the two cherubim, and they are two chariots which force the Shekhinah to dwell on earth and to speak with man.[63]

This passage suggests the ability of the breath to bring about a mystical experience, and through that the survival of the soul.[64] The two aspects of breath—that of overcoming corporeality and of strengthening spirituality—are symbolized by the two angels, Gabriel and Michael: "from his two nostrils one may recognize the two archangels, of whom it is said that the names of all the angels change in accordance with their work and their deeds and their activities,[65] [i.e.,] Michael and Gabriel."[66] In Abulafia, Michael is identified with the Active Intellect or Metatron, while Gabriel is identified with Sandalphon, to whom is encharged the corporeal realm.[67] In two other passages, we learn of the service and knowledge of God with the help of breathing: "Remember *Yah* and his activities, for He is the one who seals and makes an impress—know *Yah* through your breath.[68] "'All that has breath shall praise Yah, Hallelujah'[69] and it is said,[70] 'with each and every breath that is within you praise God.'"[71]

In conclusion, we must mention the connection between breathing and the recitation of the Name as it appears in *Rešit Ḥokmah.*[72] The sixteenth century Safedian Kabbalist, R. Elijah de Vidas, quotes therein a certain book not mentioned by title, as follows:

> There are 1080 divisions to an hour, corresponding to which the Tetragrammaton is combined and permutated in various combinations of vocalizations of the alphabet, in a total of 1080 combinations. These 1080 combinations correspond to the 1080 breaths which a man breathes, and to each breath there corresponds one letter of the name of four letters, which gives vitality to that breath. And this is alluded to in,[73] "For by every thing which comes from the mouth of God may man live." As God gives breath and life, it is appropriate that all his [man's] breaths be devoted to the service of the Creator, and to this our sages referred in Genesis Rabba [in their interpretation of] the phrase "all that has breath shall praise Yah." [Ps. 150:6]

The connection between the act of breathing and the recitation of the 1080 combinations of the Ineffable Name, with all possible vocalizations,[74] is made here, to the best of my knowledge, for the first time. It is based upon R. Eleazar of Worms' *ʿEser Hawayot* and on the quotation from *Ôr ha-Sekel,* both of which appear in *Pardes Rimmonim,*[75] the major work of de Vidas' master, R. Moses Cordovero. From a practical viewpoint, it is difficult to imagine that one may breathe 1080 times in one hour, particularly when one also needs to pronounce letters; in any event, such a pace would seem to contradict Abulafia's whole approach. However, the very occurrence of the breathing technique together with the pronunciation of letters of the Divine Name evinces the practice of an Abulafian-like technique among the Safedian Kabbalists, a fact further strengthened by other evidence.

B. Shaking of One's Head

In Abulafia, the act of pronouncing the letters is accompanied by motions of the head corresponding to the vowels of the letters pronounced. A detailed description of this practice appears in *Ḥayyê ha-ʿOlam ha-Ba,*[76] quoted here *in extenso:*

> After you begin to pronounce the letter, begin to move your heart and head: your heart by your intellection, because it is an inner [organ], and your head itself, because it is external. And move your head in the form of the vowel [-point] of the letter which you are pronouncing. This is the manner of the form of the motion: know that the vocalization which is above is called *Ḥolam*, and that alone is marked above the letter, but the other four vowel sounds are below the letter. And that [vowel] which is above the letter *Aleph*, which you pronounce with the letter *Kaf* or *Qof*: do not in the beginning incline your head either to the right or the left, nor below or above at all, but let your head be set evenly, as if it were in a scale [i.e., balanced], in the manner in which you would speak with another person of the same height as yourself, face to face. Thus, when you extend the vowel of the letter in its pronunciation, move your head up towards the heavens, and close your eyes and open your mouth and let your words shine,[77] and clear your throat of all spittle so that it not interfere with the pronunciation of the letter in your mouth, and in accord with the length of your breath shall be the upper movement, until you interrupt the breathing together with the movement of your head. And if after uttering [the letter] there is a moment left to complete the breath, do not lower your head until you complete everything.

The process described here in detail is also alluded to briefly in *Sefer Ôr ha-Seḵel*:[78]

> And your head is crowned with *tefillin*, facing east, for from there light emerges to the world, and [from] there you may move your head towards five directions. And on [the vowel] *ḥolam* begin from the center of the east, and purify your thoughts, and lift your head with the breath bit by bit until it is complete, and your head shall be facing up. And after this is completed bow down to the earth once . . . and on [the vowel] *z̲erê* move your head from left to right, and on *qamaz̲* from right to left.

As one can clearly see, the head motions are simply attempts to imitate the written form of the vowel sounds, an attempt repeated in the use of music, where the vocalization is transformed into musical notes, as we shall see in the next chapter.

C. *The Hands*

We find a description in *Sefer ha-Ḥešeq* of the hand movements to be performed during the pronunciation of the Divine Names.[79]

This description is unique in Abulafia's extant works and it reflects the position of the hands during the Priestly Blessing:

> "Let my prayer be acceptable as incense, the offerings of my hands as sweet meal-offerings."[80] And lift your eyes up to the heaven, and lift your left and right hands, like the lifting up of hands of the *kohen*, who divides his fingers, five on one side and five on the other, with two on the right and two on the left [in each hand], the two smallest fingers, *qemiẕah* and *zeret* (i.e., the little finger and the ring finger) joined together, and these two next to them also joined. And divide between them with the thumb stuck out by itself, and your hands shall also be in this form—  —and your tongue shall separate between them, like a balance stone . . . [here details of the pronunciation are given] . . . and immediately put down your hands, which you lifted before God with ease, in the image of the ten Sefirot from the right, like the image of the ten fingers, five over against five, to the right and left. And you have switched the powers and made meritorious the one who was guilty; therefore place your left hand on your heart, spread out with the five fingers, and above it place your right hand, outstretched with its five fingers, to indicate that the meritorious one has overcome him . . . and if you wish to lift your hands for a longer period of time, you are allowed to do so; but if not, you need not worry.

Thus far, we have described those actions which one is to perform while pronouncing the letters. A separate chapter will be devoted to the song or "melody," as Abulafia calls the pronunciation of the letters in different tones. We shall now turn to the third stage of the pronunciation of the Divine Name, namely, the inner activities performed in the "the heart," that is, with the powers of the soul: the intellect and the imagination.

4. The Inner Pronunciation

From the mid-thirteenth century, there appears in Hebrew mystical literature a technique, one of whose components is the imagining of the letters of the Divine Names. Evidence of such a practice appears in R. Isaac Ibn Latif, who enumerates three different stages of contemplation of the letters of the Divine Name. In his *Ẕurat ha-ʿOlam*, which was apparently written at the end of the second third of the thirteenth century, he writes:[81]

> The desired end is to strip the Name of [its] matter and to imagine

it in your mind, although it is impossible for the imagination to depict it without some physical image, because the imagination is not separate from the *sensibilia,* and most of what is attained by the activity of the imagination is performed through the contemplation of the shape of the letters and their forms and number. And it must also be understood that its letters [i.e., those of the Divine Name] are that which make it move and speak, and that the other letters move about, but one cannot image them in speech except for the letters of the Name, even though they do not become mingled and do not change their places in the squaring of the numbers. . . . And it is known to anyone who is wise of heart that when the imagination goes away, so do the letters. Therefore, the straightforward intellect must strip this Name of simple matter, and imagine it in the form of pure mind.

The subject of this passage is the letters of the Divine Name, *ʾhwy,* which enliven speech and shoe numerical counterparts (i.e., 1, 5, 6, 10) each retain their final digit when they are squared.[82] According to Ibn Latif, there are three levels of contemplation of these letters: the material, the imaginative, and the intellective. The second stage is to be understood, in my opinion, as the depicting of the letters in the power of the imagination, without the physical presence of the written letters. These imaginary letters are thereby transformed into an object of contemplation of the intellect just as, according to the Aristotelian theory of knowledge, an imaginary form is the material for intellectual activity.

Ibn Latif's words indicate that the technique which he discusses at length in several places was already in use some time before its occurrence in Abulafia. In the latter's *Ḥayyê ha-ʿOlam ha-Ba,* we read:

Prepare your true thoughts to imagine the Name, may He be Blessed, and with it the supernal angels. And visualize them in your heart as if they are human beings standing or sitting around you, and you are among them like a messenger. . . . And after you have imagined this entirely, prepare your mind and your heart to understand the thoughts whose matters are to be brought to you by the letters you have thought of in your heart.[83]

It becomes clear several pages later that this refers to the letters of the Ineffable Name, of which it is said that they are the ones portrayed "and he shall close his eyes and intend in his thought, and the first intention is that he is to imagine that there are four camps of the Indwelling, or a Tabernacle around them, and four beautiful flags in round forms surrounding the fifth camp."[84] Following this passage, Abulafia describes the image that is to be imagined: the seventy-two letters Name in the center, with the four Names of four letters in the four corners of the square. Next to the seventy-two letter Name is written thirty-two [probably an allusion to the thirty-two *netivot* mentioned in *Sefer Yezirah]*; this is an allusion to the gematria: 72+32 =104 =4 x 26 [26 is the gematria of the Tetragrammaton].

One also ought to note here the parallels to the techniques of imagining in the writings of other Kabbalists. Abulafia's younger contemporary, R. Joseph b. Shalom Ashkenazi, cites an extremely interesting quotation in the name of "the philosophers." This quotation, to be discussed below, is important in a number of different respects; I shall confine myself here to mentioning just one of them. The unidentified philosophers cited, who were presumably contemporaries or predecessors of Abulafia, proposed a technique of contemplation quite similar in several respects to that contained in the above quotations from Abulafia, though not identical with it. The following is the text of the passage:[85]

> The philosophers have already written on the issue of prophecy, saying that it is not improbable that there will be a person to whom things will appear in his imaginative faculty comparable to that which appears to the imaginative faculty in a dream. All this [could take place] while someone is awake, and all his senses are obliterated, as the letters of the Divine Name [stand] in front of his eyes, in the gathered colours. Sometimes he will hear a voice,[86] a wind, a speech, a thunder and a noise with all the organs of his hearing sense, and he will see with his imaginative faculty with all the organs of sight, and he will smell with all the organs of smell, and he will taste with all the organs of taste, and he will touch with all the organs of touch, and he will walk and levitate. All this while the holy letters are in front of his eyes, and its colours are covering it; this[87] is the sleep of prophecy.

The similarity of the content of this quotation to Abulafia's teaching is interesting, despite the fact that he is clearly not the author quoted here; the contemplation of the letters of the Divine Name as a technique for bringing about 'prophecy' is clearly parallel to Abulafia's own path. Moreover, the quotation of these words in the name of "the philosophers," despite the fact that it is mingled with ideas from *Sefer Yezirah,* fits the mixture of Maimonidean philosophy and *Sefer Yezirah* mysticism characteristic of Abulafia's own writings. Nevertheless, the presence here of a certain motif which is definitively rejected by Abulafia—i.e., "and its colors are enwrapped in it"[88]—makes it difficult for us to identify this passage with any likelihood as one of the "lost" writings of Abulafia. Yet it is precisely this conclusion, taken together with the quotation from Ibn Latif, which is significant for our understanding of the development of the teaching of this ecstatic Kabbalist. Abulafia did not create a new theory, but developed an already existing tendency, albeit one in some respects rather different from that expressed in his works.

R. Isaac of Acre, an ecstatic Kabbalist of the late thirteenth and early fourteenth century, saw the act of imagining of the letters composing the name of God as a means of achieving the life of the world to come. These are his words in *Me'irat ʿEnayim*:[89]

> I, Isaac the young, the son of Samuel, of Acre, may it speedily be rebuilt, say [as follows], to the elite as well as to the vulgus: that whoever wishes to know the secret of attaching one's soul above and cleaving one's thought to Almighty God, so that one may acquire the World to Come with that same constant thought, without interruption, and God will always be with him, in this [world] and the next [do as follows]: Let him place before his eyes and his thought the letters of the Ineffable Name, as if they are written before him in a book, in Assyriac writing, and let him visualize each letter before his eyes as great, without limits. I mean by this to say that when you envision the letters of the Ineffable Name before your eyes, [imaginatively] put your mind's eye on them but the thought of your heart be on the Infinite [*Ein Sof*], [the envisioning and the thought] both concomitantly. And this is the true cleaving of which Scripture said, "to cleave to Him."[90] "and to Him shall you cleave,"[91] "and you who cleave,"[92] etc. And so long as the soul of man cleaves to the Name, may He be blessed, no evil shall befall you, and you shall come to no error in any matter, either intellective or sensory, and you will not fall into the hand of chance, for so long as one is cleaving to God, may He be blessed, he is above all chance and rules over them.

Another sentence in the same work describes the technique of imagination:

> I, Isaac . . . of Acre, have come to write a tradition pertaining to the intention of the punctuation of the Holy Name . . . of which whosoever knows it will think in his heart of its vocalization as if it is vocalized before him.[93]

In a magical passage appearing in the manuscripts, the idea of imagination appears as follows: "Another way. *YHWH* with the vocalization of *devareḵa*. Imagine in your mind the letters of the Ineffable Name before your eyes, in a circle colored red as fire, and your thought shall perform much. From Rabbi Tanhum."[94] The expression, "your mind shall perform much," and the end of the previous passage from *Me'irat ʿEnayim*, suggest an explicitly magical direction, conveying a technique, the main element of which is the attainment of cleaving to God *(devequt)*.[95] It may be that R. Isaac of Acre combined Abulafia's teaching with a magical understanding of the imagining of the letters of God's Name which also was practiced in the thirteenth century.

In conclusion, it is worthwhile citing a few comments concerning the imagining of the letters from MS. Sasson 290, p, 648:

> You may picture the Ineffable Name like the white flame of the candle, in absolute whiteness, and the light in your looking at the candle, and even when there is no candle, remember the flame, and there you may see and look at the light, from the pure white light. And one must always imagine that you are a soul without a body, and the soul is the light, and you are always within the above-mentioned flames, by way of the pure clouds. And strive to be pure and full, and if it is daytime wearing *ẕiẕit* and *tefillin* and the ring upon your finger, and at night as well the ring upon your finger. And be accustomed to cleanliness in that house where you stand in the sanctuary of God, within His precious, holy and pure names.

I have discussed the visualization of the Divine Names at some length, because it concerns an extremely widespread technique, known to a number of different Kabbalists. However, there is one point which is critical for the understanding of Abulafia's doctrine: what he assumes to be a means, in the passages we have cited from *Ḥayyê ha-ʿOlam ha-Ba*, become (in other passages of his to be discussed in the third chapter) the goal. The letters of the Divine Name are not only a component of the method of cleaving to God; the process of imagining the letters in the first stage precedes the vision of the letters in the final stage of the ecstatic process.[96] This distinction between technique and goal is not clear in other authors, so that in their descriptions the imagining of the letters is transformed into immediate cleaving to them. Finally, let us note that the technique of imagining already appears in the early thirteenth century mystic Ibn Arabi.[97]

Another interesting element of Abulafia's technique of contemplation appears in *Ḥayyê ha-ʿOlam ha-Ba*. In several places there, he refers to a technique of recitation and contemplation connected to the three main organs of the body: the head, the belly, and the torso:

> And he should again pronounce the head of the end, which is *L*

> [*lamed*], and imagine as if you are gazing at your belly, and do not breath between pronouncing the place of your organ and pronouncing that letter which rules over that organ.[98]

Elsewhere in the same work we read:

> Again, go and mention the head of the middle of the Name. You already know that you ought to pronounce [the names of] the organs from what I have said, that there are so to speak three spots on your head: the inside, which is the head of the head; the middle, which is the inside of the head; and the behind, which is the end of the head. And likewise imagine as if there are three points on your torso, which is the place of your heart: the head, which is the center of the middle; the middle, which is the middle of the middle, which is but one point in its center; and the behind, which is the end of the end. And likewise imagine that there are three points in your belly: the front, which is the point of your navel, the head of the end; the middle, which is the point of your entrails; the middle of the end, and behind, which is the point of the end of your spine, which is the place of the kidneys where the spinal cord is completed, the end of the end.[99]

This passage is based upon the pronunciation of the letters of the Name of seventy-two letters, consisting of units of three letters, each three of which constitute one column. A unit consists of a beginning, the first letter; a middle, the second letter; and an end, the final letter. It follows from this that, by reciting a column of nine letters pertaining to the bodily organs, one thereby refers to the human head, torso, and belly. An error in the recitation of one letter is likely to bring about a change in one of the organs of the body, for which reason the name of seventy-two letters also includes the combination *Mum* [defect].[100]

What are the sources of this technique? The reference to the navel leads G. Scholem to think that there is a connection between Abulafia and the school of hesychasm, which practiced the contemplation of one's navel.[101] But it seems to me that precisely that opinion which he sees as "one which is difficult to imagine" is the correct one; namely, that this technique came about through an internal development, based upon study of *Sefer Yeẕirah*. In *Ḥayyê ha-ʿOlam ha-Ba*, it states:

> Know that there are within man three matters created by the three pillars [i.e., primary letters], *ʾmš*, combined with *yhw*, and these are the angels of fire, wind and water. Behold, the head is created by three forms of fire, corresponding to *taʿ"q* [corresponding to] fire,

> and the belly [is created of] water, corresponding to *sʿd* [corresponding to] water, and the torso, created from the wind, corresponding to *tm"d* [corresponding to] wind.[102]

This division of the human body originates in *Sefer Yeẕirah* iii, 4, where it states "[There are] three pillars [called] *ʾmš* in the soul: fire, water and wind. The head is created from fire, the belly is created from water, end the torso, which is created from wind, mediates between them." Abulafia added a new element to this division, occurring already in *Baraita de-Mazalot*,[103]in which the astrological signs are divided into three groups, each element belonging to another group: *ṭʿ"q* = *ṭaleh, Aryeh, Qešet* (i.e., Aries, Leo, Sagittarius) = fire; *tm"d* = *Te'omim, Moznayim, Gedi* (i.e., Gemini, Libra, Capricorn) = wind; *sa'ad* = *Sarṭan, ʿAqrav, Deli* (i.e., Cancer, Scorpio, Aquarius) = water. Through this, there came about the view that the three parts of the human body are likewise connected to the three letters.

Abulafia used the letters of the Name of seventy-two letters rather than the initials of the names of the constellations. Viewed in this way, it is clear that according to his approach the navel is no more than one of the nine points of the human body, and that there is no special significance to its contemplation. It is worth mentioning here the magical character of the technique of pronouncing the name of the organ and the letter appointed over it. In *Ḥayyê ha-ʿOlam ha-Ba*, Abulafia writes:

> Head and belly and torso, that is, the head, beginning inside the end. The "head" is the first point that you imagine in it; the "end" is the purpose of the head, and is like a tail to it, and the belly is likewise like a tail to the head, and is the image of the torso, wherein the heart is located. And the image that you ought to imagine at the time of pronunciation, in order to change within that image the nature of [one] part of the bodies, alone or with others, is: think in your heart the name of that thing, and if it is [composed] of two letters, such as *yam* [sea], and you wish to invert it, and the name of the reversal is *yabašah* [dry land], the companion of *yam* with *yabašah*, and this is "beginning and end, *yah*." But the middle is *me-yabeš yam;* behold, *Yah meyabeš Yam* (God makes dry the sea), for He in truth makes the sea into dry land. And pronounce in this image whatever you remember, and thus you will first say *heh*, in the middle of your head, and draw it within your head as if you were contemplating and see the center of your brain, and its central point in your thoughts, and envision the letter *heh* inscribed above it, which guards the existence of the points of your brain.[104]

We may now understand Abulafia's remarks in *Peᶜulat ha-Yez̲irah:*

> Begin at the head of your head, until there the first eight lines to preserve the head, and he shall mention the second eight lines to fulfill the first, in the first order, and he shall mention the eight third lines, the storm and the wind, and one image emerges.[105]

There is no doubt that this refers to the head, the torso and the belly, with the help of a slightly different classification: (a) the head; (b) the first [*qama;* the correct reading may be *qômah*—stature]; (c) end. As in *Ḥayyê ha-ᶜOlam ha-Ba,* the letters of the Name of seventy-two letters, which are pronounced over the organs of the body, are here mentioned in order to create the homunculus, while while in *Ḥayyê ha-ᶜOlam ha-Ba,* "in order to change nature," namely the spiritual nature of man—his psyche. It is worth mentioning that this technique incorporates two different planes of activity: the letters must be pronounced while one envisions in one's mind the place which they influence.

The magical character of this technique is manifested in R. Judah Albotini's *Sullam ha-ᶜAliyah.* Here the author copies almost word for word, the relevant passages from the two major works by Abulafia, *Ôr ha-Sek̲el* and *Ḥayyê ha-ᶜOlam ha-Ba.*[106] Prior to describing the above-mentioned technique, the author writes:[107]

> . . . that the angels were created and all creatures were made from the twenty-two letters and their combinations and their permutations, and as fire by nature warms, and water cools, so do the letters by their nature create all sorts of creatures, and [fulfill] the requests of those who mention them with wisdom and knowledge. Of this our sages said[108] that Bezalel knew how to combine the letters with which heaven and earth were created. Likewise, the other prophets and pious men in each generation, by means of the combination and permutation of letters and their movements, used to perform miracles and wonders and turn about the order of Creation, such as we find it explained in our Talmud[109] that Rabba created a man and sent him to R. Zeira.

5. Preparations for Recitation

Having described the details of the technique of reciting the Divine Name, we shall now discuss the necessary preparations related to this act. In two of his books, *Ḥayyê ha-ᶜOlam ha-Ba* and *Ôr ha-Sekel*, Abulafia describes these conditions:

> . . . At the time that you wish to recite this Ineffable Name as engraved above with its vocalization, adorn yourself and seclude yourself in a special place so that your voice will not be heard to anyone apart from yourself, and purify your heart and your soul from all thoughts of this world.[110]

Elsewhere, he writes:

> Be prepared for thy God, o Israelite! Make thyself ready to direct thy heart to God alone. Cleanse the body and choose a lonely house where none shall hear thy voice. Sit there in thy closet and do not reveal thy secret to any man. If thou canst, do it by day in the house, but it is best if thou completest it during the night. In the hour when thou preparest thyself to speak with the Creator and thou wishest Him to reveal His might to thee, then be careful to abstract all thy thought from the vanities of the world.[111]

A similar description is repeated in *Sefer ha-Ḥešeq:*

> When you wish to recite the Name of seventy-two letters, following the preparation we have mentioned, you must arrange to be alone in a special place, to pronounce the secret of the Ineffable Name, and to separate and isolate yourself from every speaking creature, and from all vanities of [the world, so as not to view them as] attributes [of God]. And also so that there not remain in your heart any thoughts of human or natural things, of either voluntary or necessary [matters], as if you are one who has given a writ of divorce to all forms of the mundane world, as one who has given a testament in the presence of witnesses in which he orders [another] to take care of his wife and his children and his property, and has relieved himself of all involvement and supervision and transferred it from himself and one away.[112]

The two main stipulations appearing here—separation from the vanities of the world and isolation in a special house for the purpose of this recitation—reappear in *Šaʿarê Ẕedeq:*

> He should also ascend to purify his soul above all other wisdoms which he has learned; the reason for this being that, as they are natural and limited, they contaminate the soul and prevent the Divine forms, which are extremely fine, from passing through it . . . therefore one must isolate oneself in a special house, and if the house is such that he will not even hear a voice, this is even better.[113]

A third preparation for the act of recitation is to adorn oneself in *ṭalit* and *tefillin:*

> And wrap yourself in a *ṭallit* and place your *tefillin* on your head and your arm, so that you may be fearful and in awe of the Shekhinah, which is with you at that time. And cleanse yourself and your garments, and if possible let them all be white, for all this greatly assists the intention of fear and love.[114]

Elsewhere, we read, "And sit enwrapped in clean white pure garments or new garments over all your garments, or over your *ṭallit,* and your head adorned with *tefillin.*"[115] To this atmosphere of mystery is added the instruction that "if it is night, light many candles, until it shall enlighten your eyes well."[116] As two contemporary students of hypnotism have attempted to show in a study,[117] to which we shall return later, these instructions constitute a method akin to, though not identical with, that inducing auto-hypnosis.

Once these conditions have been fulfilled, the one contemplating begins to combine letters according to the methods described above. The immediate goal of these combinations is to achieve a state of "warming of the heart":[118]

> And begin to combine small letters with great ones, to reverse them and to permutate them rapidly, until your heart shall be warmed through their combinations and rejoice in their movements and in what you bring about through their permutations; and when you feel thusly that your heart is already greatly heated through the combinations . . . then you are ready to receive the emanated influx.[119]

In *Sefer ha-Melamed,* Abulafia says, "but that of which I have informed you concerning the matter of the secret of combination, that when you mention the words combined, then the divine spirit shall rest upon you through the heating of your heart."[120] We read another formulation of this motif in *Šaʿarê Ẕedeq,* "all these acts must be performed with rapid motion, which warms the thought and increases the longing and joy."[121] This motif of "warming" the heart or the thought is decisive for understanding the nature of the technique suggested by Abulafia; one may easily be misled by the external similarity between the components of Abulafia's path towards the mystical experience and certain detail in Yoga or hesychasm. But beyond the details, which are clearly borrowed from outside sources, Abulafia's way is an original one in terms of the psychological mechanism by which the new consciousness that he reaches is activated. While in the other known techniques—Yoga, Sufism and hesychasm—the goal is to attain the maximum degree of concentration by means of a generally simple formula, to be repeated over and over again, Abulafia's method is based upon the contemplation of a constantly changing object: one must combine the letters and their vowel signs, "sing" and move the head in accordance with the vocalization, and even lift one's hands in the gesture of Priestly Blessing. This combination of constantly changing components is entirely different from what we know of these other techniques. Abulafia is not interested in relaxing the consciousness by means of concentration on a "point," but in purifying it by the necessity to concentrate intensely on such a large number of activities that it is almost impossible at that moment to think about any other subject. By this means, the consciousness is purified of every subject apart from the names being uttered.

The concentrated effort also assures rapid results; in *Ḥayyê ha-ʿOlam ha-Ba,*[122] Abulafia states:

> . . . it is the tradition among us that the influx comes to the complete man when he completes the first verse following the pronunciation of the twenty-four Names, whose mnemonic[123] is "My beloved is white and ruddy: the voice[124] of my beloved knocks" *(Dôdi Ẕaḥ ve-ʿadom; Qol Dôdi Dofeq).*

The point here is that, after one utters the twenty-four Names (symbolized by the *gemaṭria* of the word *dôdi),* each of which consists of three letters, it is possible to reach contact with the archangel Metatron. This intense increase in the level of mental activity at the time of pronunciation places the Abulafian experience under the category of "intense ecstasy," to use the terminology of Marganit Laski.[125] One does not find in Abulafia experiences of contemplative mysticism which are continued over a long period of time. Instead, his approach is intense; for this reason, the duration of the experience is also limited, as it is impossible for the mind to function on such an intensive level over a long period of time. Abulafia's system directs one towards short bursts into Eternal Life, followed by a rapid return to the life of this world. For this reason, the above-mentioned approach, in which Abulafia's technique is seen as a means of bringing about a state of auto-hypnosis, seems difficult to accept.[126] The decrease in the level of bodily and mental activity characteristic of the hypnotic state is absent in Abulafia. In his opinion:

> The more the sublime intellective flow is strengthened within you, the more your external and internal organs become weakened, and your body begins to tremble greatly and mightily, until you think that you shall surely die at that time, for your soul will become separated from your body out of the great joy in attaining and knowing what you have known.[127]

I would like to note one interesting side aspect of Abulafia's technique: namely, that his method is based upon the actual expression or pronunciation of the Ineffable Name, and that, in every possible combination of vocalization and of the letters themselves. According to the Mishnah, "One who pronounces the Name in its letters [i.e., as it is written] has no share in the World to Come."[128] Abulafia claims the exact opposite: that the way to attain the World to Come is precisely, and only, by pronouncing the Ineffable Name. Thus, we find here an extraordinary phenomenon: Abulafia's system is based upon the performance of an act, the recitation of the Holy Name, which constitutes a definite halakhic transgression. It is therefore quite surprising that neither Abulafia nor his opponents even mention this problem.[129] This makes an interesting contrast to a somewhat similar case in the Christian world. I refer to a religious movement which sprang up in Russia in 1913 which saw the Name of God as the principal means for connection with Him; in its view, the recitation of God's Name during worship brings about the unification of the worshipper with God Himself through the very act of pronouncing. Its opponents argued against this view that one is categorically proscribed from uttering God's name unnecessarily.[130]

In conclusion, one can mention the term used by G. Scholem to characterize the above-described path. In several places, he referred to Abulafia's path as a kind of "magic of inwardness,"[131] whose main intention is to change man's inner structure. Abulafia claimed that one could alter both man's nature and his soul.[132] For this reason, while his path ought to be identified as a magical one because it alludes at times to the possibility of changes in external nature, its main intention of influencing the soul deserves the term technique rather than magic. As against the vain attempt to change the outside world, Abulafia at least succeeded in changing his own consciousness, as did the other mystics.

Notes to Chapter One

1. Chapter 16. The text cited here is based primarily upon S. Wertheimer, *Batê Midrašot* I, 92, with minor corrections based upon the text in *Bet ha-Midraš*, III, ed. Jellinek (Chap. 14); cf. Schäfer, *Synopse*, pp. 88-89, par. 204-205. On the Divine Names mentioned in this passage, see Scholem, *Major Trends*, p. 56 and p. 363, nn. 57-58.

2. S. Mussaioff, *Merkavah Šelemah* (Jerusalem, 1921), fol. 4b; on the parallelism between this passage and the previous one, see the note by Wertheimer, *Batê Midrašot* I, 92, n. 75.

3. Printed in *Taʿam Zeqenim* (Frankfort a. M., 1855), p. 54 ff. The version cited here appears in R. Judah al-Barceloni's *Peruš Sefer Yezirah* (Berlin, 1885), p. 104. See also B. Levin, *Ozar ha-Geonim* IV, *Responsa*, p. 17; *idem.*, I, 20, n. 1; MS. New York - JTS 1805 (Enelow Collection, 712) fol. 41a.

4. Levin, *Ozar ha-Geonim* IV, *Responsa*, p. 14; Scholem, *Major Trends*, pp. 49-50. n. 33-35. Jellinek thinks that this reflects Sufi influence, but he has not given his reasons for this statement. See *Beiträge*, no. 22, p. 15. See now also Idel, *Kabbalah: New Perspectives*, pp. 89-91.

5. G. Vajda, "Ètudes sur Qirqisani," *REJ*, vol. 106 (1941-45), p. 107, n. 2.

6. *ʿAruk ha-Šalem* vol. 1, p. 14.

7. Scholem, *Jewish Gnosticism*, p. 54.

8. See his commentary on *Ḥagiggah*, fol. 14b.

9. Rashi on *Ḥagigah* 14b. Compare the *aggadah* cited in *Yalqut Šimʿoni to Genesis, sec. 44*.

10. MS. Cambridge Add. 643, fol. 19a; MS. Oxford 1574, fol. 34b; MS. Vatican 431, fol. 39a. This passage is quoted in the name of Ibn Ezra—with slight changes—in *Sefer Ketav Tammim* of R. Moses Taku, *Ôzar Neḥmad*, III, p. 85, which matches the version found in MS. British Library 756, fol. 170b-171a. On this work, see Dan, *Esoteric Theology*, pp. 143ff.

11. *Ôzar Neḥmad* III, 84. See M. Guedemann, *ha-Torah weha-Ḥayyim be-yemey ha-Bênayim be-Zarfat uve-Aškenaz* pp. 123-124, and Scholem, *Major Trends*, pp. 102-103.

12. MS. Oxford 1812, fol. 55b. On this work, see Dan, *Studies*, pp. 44-57; *idem*, "The Ashkenazi Hasidic *Gates of Wisdom*," in *Hommage a Georges Vajda*,

ed. G. Nahon - Ch. Touati (Louvain, 1980), pp. 183-189.

13. The letters of the forty-two letter Name are here interpreted as the initials of mystical Names of God. This is an ancient approach, which had considerable influence on the medieval mystics; R. Eleazar of Worms seems to have been one of the important avenues through which this approach made its way into Europe. On the subject generally, see Idel, "The World of Angels," pp. 1-15.

14. The interpretation of each of the letters as a Name in itself already appears in the Hekhalot literature; see, for example, *Hekalot Zuṭarti*, ed. R. Elior, p. 28. On the influence of this outlook on Abulafia, and of his outlook on R. Moses Cordovero and on Hasidism, see Idel, "Perceptions of the Kabbalah."

15. Based upon *Sanhedrin*, fol. 91a; see Idel, "The Concept of Torah," p. 28, n. 20.

16. On this abbreviation as a reference to R. Eleazar, see Dan, *Esoteric Theology*, pp. 118–127.

17. Chapter 41. Printed by A. Jellinek in *Kokvê Yizḥaq* 34 (1867), p. 16. The work was composed at the beginning of the second half of the thirteenth century.

18. A certain parallel to the opinion of Ibn Latif appears in the words of an anonymous author whose work was preserved in MS. Mainz - Academie 107, fol. 98a.

> And now I shall point out what the three times *YHWH* refers. Know that there are two [kinds] of comprehension which one may comprehend of Him, may He be blessed. The first is that He exists: this comprehension is the one spoken of when they say that we may understand God through His deeds, for it is impossible without there being a first cause. The second is that, even though we have not yet reached it, we are confident that in the future awesome things are to be generated, from which we may recognize the rank [*maʿalah*] of the cause which generated them, on a level greater than that which we know now, in what has been generated in the act of Creation. And albeit that this comprehension is greater than the former one, the common element of both is that through His actions one knows the Active Agent. But these comprehensions differ in that the former is a comprehension of his existence, and the latter is comprehension of his rank. But there is yet a third [kind of] comprehension, with which created beings are not involved at all, and this is the comprehension of the essence, which is hidden from all beings but God alone, who alone comprehends His essence, and none other. And these three comprehensions are alluded to in the verse, "God has reigned, God does reign, God will reign forever and ever."

The awesome deeds referred to here are evidently parallel to Ibn Latif's remarks concerning the Divine will, on the one hand, and the miracles and wonders performed by means of the supernal will, in the quotation below from R. Moses of Burgos, on the other hand.

19. For Ibn Gabirol's influence on Ibn Latif in the identification of 'will' and 'speech,' see S. O. Heller-Wilenski, "The Problem of the Authorship of the Treatise *Šaʿar ha-Šamayim*, Ascribed to Abraham Ibn Ezra" (Heb.), *Tarbiẕ*, vol. 32 (1963), pp. 290–291, and n. 74.

20. See Scholem, *Les Origines*, p. 356.

21. MS. Oxford 1580, fol. 149a. On "Torah, Wisdom and Prophecy," see also below, Chap. 4, n. 34.

22. The reference is to R. Ishmael, R. Nehunyah ben ha-Kanah and R. Akiba, "who are among the great ones of Israel among the authors, such as *Pirqe Hekalot, Sefer ha-Bahir* and *Otiyot de-Rabbi ʿAqiva*," as Abulafia explains below, in fol. 148a.

23. *Peruš Šem- ben M"B Otiyot*, printed by Scholem in *Tarbiẕ*, vol. 5 (1934), p. 56.

24. See the chapter devoted to this subject in Idel, *Abraham Abulafia*, pp. 133ff.

25. *Sitrê Torah*, MS. Paris - BN 774, fol. 156a; *Sefer ha-Ôt*, pp. 80–81.

26. *Sitrê Torah, ibid.*, fol. 157b. The verbs "combine" and "be purified" are different forms of the root *ẕrf*.

27. *Mafteaḥ ha-Raʿayon*, MS. Vatican 291, fol. 21a.

28. See the chapter on language in Idel, *Abraham Abulafia*, pp. 143–146.

29. *Ôẕar ʿEden Ganuz*, MS. Oxford 1580, fol. 161a.

30. MS. Jerusalem 8° 148, fol. 63b.

31. *Liqquṭei Ḥamiẕ*, MS. Oxford 2239, fol. 113a.

32. MS. Oxford 1580, fol. 706b.

33. *Peruš Šir ha-Širim*, MS. Oxford 343, fol. 49a.

34. MS. München 408, fols. 65a–65b, also published in *Sefer ha- Peliʾah*, fol. 35b. On the dialogic element in Abulafia's mystical experience, see below, chap. 3.

35. On *Maʿaseh Merkavah* = *šem be-šem* = 682, see Idel, *Abraham Abulafia*, pp. 179–181.

36. *Ôr ha-Sekel*, MS. Vatican 233, fol. 95a, copied in *Pardes Rimmonim*, fol. 92c, under the title *Sefer ha-Niqqud*. Compare, against this, the table appearing in *Ner Elohim*, MS. München 10, fol. 149a–149b and 150b, which differs in a number of respects from that in *Ôr ha-Sekel*. A specimen of the table of

letter-combinations which we have printed appears as well in Tocci, "Technique of Pronunciation," pp. 222, 229, which he printed from *Ôr ha-Sekel;* he likewise noted the source of the section in *Pardes Rimmonim* in *Ôr ha-Sekel.*

For similar phenomena of combinations of vowels in ancient pagan magic see P. C. Miller "In Praise of Nonsense" in *Classical Mediterranean Spirituality* ed. A. H. Armstrong (New York, 1986) pp. 482-499.

37. MS. Vatican 233, fol. 97a.

38. *ʿEser Hawayot,* MS, München 43, fol. 219a, as well as in several passages in *Sefer ha-Šem.* The section was copied from the works of R. Eleazar in *Minḥat Yehudah* by R. Judah Ḥayyat *(Maʿareket ha-Elohut,* fol. 197b) and from there to *Pardes Rimmonim,* fol. 92b. The expression, "the book of the structures [*maʿarakot*] of the living God" is an allusion to *Maʿareket ha-Elohut,* R. Moses Cordovero substituting the author for its commentary. The first Spanish Kabbalist to use an Ashkenazic system in his books was R. David b. Judah he-Hasid, in Matt *Mar'ot ha-Zov'ot,* p. 95. This source was also known to R. Moses Cordovero, who mentions him as "the author of *Sefer Ôr Zaruʿa,*" which, as is known, is the work of R. David. Compare *Pardes Rimmonim,* fol. 93b with the citation given in *Mar'ot ha-Zov'ot.* R. David's contemporary, R. Menahem Recanati, also alludes to this system in his *Peruš la-Torah,* (Jerusalem, 1961) fol. 49b.

39. See the chapter on language in Idel, *Abraham Abulafia,* sec. 3 and n. 31. Abulafia based the use of the word *noṭariqon* upon widespread knowledge in his circle. See MS. Berlin - Tübingen Or. 941, fol. 88a, which contains a text very similar to pt. 3 of *Ginnat Egoz,* in which the word *notariqon* appears with the vocalization of five different vowels.

40. On Exodus 3:15.

41. M. Steinschneider (*Hebräische Bibliographie,* vol. 21, p. 35) alludes to the possibility of the influence of *ha-ʿAgulot ha-Raʿayoniot* on the technique of circles in *Ḥayyê ha-ʿOlam ha-Ba.* However, it is difficult to substantiate such an assumption in light of the fact that Abulafia does not at all mention *ha-ʿAgulot ha Raʿayoniot,* despite the fact that this was a widespread work among the Jews.

42. MS. Rome - Angelica 38, fol. 38b; MS. München 285, f. 30a.

43. MS. München 285 fol. 102a.

44. MS. München 58, fol. 320a.

45. George Anawati, "Le nom supreme de Dieu," *Etudes de philosophie musulmane* (Paris, 1974), pp. 404–405.

46. Extensive bibliographical material on breathing and on the various techniques of pronunciation was gathered by Tocci in the notes to his article,

"Technique of Pronunciation." However, his analysis of the details of Abulafia's system of breathing is based upon a passage from *Ôr ha-Sekel* and upon the printed portion of *Ḥayyê ha-ʿOlam ha-Ba;* he was unaware of several important discussions concerning breathing technique, which we will cite below, for which reason his study is incomplete.

47. MS. New York - JTS 1897, fols. 86b–87a.

48. Avot 4:1.

49. These are the first and last letters of the Name of forty-two letters.

50. *Ševaʿ Netivot ha-Torah,* p. 25; *Ḥayyê ha-ʿOlam ha-Ba,* MS. Oxford 1582, fol. 54b.

51. J. H. Woods, *The Yoga System of Patanjali* (Cambridge, Mass.: Harvard University Press, 1966), p. 193; Yoga-Sutra II, 49.

52. The accepted interpretation of *kumbhaka* is "halting"—an interruption in the breathing activity after one draws in air. In one place only have I succeeded in finding an interpretation suitable to Abulafia as well: in the French translation of the lectures of Vivekananda on the sutra of Patanjalil, Jean Herbert, the translator, remarks that the meaning of *kumbhaka* is a halt before or after the breath. The former interpretation suits the idea of rest in Abulafia, but I cannot verify the reliability of this interpretation. See S. Vivekananda, *Les Yogas practiques* (Paris, 1939), p. 551, note 1.

53. MS. Vatican 528, fol. 71b.

54. MS. Vatican 233, fols. 109b-110a. Copied by R. Moses Cordovero in *Pardes Rimmonim,* fol. 92c-d, as *Sefer ha-Niqqud.*

55. Ibid, fols. 110a–110b.

56. The straight ones are read as *Aleph - Yod,* the inverted ones as *Yod -Aleph.*

57. MS. Oxford 1582, fol. 54b: "And between each letter you are allowed to wait aad to prepare yourself and breathe for the duration of three breaths of the breaths of pronunciation."

58. The sentence "but he is not allowed . . . together" appears twice; I have eliminated the repetition.

59. *Mafteaḥ ha-Šemot* MS. New York, JTS 1897, fol. 87a. It is worth noting that, despite the difficulty in uttering letters while breathing, such an instruction does appear among the Sufis, who make use of a technique combining pronouncing while breathing and emitting air. See Anawati-Gardet, *Mystique musulmane* (Paris, 1961), pp. 208–209.

60. In Sephirotic Kabbalah, the forty-two letter Name serves as a symbol for the attribute of *Gevurah*—the Sefirah of rigor.

61. MS. Oxford 1582, fol. 61b.

62. *G' nešimot* (three breaths) › 814 › *nešimah aḥat* › *ha-saṭan yamut -masṭinot* (one breath; Satan will die; enemies) > *ha-hasagot be-dam ha-adam* (the comprehension in the blood of man) > *sin dalet yod* (the letter of *Sadday* written out in full) › *ḥotam šeni* (the second seal) › *hemit ha-šedim* (killed the demons) › *ba-ḥotam mašiaḥ* (with the seal of Messiah) › *memit ha-dam ha-raᶜ* (kills the bad blood) › *memit middah raᶜ ah* (kills the bad attribute) › *met mi-yad yeqarah* (dies of a dear hand). There may be a connection between the positive valuation of breathing as a means of strengthening the spiritual element, and the idea of the Orphic poets, quoted and rejected by Aristotle in *De Anima* 410b, 28, that the soul is drawn in by breathing.

63. MS. Oxford 1582, fols. 54b-55a. *Y"Ḥ nesimot* (18 breaths) > *šenot ḥayyim* (years of life) > *ḥayye nešamot* (life of the soul) > *mešanney ḥayut* (the changers of vitality) › *ḥayut ha-nešamah* (vitality of the soul). *Šene neḥirim* (two nostrils) › 678 › *ᶜaravot* › *neḥire nešamah* (nostrils of the soul) › *šenaim keruvim* (two cherubs) › *šeney murkavim* (two compounded) › *makriḥe ha-Šekinah* (those who force the Shekhinah). See also MS. Jerusalem 8° 1303 fol. 55b.

64. Compare *Gan Naᶜul,* MS. München 58, fol. 322a:

> As it is said [Gen. 2:7], "And he breathed into their nostrils the breath of life," and one who weighs the letters must contemplate the secret of the recitation of the names, with the hidden breaths sealed by all the wisdoms, and in them he shall live after death.

Compare also Naḥmanides in his commentary to Ecclesiastes, *Kitvê Ramban,* ed. Chavel Jerusalem, 1963 I, 192:

> And with the unique Name [there are] letters created and revealed miracles performed in the world . . . for with His Name He spoke and the world was, and there is no chance in his words, but through them he splits the Sea and the Jordan.

See also note 67 below.

65. Abulafia derives the word *mal'ak* (angel) from *mel'akah* (labor). See *Ḥayyê ha-Nefeš,* MS. München 408, fols. 27a–b; *Imrê Šefer* MS. München 40, fol. 225b, etc.

66. *Mafteaḥ ha-Šemot,* MS. New York JTS 1897, fol. 87a.

67. See Idel, "The World of the Imagination," pp. 168–171.

68. The concluding poem of *Ḥayyê ha-ᶜOlam ha-Ba,* MS. Oxford 1582, fol. 82a.

69. Psalm 150:6.

70. *Genesis Rabba* 14:9, ed. Theodor-Albeck, p. 134.

71. *Mafteaḥ ha-Šemot*, MS. New York JTS 1897, fol. 87a. Compare also *Ôr ha-Sekel*, MS. Vatican 233, fol. 77b.

72. *Šaʿar ha-Yirʾah*, Chap. 10. The section is also quoted in *Midraš Talpiyot* of R. Elijah ha-Kohen, fol. 15b.

73. Deuteromomy 8:3.

74. The division of the hour into 1080 seconds, as well as the 1080 combinations, also appears in Abulafia, but he does not draw any connection between them in his known works, no doubt because no connection of this type exists in actuality. See: *Iš Adam*, MS. Rome - Angelica 38, fol. 5a; *Peruš Sefer Yezirah*, MS. Paris 774, fol. 60a; *Ôzar Gan ʿEden*, MS. Oxford 1580, fol. 40b; and many other places. See also the introduction to *Or Yaqar*, printed in R. Abraham Azulai's *Ôr ha-Ḥamah* (Bene Barak, 1973), III, fol. 44c sec, 73 on *Bamidbar*.

75. *Šaʿar Pirṭe ha-Šemot*, Chaps. 1–2; as is well known, R. Moses Cordovero was the teacher of R. Elijah de Vidas.

76. MS. Oxford 1582, fols. 54a–54b, printed by Scholem, *Abulafia*, p. 23.

77. *Berakot*, fol, 22a.

78. MS. Vatican 233, fols. 110a–110b; Scholem, *Abulafia*, p. 226. See also J. L. Blau, *The Christian Interpretation of the Cabala in the Renaissance* (New York, 1965), p. 69, n. 12.

79. MS. New York JTS 1801, fols. 9a–b; MS. British Library 749, fol. 12a–b, with omissions. See also *Ner Elohim*, MS. München 10, fol. 166b.

80. Psalms 141:2.

81. (Wien, 1860), p. 32. In the printed version the word *magiʿot* appears there, which I have corrected in accordance with the meaning here. Here, it refers to the letters of the Ineffable Name, which move the letters of *Alef Bet*, an idea which appears already in *Kuzari* IV:25, and was already known among the Kabbalists of Gerona, and afterwards by R. Joseph of Hamadan.

82. See Ibn Ezra's commentary to Exodus 3:15, which is also cited in the section on circles, below, Chap. 3.

83. MS. Oxford 1582, fol. 52a.

84. *Ibid*,, fols. 57b–58a. On the connection between closing one's eyes and the use of mystical technique, see Idel, "*Hitbodedut* as Concentration," *Studies*, essay VII, Appendix A.

85. Printed by Gershom Scholem, from the commentary of R. Joseph Ashkenazi to *Parašat Berešit*, in his article, "The True Author of the

Commentary to *Sefer Yezirah* attributed to the Rabad and his Works" (Heb.), *Qiryat Sefer* 4 (1927–28), p. 299; see also Scholem's remarks, *ibid.*, n. 2; Hallamish, *Kabbalistic Commentary*, p. 223.

86. *Sefer Yezirah* I:9.

87. Compare *Genesis Rabbah* 17:5, ed. Theodor-Albeck p. 156.

88. The problem of the contemplation of colors and lights in Kabbalah will be discussed in a separate work, in which I shall analyze this passage from R. Joseph from other aspects. Abulafia does not mention colors at all in his works, while elsewhere, in the epistle *We-Zot li-Yihudah*, p. 16, Abulafia criticizes the contemplation of lights as being of a lower type of Kabbalah than that which he advocates. See also the quotation alluded to below, p. 00.

89. Ed. Goldreich, p. 217; see also Gottlieb, *Studies*, p. 235.

90. Deuteronomy 11:22.

91. Deut. 10:20.

92. Deut. 4:4.

93. Ed. Goldreich, p. 89.

94. MS. Paris—Seminaire Israelite de France 108, fol. 95a, and compare MS. Oxford 1943 British Library 768, fols. 190b-191a, and *ibid.*, 771/2. MS. Paris 108 contains sections from both *Me'irat ʿÊnayim* (see fol. 92a) and an anonymous work of Abulafia (fol. 82a–89a). The forming of the letters of the Name with colors, while connecting matter to Sefirot, appears as well in MS. Sasson 919, p. 229, which also includes material from the circle of R. Isaac of Acre.

95. There is no doubt that R. Isaac of Acre's remarks were influenced by Maimonides' understanding of providence in *Guide*, III:51, albeit his intellectual approach was given a magical significance.

96. The circle used by Abulafia in his technique turns afterwards into a subject revealed in his vision.

97. Henry Corbin, *Creative Imagination in the Sufism of Ibn Arabi* (London, 1970), p. 234, n. 41–42.

98. MS. Oxford 1582, fol. 62a.

99. *Ibid.*, fols. 63a–b.

100. *Ibid.*, fol. 12b.

101. *Abulafia*, p. 170.

102. MS. Oxford 1582, fol. 12b.

103. See Gad Ben-Ami Zarfati, "Introduction to *Baraita de-Mazalot*" (Heb.), *Bar Ilan; Sefer ha-Šanah* 3 (1968), p. 67 and n. 34. This division appears

in many places in medieval literature; see Wertheimer's *Batê Midrašot* II, p. 26, and the comments of Abraham Epstein, *Mi-Qadmoniot ha-Yehudim* (Jerusalem, 1957), p. 82. Abulafia himself also used this distinction in his anonymous work in MS. Sasson 290, p. 235, and in *Ôẕar ʿEden Ganuz,* MS. Oxford 1580 fol. 81a. It is worth noting that the concept of "forms" (*ẕurot),* which appears in the section quoted from *Ḥayyê ha-ʿOlam ha-Ba,* means "constellations"; see I. Efrat, *Jewish Philosophy in the Middle Ages* (Heb.), II, pp. 93–94.

104. MS. Oxford 1582, fol. 61a.

105. Idel, *Abraham Abulafia,* p. 131.

106. Published by Scholem in *Qiryat Sefer* 22 (1945), p, 161.

107. *Ibid,,* p. 165.

108. *Berakot,* fol. 55a.

109. *Sanhedrin,* fol. 65b.

110. *Ôr ha-Sekel,* MS. Vatican 233, fol. 1O9a.

111. *Ḥayyê ha-ʿOlam ha-Ba,* MS. Oxford 1582, fol. 51b; Scholem, *Abulafia,* p. 210. English translation taken from Scholem, *Major Trends,* pp. 136–137. From this text, Ch. G, Nauert, *Agrippa and the Crisis of Renaissance Thought* (Urbana, Ill., 1965), p. 289, n. 7, concludes that there may have been some connection between Abulafia and Agrippa, although at present there is no evidence to support such an opinion. Compare the words brought in the name of R. Elijah of London, quoted below in n. 129.

112. MS. New York JTS 1801, fol. 9a; MS. British Library 749, fol. 12b.

113. MS. Jerusalem 8° 148, fols. 71b–72a. This is the source for the description in *Sullam ha-ʿAliyah* of R. Judah al-Botini; See Scholem *Kabbalistic Manuscripts,* pp. 226–227. The language is more similar to *Šaʿarê Ẕedeq* than to *Ḥayyê ha-ʿOlam ha-Ba,* as thought by Scholem, *ibid.,* n. 5, even though Abulafia's book greatly influenced the quotation from *Sullam ha-ʿAliyah.*

114. *Ḥayyê ha-ʿOlam ha-Ba,* MS. Oxford 1582, fol. 51b; Scholem, *Abulafia,* p. 210; and *Sefer Sullam ha-ʿAliyah,* printed in his *Kabbalistic Manuscripts,* p. 227. The motif of the "white garments" appears in a number of texts connected with the recitation of the Divine Name. The recitation of the Ineffable Name is described in a work entitled *Šimuš Rišon le-Girsat ha-Sefarim ha-Ḥiẕoniim,* MS. Bologna, University No. 2914, fol. 55a. Among the actions which precede this recitation are immersion in a ritual bath, fasting, and wearing white clothes, See also the ceremony of creating the *golem,* in the section quoted by Scholem, *On the Kabbalah,* p. 185, Compare his words quoted in the name of R. Elijah of Londres (London) in MS. Sasson 290, p. 381:

When you wish . . . to make your question, turn your heart from all other involvements, and unify your intentions and your thoughts to enter *Pardes.* Sit alone in awe, wrapped in *ṭallit* and with *tefillin* on your head, and begin [to recite] 'Mikhtam for David' [Ps. 16], the entire psalm . . . and read them with their melodies.

115. *Ôr ha-Seḵel,* MS. Vatican 233, fol. 109a.

116. *Hayyê ha-ʿOlam ha-Ba,* MS. Oxford 1582, fol, 52a; Scholem, *Kabbalistic Manuscripts* p. 227.

117. M. Bowers - S. Glasner , "Autohypnotic Aspects of the Kabbalistic Concept of Kavanah," *Journal of Clinical and Experimental Hypnosis* 6 (1958), pp. 3–23. The authors rely almost exclusively upon the material appearing in G. Scholem on Abulafia and his disciples, and also analyze phenomena pertaining to the Hekhalot literature and to M. H. Luzzatto. It should be noted that the assumption that the ecstatic situation of the "descenders to the Merkavah" is the result of self-hypnosis already appears in the article by Yitzhak Heinemann, "Die Sektenfrommigkeit der Therapeuten," MGWJ 78 (1934), p. 110, n. 1.

118. On the sensation of heat among various mystics, see C. Rowland, "The Visions of God in Apocalyptic Literature," *Journal for the Study of Judaism,* vol. 10 (1979), p. 141, and n. 10.

119. *Ḥayyê ha-ʿOlam ha-Ba,* MS. Oxford 1582, fol. 52a.

120. MS. Paris - BN 680, fol. 293a.

121. MS. Jerusalem 8° 148, fol. 73a.

122. MS. Oxford 1582, fol. 53a.

123. Song of Songs 5:10.

124. *Ibid.*, v. 2.

125. M. Laski, *Ecstasy* (New York, 1968), pp.47 ff.

126. See above, n. 117.

127. *Ḥayyê ha-ʿOlam ha-Ba,* MS. Oxford 1582, fol. 52a.

128. *Sanhedrin,* fol. 90b.

129. Compare the things attributed to R. Elijah of London (see above, n. 114), who writes, after what is cited there:

Thereafter he should bow on his knees with his face to the east and say as follows . . . and think of the Name which is written before him, but not utter it with his lips . . . and the Name of four letters, which is divided on the the perfection of the vocalization into thirty-eight sections, and they are not to

> be pronounced, but he is only to direct his thoughts to them. (MS. Sasson 290, p. 381).

And compare to MS. Sasson 919, p. 210:

> I, R. Isaac of Acre, felt in myself a great longing to gaze at the *milui* [i.e., the plene writing of each letter] of the Ineffable Name in all its ways, for I already knew that the ways of *heh* and *waw* four and four, thus, *h ha hh hy w ww waw wyw*. But the first one has only one *milui*, thus, *ywd*. But now guard yourself and guard your soul lest you read the letters *hhwyh*, and do not read them, for whoever pronounces the Name by its letters as they are written has no portion in the World to Come. See this and ask your soul, but contemplate them.

See also below Chap. 3, pp. 304–305.

130. R. Fulop-Miller, *The Mind and Face of Bolshevism* (London, New York, 1927), pp. 258–260. The author, who points out the origins of this movement in Mt. Athos in Greece, and sees a continuation thereof in hesychasm, which is likewise based upon the recitation of the name of Jesus, claims (p. 260) that the source of his approach lies in "Jewish Kabbalah," but there is no proof for such a connection.

131. Scholem, *Major Trends*, p. 145.

132. See Idel, *Abraham Abulafia*, pp. 129–133.

Chapter Two

Music and Ecstatic Kabbalah

There are two main aspects to the association between mystical ecstasy and music in the ecstatic Kabbalah: on the one hand, music served as an analogy for the technique giving rise to ecstasy and the ecstatic experience; on the other, it was an important element of the actual technique of Abulafia and his students. We shall first consider music as an analogy.

1. Analogy for Ecstasy-Evoking Techniques

In *Gan Na^cul,* we find a passage containing a comparison between the influence exerted by music and the combination of letters:[1]

> Know that [letter-] combination is like the hearing of the ears, for the ear hears and the sounds are combined according to the form of the tune and the sound-enunciation.[2] Witness the (stringed instruments) *kinnôr* and *nevel;* their sounds are combined, and with the combination of the sounds the ears hear variation and exchange[3] in the pangs of love.[4] The strings which are struck with the right hand and with the left hand vibrate, bringing the sweet taste to the ears, from which sound moves to the heart, and from the heart to the spleen.[5] In the meantime, joy is renewed through the pleasure of the variation of the tunes, which can only be renewed by the form of the combinations. That is, the player plucks the first string, which is analogous to the letter *alef,* for example, and it moves from there to one string,[6] to *bet, gimel dalet,* or *hê*—that is to say, a second, third, fourth, or fifth string, as we are using five as an

> example. From there the pluckings are transposed, and by means of transposition tunes and melodies are brought about which transpose the heart by means of the ears. Thus also is the matter of combining letters from the outside with the pen, in the form of the combinations of the letters (*ʾalef mem šin*), as follows: *ʾmš, ʾšm, mšʾ, mʾš, sʾm, šmʾ*; thus all cognates and similar things.

There are parallels between music and the technique of combination in three areas: 1) Music-making and letter-combination operate by means of the harmony which is produced by the conjoining of two different principles: two different instruments (*kinnôr* and *nevel*), two different tones from the same musical instrument, or the joining of two different letters in the process of combination. The movement from one string to another described by Abulafia is similar to a certain technique of combination which begins with a particular letter and either moves to the adjoining letter or skips over one or more letters: i.e., *A-B, B-G, G-D*, etc., or *A-G, B-D, G-H*, etc.[7] 2) Letter-combination, like music, gladdens the heart; it does so by means of the "hidden things which are found in the transposition of the letters," wherein the joy comes from uncovering the secrets. 3) Like music, letter-combination is an activity which takes place outside the soul, influencing the soul inwards.

This parallel between music and letter-combination is repeated in *Sefer ha-Ḥešeq*. There, Abulafia writes:

> You must first verify in your heart, anyway that you can verify it, that the letters are in essence signs and hints in the image of characters and parables, and were created because they are instruments by which man is taught the way of understanding; and to us they are in the image of the strings of the *kinnôr*. For by means of the production of sound when it is plucked on the string with the plectrum with the shift of the plucking from string to string, and with the combination of the sound-enunciations which are produced by it, the soul of the man wishing to be joyous is awakened to joy, happiness, and gladness, and it receives from this its pleasure and much benefit to the soul.[8]

Abulafia's student, the anonymous author of *Šaʿarê Ẕedeq*, largely follows in the footsteps of his teacher when he writes:[9]

> And how the letters transpose, change, conjoin, separate, and jump about in the first letters, in the middle of the word, and at the end of the word, and the whole word, and the kind of the form of combination of vowel points, and their pronunciation, and these are carried over to the second degree, which is the form of the sound

> and melody, until its melodic sound is made to be like *kinnôr*, putting in motion his soul to the fineness of the melody and its variation. Then the true pronunciation of the letter is revealed to him, according to their special natures which function by means of the variation of melody, in a motion working in his soul. Just as music affects the [proper] balance [10] of the body, so has this an effect on the soul by the power of the Name.

When we pronounce the various combinations of the letters, we affect the soul alone, whereas the influence of music is perceptible both in the soul and in the body. There is an important distinction to be added between the citation from *Gan Naᶜul* and that from *Šaᶜarê Ẕedeq:* the influence of the revelation of the secrets—that is, the intellectual principle behind the process of letter-combination—in the latter passage turns into an influence on sensation: the voice of the one uttering the letters of the Name is pleasant, as is the sound of the harp, and thus influences the soul.[11] Music is also used as an analogy for 'prophecy' itself.

2. Analogy for 'Prophecy'

The comparison between the mystical experience and the hearing of music[12] (a motif which often appears in mystical literature) serves to describe the actual occurrence in terms of a non-verbal medium, which makes it possible to compare the sensation at the moment of the experience with something familiar from everyday experience. Abulafia's approach is different: in his view, the analogy of music serves to describe the mechanism of the coming about of 'prophecy' itself. In *Mafteaḥ ha-Raᶜayon,* we read:[13]

> It is known that sound is heard more loudly in a place which is hollow or pierced, due to the purity of the spiritual air which enters therein, as in the case of the *kinnôr* and similar musical instruments, which produce sound without any speech, and so also the concavities of the upper stories, caves, mountains, bathhouses, ruins, etc., whose interior is hollow. Notice that from them there is also produced a sound like the sound of one who is speaking. By means of this secret you will understand the meaning of 'Moses spake and God answered him by a voice' [Ex. 19:19], i.e., in a voice similar to that of Moses.[14] You must know that the body of man is full of holes and cavities, from which you may understand how the Shekhinah dwells in the body which is pierced and [contains] cavities and which produces speech.

Here, Abulafia compares the body to the *kinnôr* or some other musical instrument, as the human body is filled with cavities and holes which are apt to produce a sound when a wind blows. This process is similar to the Holy Spirit—the Shekhinah—moving in the human body, giving rise to prophecy. The analogy of the human body to the *kinnôr* appears in *Imrê Šefer:*[15]

> Just as the owner of a garden has the power to water the garden at will by means of rivers, so does the one making music with the Name have the power to water at will his limbs by means of his soul, through the Almighty, Blessed Name; and this is [the meaning of] "and it came to pass, when the minstrel played, that the hand of the Lord came upon him" [II Kings 3:15]—this is the *kinnôr* hung above David's bed, which used to play of itself and praise Him with the *nevel* and *kinnôr* [Ps. 150:].[16] But this would only be after receiving the divine effluence, which is called the seventy-two letter name, together with the understanding of its paths.

It seems to me that the analogy of the garden to the body also extends to the *kinnôr:* just as the garden and the body are passive, receiving the action of the gardener and the musician with the Name of the seventy-two letters, so also does David's *kinnôr* play "of itself" when the divine effluence reverberates within it. Abulafia here appears to suggest that David's *kinnôr* resembles the human body: like the *kinnôr,* man also makes music "of himself" when the wind blows. Possible support for this interpretation may be found in *Ḥayyê ha-ʿOlam ha-Ba*:

> The body is like a garden, which is the master of vegetation, and the soul is Eden, which is the master of delights: and the body is planted in it. The secret of *gan ʿeden* [Garden of Eden] is *ʿad naggen* [through playing] for prophecy dwells when *ʿeved naggen* [the servant plays?], e.g., when the minstrel played [II Kings 3:15], as in the case of Elisha.[17]

If we have deciphered Abulafia's meaning correctly, then we are confronted with the widespread analogy of man to the *kinnôr* or *nevel* upon which God plays music. This motif is hinted at as early as Philo;[18] since Montanus[19] it appears explicitly several times in mystical literature,[20] nor is it absent from Hebrew literature. The Midrash[21] speaks of prophets as those "who were like an instrument full of speech." R. Judah the Hasid describes the Glory as a *nevel* upon which God plays in order to arouse the prophet to prophesy.[22]

This topic appears several times in Kabbalistic literature.[23] The motif later reached Hasidism, which spoke of converting the musician to a musical instrument, and of the analogy of the shofar, which produces a sound when one blows into it, with the prophet, who prophesies only when God dwells within him.[24]

3. Music as a Means of Attaining 'Prophecy'

In the above-cited passages, music does not play any part in the manifestation of 'prophecy', although such a function is among the most ancient ascribed to it. It fulfills such a role in the Bible,[25] in the Talmud,[26] and in the medieval literature.[27] In the latter period, there was a widely-held view that music performed a two-fold function: through its mediation, 'prophecy' descended directly upon the individual; moreover, it was within the capacity of music to prepare the intellect, the instrument of 'prophecy', and thereby facilitate its reception. Medieval authors considered music as an integral part of their theoretical education and as a means of strengthening their intellectual powers. Isaac ibn Latif writes:[28] "The science of music is a propaedeutic one, leading to improvement of the psychological disposition as well as to understanding of some of the higher intellectual principles." On the other hand, Solomon ibn Adret writes:[29]

> With the increase in joy, the intellectual power which resides in the soul is fortified and is better prepared to grasp the intelligibles, as was the case with Elisha, "bring me a minstrel." As our Sages of Blessed Memory taught,[30] "The Shekhinah does not dwell as a result of inaction or sadness, but rather through a joyous thing."

Joseph ibn Caspi states:[31] "Poetic words: the whole art of song-making performed on musical instruments which have the effect of rousing the intelligent soul, and which was termed in ancient times music." The author of *Ôr ha-Menorah*, who belonged to Abulafia's school, wrote in the fourteenth century:[32]

> If he shall praise with [his] voice he is more likely to bring pleasure to the soul and lead it to the Holy Spirit, as it is said, "with *nevel* and *tof* and *ḥalil* and *kinnôr* before them, and they shall prophesy"[I Sam. 10:5], and so also in the matter of Elisha [II Kings 3:15] "but now bring me a minstrel." You likewise find that in the Eternal House [i.e., the Temple] they played and performed upon musical instruments. You know their saying, "the most important music

> was by means of instruments," although some said, "the most important music was vocal."[33] It was all through the enunciation of sound alone, rising and falling. The main intention was to arouse the soul to make use of all of its glorious power, which is the power of intellectual attainment.

Another interesting testimony is given by an early fourteenth century Byzantine kabbalist, R. Isaiah ben Joseph, who writes:

> Know that the prophet, when he wishes to prophesy, must first isolate himself for a determined period of time and perform his ablutions. Afterwards he settles into his special place, and he then summons musicians on various instruments who play for him and sing spiritual songs, and he will deal with certain chapters of this book. . . . Afterwards the musicians will begin to play, as we explained in the eighth chapter of *Sefer ha-Hašgaḥah,* which is the fourth part of our treatise *Hašqafat ha-Sekel,* and there is no need to repeat it here.[34]

These are the views of some savants of Abulafia's period. We find a different point of view on music in the writings of two other contemporaries, both of them mystics. One of them, Isaac ben Jacob ha-Kohen, maintains that the science of music was known to those who served in the Temple and to the prophets, who employed it in order to receive the Holy Spirit:[35]

> Those who served in our glorious Temple were expert in the subtleties of the *nequddôt*[36] which went forth from their mouths when they made music, with the known measure and references to the musical instruments of David, "the most pleasant of Israel's singers," of blessed memory. At the moment when [the melody] emanates from their mouths with awe, reverence, holiness and pleasant voice, rising and falling, extending and shortening,[37] by the Holy Spirit, of specified measure according to the prophets of blessed memory, and on the basis of the pattern of the notes *(nequddôt)* drawn according to the melodic [evolution] of the rising and falling sounds . . .[38] some of them of high [pitch] and others of low [pitch],[39] some are small and others large [rhythmic values?]. The measures and the drawings [of the notes according to] the melodic [evolution] of the sounds are all based upon and directed to the inner spiritual qualities—then the Holy Spirit awakens, sparkles,[40] and craves.

We find similar remarks in *ha-ʿAmmud ha-Smali* [Treatise on the Left Emanation] of Isaac ha-Kohen:

> The High Priest . . . knows how to fully direct his concentration on all inner and outer emanations, in order to exert influence by means of the secret of the holy Seraphim; his elevation is according to either his closeness or remoteness, and his power is awakened by the sweetness of the song and the pure prayer. So do the musicians direct their fingers, according to their elevation and understanding, [placing them] on the keyholes of [wind instruments] *kinnôrôt* [!] and [on] strings, arousing the song and the melody to direct their hearts toward God. Thus the Blessing is aroused and the Shekhinah resides in them, each one according to his performance and according to his understanding.[41]

The first passage had an influence on Isaac ha-Kohen's follower's student, Isaac ben Solomon ibn Abi Sahula, who studied Kabbalah with Moses of Burgos.[42] In his commentary on Song of Songs, Isaac ibn Abi Sahula writes:[43]

> Properly speaking, the Sage should have called it "Song of Songs" and no other name, because of the science of song which was known among that nation in that period. The Levites used to perform according to it in the Temple at the time of service, as it is written, "he shall minister in the name of the Lord his God," [Deut. 18:7] and we learned in our tradition: "What service is it which is in the name of God? One must say that it is that of song."[44] This singing was a great and awesome matter, "a crown of glory and a diadem of beauty" [Isa. 28:5]. By means of the melodic song, both vocal and instrumental, the soul is awakened and the Holy Spirit shines within it and it is elevated, understanding things far more sublime that it had understood beforehand. This praiseworthy song is the sound emanating from the musicians' mouth with awe, reverence, and holiness, rising and falling, extending and shortening as if it were emanating from the song of the heavenly angels. By moving[45] in known measures, which are understood by the pattern of the notes [*nequddôt*] which are drawn according to the melodic [evolution] of the sounds, they are directed towards the spiritual degrees, as is explained in the science of music. . . . Among the holy musicians there were some who were superior to others in this science, as they said:[46] Hogras ben Levi had a chapter of song, i.e., more than the chapters which his fellow musicians had. This indicates that they had books composed on the tradition of song, arranged like the chapters of the Mishnah. All this was intended to awaken the soul to its loftiness, in order that it arrive at its true character. Then the Holy Spirit arises, sparkles, and craves with fondness, care, and great love, and then it achieves an even greater degree.

There is a close connection between this passage and the first citation from Isaac ha-Kohen; one might even say that ibn Abi Sahula expanded upon what was said by Isaac ha-Kohen. With regard to our subject, these passages may be summarized as follows: 1) There is a connection between the science of music, though it is now lost, and prophecy; 2) The singing of the Levites and of the prophets was connected with the Name of God; 3) The somewhat ambiguous use of the term *nequddah* (musical note/vowel-point) seems to indicate a connection between the song of the Levites and vowel points.

These ideas appear also in the *Sôd ha-Šalšelet*. It is difficult to determine exactly when this work was written, but it appears to date from the end of the thirteenth or the beginning of the fourteenth century.[47]

> The secret of the *šalšelet:* In a few places in the Torah there is a cantillation note called *šalšelet*, whose form is: . It is found on the words *wa-yitmahmah* ("and he lingered") [Gen. 19:16], and [*wa-y*ᶜ*omar* ("and he said") in the verse] "and he said, 'O Lord, God of my master Abraham' " [Genesis 24:12], and also in the Hagiographa and in the Psalms. The Kabbalists say that this note is like the lovely music which the angels sing and play before God, and that David received some of this music by means of the Holy Spirit. So also with the Levites, who performed the holy songs in the Temple, that is, the Psalms. They made their voice pleasant by singing the song in a lovely, pleasant, clear, and good voice. They pronounced their speech with a significant melodic movement, with that same suspended pronunciation as with the great *šalšelet*, in order to elevate that speech with the note of the *šalšelet*, which is made at the beginning of the word, and before he ends that particular word, he makes a lovely turn with the small *šalšelet*. He would thereby elevate his tune higher, and then lower it a little, as, for example, in chanting according to the science of music. He would make this pronunciation while performing the good and pleasant song which he knows by tradition to be fit for the *šalšelet*. If he has received no tradition, and he knows how to innovate a pleasant tune on his own—a tune which will have a pleasant cantillation and a pronunciation similar to the enunciation of the *šalšelet*—then he must pronounce the Name in this order and with this sound, for this is what the High Priest used to do. He used to proclaim the Name with this tune while in the Holy of Holies, and he would vocalize it while employing a tune according to the rule of the *šalšelet*, so that he would swallow the letters of the Name. This was so that all those listening heard the pleasant melody and did not need to understand the letters of the Name, so much were their souls enjoying listening to the melody. This can be done also by one graced by God to proclaim Names, by

> one who knows how to do this, and who directs the letters and performs the necessary activities, and this is the secret of "He within Whose dwelling there is Joy."[48] Joy comes only from the joy of music, and the joy of music comes from the Holy Spirit, as it is written, "and when the minstrel played, the power of the Lord came upon him." [II Kings 3:15] Such also was the incident of the two young French girls in the city of Montpellier [49] in ancient times, who knew how to perform music, and had pleasant voices, and excelled in the science of music. They began to recite [Psalms 45:1]: "to the chief musician upon Šošannim, for the sons of Korah, Maschil, A Song of Loves." They chanted according to the straight path, and they fused with the higher [entities], and they were so absorbed in song that before they finished half the psalm, God rejoiced at hearing the song from their mouths, as is His way, that the tune rose upwards, they achieved union, and their souls ascended to Heaven.[50] See how God rejoices at hearing a tune done correctly, and how much power there is in good music! As proof, notice that when the cantor has a good appearance, a pleasant voice, clear speech, and good melodies, the congregation rejoices with him, and for this reason the souls, which are sublime, take pleasure. Souls come from God, and thus God rejoices along with them, concerning which they say,[51] "making happy God and men."

In this passage we find some of the ideas which we found in the circle of Isaac ha-Kohen. Music is described as a science which, in ancient times, was known to the High Priest; it leads to devotion and is connected with the pronunciation of the Name. However, in the passage quoted above, music is described as still effective, and not as a lost science. It seems that this science was preserved in the circle of Abraham Abulafia, who was closely associated with one of the disciples of Isaac ha-Kohen, namely, Moses b. Simeon of Burgos.[52]

4. Music as a Component of the Abulafian Technique

In striking contrast to the philosophers and kabbalists, Abulafia says very little about the theoretical aspects of the connection between music and 'prophecy.' In his writings one only finds instructions concerning music-making while pronouncing Divine Names, which is the path by which we arrive at 'prophecy.' In his book *Ôẕar ʿEden Ganuz*, we read:

> The proof that song indicates the degree of prophecy is that it is the way of song to make the heart happy by means of tunes, as it is said, "And when the minstrel played, the power of the Lord came upon

him," [II Kings 3:15] for prophecy does not dwell in him [unless there is] joy [see *Šabbat* 30b]. This was already hinted at in two words appearing at the end of Ecclesiastes [12:13], where he says, "The end of the matter, all being heard: Fear God, and keep his commandments, for this is the whole duty of man." Join *yarê* (fear) with *šamar* (keep), and you find *šir amar* (i.e., "say a song"). There ia a hint [of this] in [Numbers 6:27] "and they shall put my name upon the children of Israel, and I will bless them"—*yarê samar, et šemi.*[53]

Elsewhere, Abulafia speaks of music in terms of practical instruction. We read in his book *Ḥayyê ʿOlam ha-Ba:* "In this manner he should transpose each letter frontwards and backwards, using many tunes."[54] In another place he says:

Make that special breath as long as you can, according to your capacity for taking one long breath, as long as you can possibly make it, and sing the *alef* and every other letter which you proclaim with awe, fear and reverence, until the joy of the soul is combined with its understanding, which is great. The form of the tune for each letter should be in the image of the vowel points. It should be in the form of the *ḥôlam* upwards.[55]

Again, in *Ôr ha-Sekel* we find: "Until you say *he* properly, and in the image of the *ḥôlam* which extends upwards, play the *ḥiriq* which extends downwards."[56] Similarly, in *Ôzar ʿEden Ganuz:* "Your tongue should always speak with a pleasant and pleasing tune, and very gently."[57] On page 70 of *Sefer ha-Ôt,* music is mentioned as an additional element of the sacred text along with letters and vowel points. The parallel between music and vowel points emerges from these citations. The vowel point serves as a sort of note which gives the pitch to the one proclaiming the Name: *ḥolam* indicates a high pitch, and *ḥiriq* a low pitch. This usage calls to mind the lost science of music mentioned by Isaac ha-Kohen. Both he and Abulafia hold that this science leads to 'prophecy.' There is no doubt that the remarks of the anonymous author of *Ner Elohim*[58] also represent in essence a description of a technique which was employed in practice, and not a "lost" science:

The *niggun* [i.e., music] is the beauty of pronunciation and indicates the production of sounds, with reference to five matters, because of the five varying pronunciations of the vowel points.[59] Moreover, the lute *(kinnôr),* which has five strings, encompasses all music.[60] The philosophers call this science *muziqa* in Greek, because the word *kinnôr* [is equivalent to] music.[61] We also call it *noʿam* and *ṭaʿam,* as with the cantillation accents *(ṭeʿamim),* which are *zarqa, tarsa, tevir,*

> *reviʿa, gereš*, etc., because by means of them the entire recitation is made more beautiful and more pleasing to those listening to it. It [the recitation] climbs up, becomes longer, and then turns backwards.[62]

Further evidence of the integration of music into the technique of Abulafia's students is found in *Šaʿarê Ẕedeq:*

> He should then continue with a pleasant voice and with melodies in the verses of praise and out of love of the Torah, for the joy of the living soul which is partnered to the rational [soul].[63]

Based upon this passage, Judah al-Botini writes in *Sullam ha-ʿAliyyah:*

> He should continue to play on all sorts of music[al instruments] if he has such or if he knows how to play on them; if not, he should make music with his mouth, by means of his voice, [singing] the verses of praise and out of love for the Torah, in order to gladden the living soul which is partnered to the speaking, intellectual soul.[64]

Music's sphere of influence is the living soul. Its task is to make this soul happy, so as not to interfere with the proper functioning of the intellectual soul, or the intellect.[65] This view also appears in *Yesod ʿOlam*, written at the end of the thirteenth century by Elḥanan ben Abraham Eskira, who belonged to a circle close to the views of *Ginnat Egoz* and the *Sefer ʿIyyun*. There we read:[66]

> When the soul craves for solitude and to regale itself in the luxuries of the intellect, were it not that Nature stands in its way with a temptation of images, it would separate itself from the body. For this reason, the *kinnôr* was struck in front of the altar at the time that the sacrifice was offered.[67] When the priest entered the Holy of Holies, which is the solitude, his garment produced sounds from the thirty-two bells, as it is written, "and his sound shall be heard when he goeth in unto the holy place . . . that he die not"[Ex. 28:35]. It is known to those who speak of the science of music that music is intermediate between the spiritual and the material, in that it draws forth the intellect at the time of its imprisonment, as it is written, "but now bring me a minstrel" [II Kings 3:15], and as it is written, "awake *nevel* and *kinnôr*" [Ps. 57:9]. Nature drags the intellect, so to speak, to leave the intellectual [world] and to amuse itself with material things.

In another work written at the same time, Joseph ben Shalom

Ashkenazi's commentary to *Sefer Yeẕirah,*[68] the entry of the High Priest into the Holy of Holies is also seen as a symbol of mystical experience connected with music:

> The letters go out in the ways of the paths through the way of music, and this is the secret of the cantillation accents *(ṭeʿamim)* of the Torah, for they come in and go out with the sound of singing. The secret of this is the golden bell and pomegranate with which the High Priest used to enter the Holy of Holies, so that its sound may he heard. From this you will understand the secret of the Holy Spirit which resides in prophets in the manner of music.

The author of the *Sefer ha-Peli'ah* combines the views of *Yesod ʿOlam* with those of the *Commentary to Sefer Yeẕirah* when he writes:

> He should draw the spirit of the Living God by means of known melodies which are the thirty-two melodies according to which the Torah is transposed. They say that those melodies are the cantillation accents of the Torah *(ṭaʿame torah).*[69]

Finally, let us quote the remarks of Ḥayyim Vital, who in the fourth part of *Šaʿarê Qedušah* writes:[70]

> And this is the secret of the "sons of the prophets," before whom went the drum and the flute, etc. For by means of the sweetness of the sound of music, dumbness [of senses][71] descends upon them with the pleasantness of the sound. They withdraw their souls,[72] and then the musician stops playing, and the "sons of the prophets" are left with this supreme union and prophesy.

Notes to Chapter Two

1. MS. München 58, fols. 324a–b; MS. British Library Or. 13136 fols. 7a–b. The passage was printed in *Sefer ha-Peli'ah* (Koretz, 1784), fol. 52a–53a, and appears again in the anthology of Abulafia's works by Joseph Ḥamiẓ, MS. Oxford 2239, fol. 114b. Joseph ben Joseph copied it in *Sefer Maʾamarim,* MS. Musayoff 30, fol. 19a, from *Sefer ha-Peli'ah.* For the edition of the Hebrew text, with textual variants between MS. München 58 and *Sefer ha-Peli'ah,* cf. Adler, *HWCM,* pp. 35–36.

2. For the musical connotations of the term *havarah,* see Adler, HWCM, index, p. 359.

3. For the musical connotations of these terms, see Adler, *HWCM,* index, p. 360; *ḥilluf qôl* (mutation), *hitḥallefut ha-Qôlot* (modulating [?] voice): see also

the term *tamrur, ibid.*, 250 Simeon Duran. B. 3 (p. 134).

4. I have not found this metaphorical usage prior to the period of Abulafia. This author uses the combination 'pangs of love" ("and the spirit of his love is drawn out with the pangs of true love") in another work, *Sefer ha-Ôt*, p. 78. This phrase appears a few years later in the work of the Kabbalist known as Joseph of Hamadan, *ṭaʿame ha-Mizwot*, MS. Jerusalem 8B 3925, fol. 82b.

5. This connection between the spleen and joy stems from a misunderstanding of the saying in *Berakot* 51b dealing with the "grinding (*šoḥeq*) spleen." The reference in the Gemara, as in parallel sources such as *Ecclesiastes Rabbah* 7:37 and others, was to the action of grinding (*šeḥiqah*) and not to laughter (*seḥôq*). However, in the Middle Ages the verb *ŠḤQ* was understood to mean the same as *SḤQ*; cf. the sources gathered by Wertheimer in *Batê Midrašot*, II, p. 378, n. 111. Add to them *Šaʿar ha-Šamayim* of Gershom ben Solomon (Warsaw, 1876), fol. 33c, and *Ševilê Emunah* by Meir Aldabi (Warsaw, 1887), fol. 44a.

6. Instead of *yeter ʾeḥad* perhaps read *yeter ʾaḥer*, giving the translation: "moves from there to another string, such as *bet, gimmel*."

7. Cf. *Commentary to Sefer Yezirah* by Eleazar of Worms (Premisla, 1883), fols. 5b–d. This theory of combination appears in Abulafia's epistle known as *ha-Seder ha-mithappek*, MS. British Library 749, fols. 30a–31a, and in several other places.

8. MS. New York JTS 1801, fol. 31b.

9. MS. Jerusalem 8° 148, fols. 48b–49a, and MS. New York - Columbia X 893 Sh. 43, fol. 19b.

10. On the influence of music on the body, cf. Adler, *HWCM*, index, p. 361, "influence of music."

11. Another new principle found in *Šaʿarê Zedeq* is that of the vocalizations or vowel-points which allow for the pronunciation of the consonants. Cf. below, Chap. 4.

12. Cf. e.g. Underhill, *Mysticism*, pp. 76–78, 90–93.

13. MS. Oxford Heb. e 123, fol. 64b.

14. Cf. *Tanḥuma ha-Yašan* (ed. Buber), Genesis, p. 3. The combination "in the voice of Moses" appears several times in the work of Abraham Abulafia, in order to emphasize the inner source of prophecy. Cf. e.g. *Ôzar ʿEden Ganuz* MS. Oxford 1580, fol. 12a; *Sitrê Tôrah*, MS. Paris - BN 774, fol. 140a.

15. MS München 40, fol. 246b; in the anthology of Joseph Ḥamiz, MS. Oxford 2239, fol. 130a.

16. The combination of the legend of David's harp with the verse in II

Kings 2:3 appears in several places. Cf. *Pesiqeta de-Rav Kahana* (ed. Buber), chapter 7, fols. 62b–63a, and Buber's notes ; also L. Ginzburg. *The Legends of the Jews* (Philadelphia, 1946), VI, p. 262 , n. 81–83.

17. MS. Oxford 1582, fol. 7a. "*Gan ʿeden* in *gemaṭria* equals *ʿad naggen*, and *gan ʿeden* in *gemaṭria* equals *ʿeved naggen.*"

18. *De Virtutibus*, 39, 217; cf. also H.A. Wolfson, *Philo* (Cambridge, Mass., 1947), II, p. 29.

19. M.J. Rufus, *Studies in Mystical Religion* (London, 1919), p. 40.

20. Cf. the material collected by A.J. Heschel, *The Prophets* (New York, 1962), p. 341, n. 28–29, and Meyerovitch, *Mystique et poésie*, pp. 78, 88.

21. Cf. *Mekileṯa* on Exodus 18:19; cf. also B. Cohen, *Law and Tradition in Judaism* (New York, 1959), p. 24, n. 70.

22. Cf. Dan, *Studies* p. 179:

> It cannot be that the Glory speaks of His Own accord in the same way that man speaks of his own accord. Take the *nevel* as an example; the man plays on it, and the sound is not of the *nevel's* own accord.

R. Judah transfers the analogy from the sphere of the God-man connection to the sphere of God-glory, given that the Glory is the source of prophecy and the place of its occurrence.

23. Heschel, *Theology of Ancient Judaism*, II, pp. 264–266; Werblowsky, *Joseph Karo*, p. 260, nn. 7–8.

24. J. Weiss, "Via passiva in early Hassidim," *JJS* 11 (1960), pp.140–145. See also R. Shatz-Uffenheimer, *Quietistic Elements in 18th Century Hasidic Thought* [Heb.] (Jerusalem, 1968), p. 112.

25. I Samuel 10:5: II Kings 3:15. The latter verse became the scriptural support of all those who connect prophecy to music.

26. *TB Pesaḥim* 117a, *Šabbat* 30a, and other places.

27. *Hilkot Yesodê ha-Torah*, 7:4: *Sefer ha-'Yiḥud* attributed to Maimonides (Berlin, 1916), pp 20–21, and also in *Peraqim be-hazlaḥah* attributed to Maimonides (Jerusalem, 1939), p. 7. See also Adler, *HWCM* index, pp. 378–379, "prophetic inspiration aroused by music."

28. *Ginzê ha-Meleḵ*, chap. 15 (Adler, *HWCM*, p. 171, sentence 1): cf. the translation by Werner & Sonne, *HUCA* 16 (1941), pp.283–284, and see also *Musarê ha-filosofim*, chap. 18: "He says to the musician: awaken the soul to its honorable power from modesty and righteousness . . ." (Adler, *HWCM*, p. 148, sentence 6). Cf. also the remarks of the anonymous author of *Toledot ʾadam*, written in 1444 (MS. Oxford 836, fol. 184a):

> The experts in this art call these six notes, in their language, [u]t, mi[!] re fa sol la, and there is another fine note which joins in with them all, together and equally, and it is the song of [all] songs, "a great sound which did not cease." It is possible that David of blessed memory alluded to this art with the seven sounds, firstly, the "sound on the water" to instruct us in the Name. This art is truly material and spiritual, and therefore it arouses the perfection of the qualities by which prophecy sets in, as it is written, "But bring me now a minstrel, and when the minstrel played."

This work was written under the influence of Abulafia's theory.

29. Quoted from the *Peruš ha-Torah* by Baḥya ben Ašer on Genesis 1 (ed. Chavel, Jerusalem, 1966), p. 39. Cf. also the commentary by Solomon ben Adret on *Bava Batra* 74b (ed. L. A. Feldman, in *Bar-Ilan; annual of Bar-Ilan University*, vols. 7–8, 1970), p. 141.

30. *Šabbat* 30b.

31. *Sefer Adnê Kesef* (London, 1912), vol. 2, p. 120.

32. MS. Jerusalem 8° 1303 fol. 47b.

33. The two views are found in *Sukkah* 50b.

34. *Ôẕar ha-Ḥokmah*, MS. Musayoff Jerusalem 55, fol. 84a. On this author and his times, cf. Scholem, *Kabbalistic Manuscripts*, pp. 42–43.

35. This passage is cited in the name of R. Isaac in *Sefer ha-Emunot* by Shem Tov ben Shem Tov (Ferrara, 1556), fol. 94a, published by G. Scholem in *Maddaʿe ha-Yahadut* II (1927), p. 277. Cf. *Pitḥê ʿOlam* by Solomon ben Samuel (who apparently lived at the end of the fourteenth century), Adler, *HWCM*, p. 301, s [1] n. 1:

> The tenth gate: the musical service in the Temple, vocal and instrumental, in order to draw hearts towards Blessed God, and to lift the souls to the supreme world, the spiritual world. This is the issue of the pleasantness of voice [required] in the synagogues for prayers, *qerovot* and *piyyutim*, and in the Temple they had proper command of the science of music.

Cf. also *ibid.*, pp. 300–301.

36. *Nequddôt*, usually denomination of vowel points; here, the term was probably used in the sense of musical notes. Cf. Adler, *HWCM*, p. 172 (the pref. of 360 / *Ibn Sahula*) and p. 173, sentence 3. see also *ibid*, index, p. 375: *nequddah*.

37. For an identical formulation of the melodic and rhythmic evolution of the song of the Levites, see the reference to Adler, *HWCM* in the preceding note; see also the text by Ibn Sahula below.

38. In ed. Ferrara and MS. Paris-BN Heb. 745: *ha-beṭen:* Scholem suggests the correction *ha-biṭṭuy:* the original version may have been a Hebrew transcription *(laʿaz)* of the term *notes,* such as, *ha-noṭi.*

39. For these denominations of high and low pitch, see Adler, *HWCM,* index, p. 354 *(daq)* and p. 82, sentence 2, n. 1 *(gas).*

40, Ed. Ferrara and G. Scholem read *"mitnoseset,"* but see below the corresponding passage of Ibn Sahula, and see also the commentary *ṭaʿamê ha-Nequddôt we-Ẕuratan* in *Maddaʿe ha-Yahadut* II (1927), p. 267, 1. 18; we therefore adopt the correction *mitnoẕeẕet.*

41. Published in *Maddaʿe ha-Yahadut* II (1927), p. 247.

42. Cf. Scholem, *Maddaʿe ha-Yahadut* II (1927), p. 169.

43. MS. Oxford 343, fol. 38b. On this work and its relation to the Kabbalah of the *Zohar,* cf. G. Scholem, *Peraqim be-toledot Sifrut ha-Qabbalah* (Jerusalem, 1930/31), p. 62. I have omitted the passage dealing with music indicated by dots, which deals with music from *Midraš ha-Neʿelam,* which Scholem published there. Cf. also Adler, *HWCM* pp 172–174.

44. *Numbers Rabbah* 6:10. Cf. Adler, *HWCM* pp. 173–174, sentence 1, n. 2.

45. *Tenuʿah,* (musical) motion; for the various musical meanings, see Adler, *HWCM* index, p. 380 *(tenuʿah),* p. 376*(nuʿ nuʿ a);* see also Werner-Sonne, in *HUCA* 16 (1941), 306, n. 183, and 17 (1942-43), 537.

46. *Mišnah, Yoma* 3:11. The idea that the science of music had originated with Israel and was then lost also appears in the passage cited above from *Adnê Kesef,* and also in the important musical discussion of Moses Isserles in *Torat ha-ʿOlah,* pt. 2, chap. 38: "the science of music which, due to sin, has been forgotten by us from the day on which the song-service ceased to exist." Cf. also I. Adler, "Le traite anonyme du manuscrit Hebreu 1037 de la Bibliotheque Nationale de Paris," *Yuval* 1 (1968), 15–16.

47. *Sod ha-Šalšelet,* found in *Sodot,* MS. Paris - BN 790, fols. 141a–b; cf. Gottleib, *Studies,* p. 120, n. 57.

48. The expression "in whose dwelling there is joy" appears twice in connection with music in *Sod Ilan ha-Aẕilut,* from the circle of *Sefer ha-Temunah;* G. Scholem published this small treatise in *Qovez ʿal Yad* (n. s.) 5 (1950); cf. *ibid.,* pp. 83, 97. There is question that there is a very close connection between the conception of music found in *Sôd ha-Ŝalšelet* and that found among members of the circle of the *Sefer ha-Temunah.* I hope to write at length elsewhere on the conception of music in this circle.

49. Cf. H. Gross, *Gallia Judaica,* p. 322.

50. On death due to religious excitement caused by singing, see D. B. Macdonald, "Al-Ghazzali on Music and Ecstasy," *JRAS* (1901), p. 708, n. 3.

51. Cf. G. Scholem, *Tarbiz̲* 3 (1932), 260.

52. See A. Jellinek, in *Bet ha-Midraš*, III, p. 21.

53. MS. Oxford 1580, fol. 62a. This passage is based upon the *gemaṭria* of 751, by which *yarê šămar*=*et šemi.*

53. MS. Oxford 1582 fol. 11b. In this manuscript, as well as in several other manuscripts of this treatise, there is an addendum which explains that the term *niggunim* is used in the sense of *niqqudim;* this is also the case in our following quotation from *Ôr ha-Sek̲el.*

56. *Ibid.*, fol. 110b.

57. MS. Oxford 1580, fol. 163a.

58. MS. München, 10, fol. 142a–b.

59. The author refers here to the five long vowels which were accepted in Hebrew grammar from the time of Joseph Qimhi and which appear in Abulafia's books. Cf. also *Ḥayyê ha-ʿOlam ha-Ba.* MS. Oxford 1582, fol. 53b.

60. The four-stringed *ʿud* (short-necked lute), considered by the Arabs to be the musical instrument *par excellence* ("instrument of the philosophers"), was liable to be supplemented by an added fifth string *(had);* see, for instance, Adler *HWCM* p. 26 (sentence IVb, 31), p. 38 (sentence 16); A. Shiloah, *The Theory of Music in Arabic Writings* (München, 1979), no 272. Of particular interest as regards our text is the source quoted (after H.G. Farmer) by Werner-Sonne, *HUCA* 16 (1941), pp.275–276, referring to the analogy of the four strings with the four elements, and associating the added fifth string with the soul. This may be related to the following quotation from *Ner Elohim* (fol. 137a):

> Indeed man is made up of five elements which encompass the whole body. One element is simple and heavenly, and it is one of the heavenly forces, and it is called in its entirety soul *(nefeš)*, spirit *(ruaḥ)* or higher soul *(nešamah)*" (see also *ibid.*, fol. 135b).

See also the references to the five stringed *kinnôr* in the *Tiqqune Zohar;* cf. *Inventory of Jewish Musical Sources*, series B, vol. I: *Music Subjects in the Zohar* . . . by A. Shiloah and R. Tene (Jerusalem, 1977), *tiqqun* 10 (p. 119, no. 175, 2), *tiqqun* 12 (p. 121, no. 178, 4 and 11). *tiqqun* 21 (p. 128, no. 181, 21).

61. The author probably has in mind the equivalence *kinnôr* = *ʿud* = the musical instrument *par excellence*, thus arriving at the equivalence *kinnôr* = music (cf. the beginning of the preceding note).

62., The last five words of this quotation perhaps refer to names of the *ṭeʿamim* (such as *ʿoleh we-yored, maʾarik̲).*

63. MS. Jerusalem 8° 148, fols. 72a–b, On this treatise, see note 9 above.

64. Published in part by Scholem in *Kabbalistic Manuscripts*, p. 227.

65. Averroes wrote on the connection between the animal soul and sounds in his *Epitome of Parva Naturalis* ed. D. Blumberg. (Cambridge, Mass., 1954), p. 11, ll. 6–9:

> The animal soul found in the living being does not deny the action of nature, but rather rejoices in the colors and sounds which nature produces, for they exist potentially in the animal soul. . . .

Cf. Johanan Alemanno's view in *Ḥey ha-ʿOlamim,* Mantua Biblioteca comunale, MS. ebr. 21, fol. 56a:

> At most times of the day which are the times of solitude, in the morning and in the evening, he should sit in the garden which delights the soul, which [soul] feels through the five senses that there exists a beauty of variety of sights—the flowers, roses, and the sight of the fruit—and a beauty of the variety of sounds—various songs with which the birds, while nesting, make pleasant melodies . . . in this manner his sensitive soul will not be sad at the beginning of solitude.

The sensitive soul of Allemanno is the animal soul of Averroes and the living soul of *Šaʿarê Ẕedeq*. It is worth addressing the difference between *Šaʿarê Ẕedeq* and *Sullam ha-ʿAliyah:* in the latter book, primarily instrumental music is discussed, and we may here be encountering the influence of the Sufi practice of *samaʿ*, which was based upon instrumental music. Cf. Meyerovitch, *Mystique et póesie,* p. 83 ff. and bibliography, as well as F. Rosenthal, "A Judeo-Arabic work under Sufi Influence," *HUCA* 15 (194O), pp. 433–48, esp. pp. 478–469.

66. MS. Moscow - Gunzburg 6O7, fol. 8a. This passage seems to be an adaptation from *Musarê ha-filosofim,* I, 18 (8); see Adler, *HWCM,* p. 148; see also the emendations of the sequence of this passage in Werner and Sonne, *HUCA* 17 (1942–43), p. 515–516 and p. 525 (English translation). For the connection between music and sacrifices, see Ibn Falaquera's *Sefer ha-Mevaqqeš* (based on the music epistle of the Iḥwan al-Safa); cf. Adler, *HWCM,* p. 165, sentence 3.

67. The phrase, "the harp was struck in front of the altar" seems to be based on the Mishnaic phrase "the *ḥalil* (flute) was played in front of the altar," in *ʿAraḵin* 2:3.

68. Ed. Jerusalem, 1965, fol. 31b. It would be superfluous to point out that the connection between High Priest and ecstasy appears as early Philo, and from there moved on to Plotinus. It a1so appears in the *Zohar*. Cf. Scholem, *Major Trends,* p. 378, n. 9.

69. Ed. Koretz, 1784, fol. 50c. In the matter of the number of bells, there is a clear parallel between *Yesod ʿOlam* and *Sefer ha-Peli'ah;* the number thirty-two does not appear in *Zevaḥim* 88b, where thirty-six or seventy-two, but not thirty-two, bells, are spoken of.

70. The text, still unpublished, is preserved in MS. British Library 749,

fol. 15b. Vital himself admits that his conception of prophecy was influenced by Abulafia whom he quotes (among others) in chapter 4.

71. *Hitbodedut:* here the meaning is not "solitude" or "isolation," as in the usual connotations of this term. See M. Steinschneider, *MGWJ* 32 (1883), p. 463, n. 8 and *Hebräische Übersetzungen* (Berlin, 1893), p. 74. The interpretation of *hitbodedut* as dumbness of the senses also seems plausible in Pseudo Ibn-Ezra, *Sefer ha-ʿAẕamim* (London, 1901), p. 13.

72. *Mafšitin nafšam:* for the meaning of this "withdrawal", see Werblowsky, *Joseph Karo*, pp. 61–62, 69.

Chapter Three

The Mystical Experience

Abulafia's system of thought is dominated by two major concepts: the intellect and the imagination. The literal meaning of the Torah is associated with the imagination, while its esoteric meaning is associated with the intellect.[1] These concepts also provide a key to understanding his visions and their hidden meaning. The allegoric approach characteristic of his scriptural hermeneutics will thus assist us in understanding the meaning of his own visions. While Abulafia's Biblical interpretation is a clear example of allegorization of the text—that is, the introduction of an allegorical meaning into a text in which there is *ab initio* no such significance—his interpretation of his visions is not subject to such a clearcut definition. On the one hand, Abulafia attempts to interpret personal experience through the use of concepts inappropriate to the type of material which they are meant to interpret; on the other hand, those concepts which Abulafia made into cornerstones of his thought may be expressed allegorically in his visions, so that the interpretation itself is not so much an allegorization as an uncovering of the allegorical element inherent within the vision. We will not attempt to decide this question at this point, but it is worth citing here Abulafia's own words concerning the need for an interpretation of his visions. In *Sefer ha-Ôt*, p. 85, he writes of his vision: "This is the meaning revealed to all, but the hidden meaning may only be understood by one who comprehends it by himself."

One may ask why Abulafia felt such a great need to interpret his visions. The answer to this question is embedded in his prophetic-mystical approach. Following Maimonides, Abulafia states that prophecy is impossible without the imaginative faculty,[2] through which the flow of the intellect is transformed into visual images and sounds. The function of interpretation is to return to the intellective influx, which contains within itself the intellectual contents of the revelation. Abulafia saw himself as a prophet in every respect, as we may see from his *Sefer ha-Haftarah*, which he asked to have read every Sabbath in the synagogue[3]; consequently, his visions include an intellectual message in imaginative garb. Our discussion must therefore be divided into two: one part will concern the sensual-imaginative aspect of his experience, and the other, the interpretive and "intellectual" part. The tangible part of Abulafia's experience is not subject to interpretation; the feeling of joy or of mission, the fear which pursues the prophet, and similar feelings, are well-known signs accompanying a message in visual or verbal form.

1. Sensations and Feelings

The connection between mystical experience and related phenomena—such as foretelling the future, magic, and extraordinary physical sensations and emotional feelings—was well known from ancient times.[4] During the Middle Ages, these phenomena continued to be viewed as epi-phenomena of prophetic experiences; Maimonides characterizes all the prophets, with the exception of Moses, with the phrase that, at the time of prophecy, "his powers would fail; he would be overcome with dread, and nearly lose his mind."[5] Elsewhere, Maimonides compares the magician to "one who falls sick," and goes on to offer an explanation of the connection between prophecy and various physical and psychic phenomena in terms of the major role played by the imaginative faculty. In *Sefer ha-Mizwot*, he writes:

> It is impossible for those possessing these imaginative powers not to perform one of those acts by which this power is actualized and brought to light. And among these are those who strike upon the ground many times with a stick which is in their hand, or scream out in strange cries and abandon their thoughts and gaze at the earth a long time until they find it, as in the matter of falling sickness [epilepsy], and will relate what is to occur in the future.[6]

Maimonides is saying here that the strengthening of the activity of the imagination is inevitably accompanied by various external manifestations. Ibn Rushd (Averroes), on the other hand, holds that the fullest activity of the imagination is contingent upon silencing the activities of the senses. In his *Epitome of Parva Naturalia,* we read:

> It is fitting that the power of the imagination act more completely and more spiritually in sleep, for at the time of sleep the soul has already nullified the senses of sight and its organs, and has turned them towards the inner sense. And the proof that the inner powers act more perfectly when the external senses are at rest is that, when the thought of the people does greatly, they turn their powers of feeling towards within the body until they faint from sleep, and they will intend to rest the external senses in order to improve the thought. And for this reason . . . prophecy indeed necessarily comes about in a similar matter. And that is because, when these inner powers move a strong movement, the external [organs] contract until at times there occurs in this something similar to fainting.[7]

Both of these opinions appear in Abulafia—that claiming a strengthening, and that asserting a diminution, of external activity simultaneous with the strengthening of the imagination, while only the latter view appears among the members of his circle. In *Sitrê Tôrah,*[8] he states:

> Know that so long as you combine letters rapidly, and the hairs of your head do not all stand up in trembling, you have not yet attained one of the levels of the spirit in which all of the limbs [of the body] are moved, and you have not known even His existence, let alone His essence. But the beginning of that apprehension is the whirlwind, of which it is said,[9] "and I looked, and behold, a whirlwind coming from the north." And it is said,[10] "and God answered Job out of the whirlwind."

The "storm" refers here to the storm of the limbs, as Abulafia describes it in *Oẕar ʿEden Ganuz*[11]:

> *The hairs of your head will begin to stand up and to the storm.* And your blood—which is the life blood which is in your heart, of which it is said[12] "for the blood is the soul," and of which it is likewise said,[13] "for the blood shall atone for the soul"—[this blood] will begin to move out because of the living combination which speaks, and all your body will begin to tremble, and your limbs will begin to shake, and you will fear a tremendous fear, and the fear of God shall cover you. . . . And the body will tremble, like the rider who races the horse, who is glad and joyful, while the horse trembles beneath him. [Emphasis added.]

The meaning of this trembling is explained in the previous page of that same work, where we read:

> And his intellect is greater than his imagination, and it rides upon it like one who rides upon a horse and drives it by hitting it with [a whip] to run before it as it wills, and his whip is in his hand to make it [i.e., the imagination] stand where his intellect wills.[14]

Another description of the trembling which overcomes one who meditates at the time of the 'prophetic' experience appears in *Ḥayyê ha-ʿOlam ha-Ba:* "By his concentration he again brings upon himself fear and trembling, and the hairs of his head stand, and all his limbs tremble."[15] Abulafia's disciples likewise testify to such a feeling; the anonymous author of *Šaʿarê Z̲edeq* writes, "great trembling seized me, and I could not gather strength, and my hairs stood up."[16]

A second element manifested in the descriptions of Abulafia's experience is "spirit"; further on in the above-cited passage from *Siṭrê Torah,* we learn that "the second apprehension is that of spirit, not like the spirit of God."[17] In *Oz̲ar ʿEden Ganuz,* Abulafia explains the subject of this spirit as follows:

> And you shall feel another spirit awakening within yourself and strengthening you and passing over your entire body and giving you pleasure, and it will seem to you that balm has been poured over you from the crown of your head to your feet, once or many times, and you shall rejoice and feel from it a great pleasure, with gladness and trembling.[18]

The feeling of pleasure and relief following the trembling is also depicted in *Ḥayyê ha-ʿOlam ha-Ba:*[19]

> Afterwards, should you merit it, the spirit of the living God shall pass over you,[20] and there shall dwell upon you the spirit of God, the spirit of wisdom and understanding, the spirit of knowledge and fear of God, and one will imagine that it is as if one's entire body has been anointed with anointing oil from head to feet, and he will be the Messiah of God and his messenger.

In *Šaʿarê Z̲edeq,* the disciple writes in the identical manner as does Abulafia:

> Behold, I was anointed from head to foot as with the anointing oil, and we were surrounded with great joy, and *I do not know how to*

compare to it any image because of its great spirituality and the sweetness of its pleasure; all this occurred to your servant at the beginning.[21] [Emphasis added]

Abulafia's disciples testify to the absence of sensation following "the storm of the organs." In the same work, the author states: "And I immediately fell down as if I were not in the world, for I did not feel any strength in any organs,"[22] while R. Judah Albotini writes: "until all of the physical powers were taken away from me, and his intellect also departed him (sic), like [the will] to act, and he falls to the earth as if dead, and lies down and falls asleep."[23] These texts, which in at least some cases reflect personal experiences, are quite rare in Jewish mysticism, and constitute important evidence of ecstatic moods and tendencies accompanied by distinctive bodily phenomena.

2. The Light

In *Siṭrê Torah,* Abulafia goes on to describe the various stages of mystical experience. We have already noted above his words referring to the storm and the wind as two primary "comprehensions." Let us now proceed to the other stages:[24] "and the third is the tumult,[25] and God was not in the tumult"; and the fourth, fire: "And God was not in the fire, and after the fire there was a still small voice." Like the first two, the third and fourth stages are defined by means of scriptural verses. The significance of the third stage—the tumult—is not clear to me, and it may be connected with the movement of the limbs referred to above. We must examine the fourth level carefully, as it includes two different elements: fire, that is, the visual element; and speech, the verbal element. The order in which these two elements are cited is determined by the verse from the book of Kings, but this order would seem in fact to reflect the preference of hearing over seeing. In his letter to R. Judah Salmon, Abulafia writes:

> But all of the early ones of the Kabbalists mentioned are called "prophets for themselves," and those who know God from his actions [i.e., the philosophers] share with them to an extent this title. Those called prophets in terms of this aspect speak within themselves alone, and the light of God illuminates part of their thoughts at some of the times [by] a small light, and they themselves recognize that this light is not from themselves, but no speech comes to them that they might recognize that it is speech, but rather light.[26]

In this passage, as in the verse cited from *Siṭrê Torah,* a distinction is drawn between the visual and verbal element, with preference given to the latter as a higher level of prophecy. According to Abulafia, the revelation of light is characteristic of 'prophetic' experience among the Kabbalists who followed the Sephirotic system. There is extensive basis for this statement; in the writings of R. Isaac the Blind, and particularly in those of R. Azriel of Gerona, we find an abundance of symbols related to light.[27] Later on, in a passage from *Šaʿar ha-Kawwanah* (attributed to R. Azriel), we read:

> Whoever fixes a thing in his mind with complete firmness, that thing becomes for him the principle thing. Thus, when you pray and recite benedictions or [otherwise] wish to direct the *kawwanah* to something in true manner, then imagine that you are light, and all about you is light from every direction and every side, and in the midst of the light a stream of light, and upon it a brilliant light, and opposite it a throne, and upon it the good light. . . . And turn to the right and you find [there] pure light, and to the left and you will find an aura, which is the radiant light. And between them and above them the light of the glory, and around it the light of life. And above it the crown of light that crowns the objects of thought, illuminates the paths of ideas, and brightens the splendor of visions. And this illumination is inexhaustible and unending.[28]

The first sentence is the most important one for understanding this passage: by concentrating his thought upon a particular subject, man is able to enter into a world whose structure is dictated by the contemplator: the "thing" which the contemplator "fixes . . . in his mind with complete firmness." In our passage, this is the light which he "makes the main thing" in wake of his spiritual effort. Evidence for the connection between the light and prophecy appears already in R. Ezra of Gerona, who writes, "for he sat and learned, and would connect his thoughts on high . . . for all light requires the supernal light which is above it, and to be drawn to it, for each light is in accordance with the subtlety of its inwardness."[29]

These passages, and others which we could have brought,[30] indicate that the light was an important focal point to the early Kabbalists, and that it continued to be an important source of symbols for the Kabbalah of R. Moses de Leon as well.[31] From this, it follows that Abulafia's distinction concerning the Kabbalists who experience light visions and those who have a "speech" experience is in many cases correct. His second statement is likewise true: the early Kabbalists were "prophets to themselves"—that is, their experiences remained confined to restricted circles, and those who underwent these experiences deliberately refrained from making them widely known. From this point of view, Abulafia argues, the early Kabbalists were similar to the philosophers, who sufficed with knowledge of God in terms of His actions, and did not generally attempt to disseminate their teaching in public. Abulafia's third statement, that the Sefirotic Kabbalists do not receive "the word," is likewise correct; as against the great number of sources dealing with light, there are very few Kabbalists who claim to have heard voices or speech.[32] To Abulafia, the receiving of light seems connected with the Sefirotic system,[33] for which reason it is a lower level of prophecy. In the continuation of the passage brought above from the epistle *We-Zot li-Yihudah,* he says of the practitioners of the Kabbalah of Names, who are designated there by the term "second," that "they are all prophets who are beginning to see light in the light of life, and from there to ascend from light to light through the course of their thoughts, which are compounded and sweet. . . ." We may infer from this that the revelation associated with light is a first stage in the path of prophecy, which also appears among those who follow Abulafia's path. Study of Abulafia's works indicates that the light has no significant function in his phenomenon of prophecy; this can be explained on the assumption that Abulafia's books are only concerned with the more advanced stage of mystical-prophetic experience, disregarding the initial stages. Abulafia thought of himself as one who had reached the highest level, for which reason it was natural that the light would no longer occupy such a prominent place in his system. On the other hand, one of Abulafia's students, the author of *Šaʿarê Ẕedeq,* comments that at the beginning of his path he experienced the appearance of light, and only later did he experience speech, exactly as described in Abulafia's above-mentioned comment. In the description of his first mystical experience, the anonymous author writes as follows:

> The third night, after midnight, I nodded off a little, quill in hand and paper on my knees. Then I noticed that the candle was about to go out. I rose to put it right, as oftentimes happens to a person awake. Then I saw that the light continued. I was greatly astonished, as though, after close examination, I saw that it issued from myself. I said: 'I do not believe it.' I walked to and fro all through the house and, behold, the light is with me; I lay on a couch and covered myself up, and behold, the light is with me all the while.[34]

There is no reference here to speech in this first revelation, which appeared after a number of days, after the author had progressed in the path of the Kabbalah of Names. One ought to point out that the system of *Ša'arê Zedeq* presents a synthesis between the Sefirotic Kabbalah and that of Names, a point on which it differs from that of Abulafia. In a passage preserved in *Šošan Sodot,*[35] the author of *Ša'are Zedeq* stresses the role of letter-combination in the appearance of light: "and by the power of the combination and the meditation, there happened to me that which happened with the light which I saw going with me, as I mentioned in *Ša'arê Zedeq.*" The two passages by this author are characterized by the fact that the source of the light is inside the person's own body. Interestingly, this same phenomenon also appears in a mystical school which emerged in Greece contemporaneously with Abulafia and his disciples. In the biography of Symeon the New Theologian, the eleventh-century thinker who greatly influenced the shaping of hesychasm in Greece in the thirteenth century, we find a description of the uniting of Symeon with the light which he saw:

> And as the light became stronger, and was bright as the sun at noon-time, he saw himself in the center of the light, and the sweetness which penetrated to his entire body caused him joy and tears. He saw the light adhering to his body in a manner which would not be believed, and gradually penetrating to all his limbs . . . and the light gradually penetrated into his entire body, to his heart and his inwards, and transformed them into fire and light.[36]

This passage also influenced *The Book of the System of Holy Prayer and Concentration,* the first work of the hesychastic school composed, according to scholars, in the thirteenth century, in which it states: "When you seek the place of the heart in your insides, you shall attain the vision of the light, which will transform you into a being completely shining, and you shall feel a great joy which cannot be described."[37] The experience of light surrounding a holy thing or a mystic is, of course, not in itself extraordinary.[38] However, the appearance of two cases of a mystic enwrapped in light during the same period cannot be merely coincidental, given the feasibility of contact between the two schools in terms of geographical proximity. While *Ša'arê Zedeq* was evidently written in the land of Israel, it may be that the events described therein occurred elsewhere: Abulafia testifies that he had disciples in both Greece and Sicily,[39] so we cannot disregard the possibility that the similarity in the appearance of light is the outcome of actual historical contact.

The vision of light continued to be a form of experience among those Kabbalists who used Abulafia's system. R. Isaac of Acre wrote in *O̲zar Ḥayyim:*

> Moreover, in the third watch, when I was half asleep, I saw the house in which I was sleeping full of a light which was very sweet and pleasant, for this light was not like the light which emanates from the sun, but was [bright] as the light of day, which is the light of dawn before the sun rises. And this light was before me for about three hours, and I hastened to open my eyes to see whether the dawn had broken or not, so that I might rise and pray, and I saw that it was yet night, and I returned to my sleep with joy, and after I rose from my bed in order to pray, I suddenly saw a secret of the letter *Alef.*[40]

As in the case of the author of *Šaʿarê Z̲edeq,* the light appears to R. Isaac of Acre in a state in which he was half-asleep, in the middle of the night. Let us now turn to the account of R. Shem Tov b. Abraham ibn Gaon: This Kabbalist, who at the beginning of his literary activity was involved with copying manuscripts and had contact with Kabbalists such as R. Solomon ibn Adret and R. Isaac Todros, later changed his path: among other factors were his meetings with the Kabbalists R. Abraham, author of *Sefer Yesod 'Olam* and his son R. Hanannel of Esquira. This change is seen in the study of *Sefer Yez̲irah,* a book which did not enjoy an important position in the circle of Ibn Adret. In *Badde ha-Aron,* [41] which was also written on the basis of a different approach than that of R. Solomon ibn Adret, [42] R. Shem Tov states that when the Kabbalist:

> . . . has no companion to himself within his heart he shall sit in silence and be still, for it has come upon him,[43] and he shall begin to write what he sees in his mind, like one who copies from a book that is written before him . . . a ball like the sun in true drawing, for the light has appeared to him at that hour.

A similar statement of R. Shem Tov ibn Gaon appears in *Šošan Sodot,* where R. Moses of Kiev states that

> . . . also at the time we composed this book, when we would articulate the Ineffable Name, things came into our eyes from verses in the image of red fire towards evening, until we were astonished by them and we left them. And this happened to us several times [while we were] writing.[44]

It seems to me that we may summarize the passages concerning the appearance of light among Jewish authors in terms of two main characteristics. First, light appears in connection with the activity of writing or of combining the letters of the Ineffable Name in writing. Even though this is not explicitly stated by our authors, from our knowledge of the technique of the author of *Šaʿarê Z̲edeq* and of R. Isaac of Acre there can be no doubt that they followed Abulafia's path in combining the letters of the Ineffable Name; among other authors, R. Shem Tov and R. Moses of Kiev, this is explicitly stated. Second, the appearance of light comes about unexpectedly; the light appears suddenly, and not as the result of a deliberate attempt to bring about an experience of light. Unlike the description in *Šaʿar ha-Kawwanah,* in which the experience of light is the result of a deliberate effort, the above-cited authors are astonished by the appearance of the light. An additional difference between them and the anonymous Kabbalist lies in the nature of the experience: from the description in *Šaʿar ha-Kawwanah,* the vision of light seems to be a pneumatic vision, while the other authors stress that this is an actual sensory phenomenon; they even attempt to describe the color of the light or the feelings which accompany the light. An additional distinction concerns the magical possibilities inherent in the lights appearing to the anonymous Kabbalist. These lights constitute a kind of world in itself to which one may turn with "requests," something for which there is no parallel among other authors.

In conclusion, I would like to cite the statements of two scholars who attempted to understand the phenomenon of light in mystical experiences, whose explanations remind one of the difference between *Šaʿar ha-Kawwanah* and Abulafia's circle. Their main claim is that the perception of light is the result of the liberation of spiritual energy that had been stored in the brain; the liberation of this inner energy brings about a stimulation of the visual nerves (for which there is no external cause), as a result of which the sensation of light is transferred to the brain. In the above-cited cases, we may refer to an intellectual effort which preceded the appearance of light: writing or the combining of letters, or a deliberate and channeled effort on the part of the anonymous Kabbalist who wrote *Šaʿar ha-Kawwanah.* We shall begin with Deikman's comments:

> The concept of sensory translation offers an intriguing explanation for the ubiquitous use of light as a metaphor for mystic experience. It may not be just a metaphor. "Illumination" may be derived from an actual sensory experience occurring when in the cognitive act of unification, a liberation of energy takes place, or when a resolution of unconscious conflict occurs, permitting the experience of "peace,"

> "presence," and the like. Liberated energy experienced as light may be the core sensory experience of mysticism.[45]

While Deikman's description is closer to that of Abulafia's circle, in the words of Staudenmaier, as quoted by H. Zimmer, we find an explanation closer to that given in *Šaʿar ha-Kawwanah.*

> In seeing, hearing, smell, touch, etc., the specific stimulus is transmitted centripetally from the peripheral organs, the eye, ear, etc., to the higher centers in the brain and finally to consciousness. In the production of optical, acoustical, and other hallucinations, one must learn to transmit the specific energy in the reverse direction from the higher brain centers to the periphery.[46]

While Deikman deals with sensations appearing without any intentionality on the part of the mystic, Staudenmaier speaks of the results of deliberate efforts, whose primary purpose is magical.

3. Speech

We shall now return to Abulafia's remarks in his letter to R. Judah Salmon. Following his remarks about light, he says the following regarding the devotees of the Kabbalah of Names:

> . . . and they ascend from light to light . . . to the union, until their inner speech returns, cleaving to the primordial speech which is the source of all speech, and they further ascend from speech to speech until the inner human speech [is a] power in itself, and he prepares himself to receive the Divine speech, whether in the aspect of the image of speech, whether in the aspect of the speech itself; and these are the prophets in truth, in justice and righteousness.[47]

Unlike light, which is the source of "personal" prophecy, speech is the source of true prophecy—that is, that prophecy which is directed both to the prophet himself and to his fellow man. In Abulafia's doctrine, prophetic speech refers, among other things, to the flow received by the power of the imagination, that is, the voice which is heard at the time of prophecy.[48] In order for the mystic to receive the speech, he must strengthen his intellect, that is, according to the medieval Aristotelian epistemology, "the inner speech," so that he may receive the flow—"the Divine word"—whose source is in God or in the Active Intellect: i.e., in "the primordial speech." The perception of speech is accomplished in two ways: either within the

Active Intellect, that is, by means of speculation concerning the contents of prophetic flux, or by means of "speech itself"—apparently by hearing voices.

Besides this theoretical description of speech, in which it is seen as the outcome of the power of the imagination—for which reason it does not originate in the organs of speech—one also finds other opinions on this subject in the writings of Abulafia and his disciples. The prophet not only delivers the prophecy by means of his voice, but also receives it "into his throat." There was a wide-spread belief among the Sages that the Shekhinah spoke through the instrument of Moses' voice,[49] while the saying, "the Shekhinah speaks from his throat" was known at least from the time of Rashi's commentary on the Pentateuch.[50] The sages based this upon the Biblical verse, "Moses spoke and God answered him with a voice."[51] So long as God was able to answer with a voice, the verse did not constitute an exegetical problem; however, with the emergence of Jewish philosophy, which developed the doctrine of the incorporeality of the Divine, those thinkers who saw God as a spiritual entity found it difficult to interpret this verse literally. In order to remove the difficulties entailed in this, R. Abraham ibn Ezra writes, "The one speaking is man, and the one hearing is man,"[52] alluding to the fact that God does not speak with the help of voices, but that He conveys the intellectual content through the instrument of spiritual speech addressed to the soul, whereafter the soul itself transforms this contents into speech which another human being is able to hear. The Divine voice is thus removed from prophecy, and in its place comes the voice of the prophet.

In *Ozar ʿEden Ganuz,*[53] Abulafia writes:

> With this voice came wondrous verses from the Torah, the Prophets and the Writings, and of this it is said, "Moses spoke and God [*Elohim*]—which is the full name[54]—answered him with a voice," and they said,[55] "with the voice of Moses." And behold, the voice of the living God speaks from within the fire, and it dwells within the heart, and thus is the speech there.

Here it states explicitly that the source of the Divine voice and speech is in man's heart, and not in the fire of the bush.[56] In another work of Abulafia's, we read:

> For this speech which comes from the Holy Spirit only comes to the prophet by means of human speech, and the evidence for this is "Moses spoke and God answered him with a voice"; and they

> revealed its secret when they said "with a voice'—this was the voice of Moses."[57]

The speech issuing from man's inner being is also mentioned in *Šaʿarê Zedeq*. In describing the latest phase of his experiences, the anonymous author writes:

> Behold, like the speech which emerges from my heart and comes to my lips, forcing them to move; and I said that perchance, God forbid, it is a spirit of folly which has entered me, and I perceive it speaking wisdoms. I said that this is certainly the spirit of wisdom.[58]

Elsewhere, he writes, "and a voice went out from me."[59] A similar idea occurs in R. Isaac of Acre, who writes in his *Commentary to Sefer Yezirah*,

> For the one who speaks with the Holy Spirit does not hear that voice, but that spirit comes within him and speaks by itself, as it comes from a high place, that from which the prophets draw [which is] in *Nezah* and *Hod*. . . . And there is no bringing together of lips there nor any other thing.[60]

The idea of human speech as an expression of the reception of prophecy again appears in the writings of R. Ḥayyim Vital, who writes in *Sefer ha-Gilgulim*:[61]

> Behold the secret of prophecy: it is certainly a voice sent from above to speak to that prophet, and the Holy Spirit is likewise in that manner. But because that voice is supernal and spiritual, it is impossible for it alone to be corporealized and to enter into the ears of the prophet, unless it first be embodied[62] in that same physical voice which emerged from that person while engaged in Torah and prayer and the like. It then embodies itself in it and is connected to it and comes to the ears of the prophet, so that he hears; but without the human voice it cannot exist. But there are many changes, as is said, for that selfsame supernal voice comes and is embodied within his voice. . . . The supernal voice of the prophet and that voice mentioned come and combine themselves with the voice of that man at present, which emerges from him when prophecy rests upon him, as is said, "the spirit of God spoke within me, and His word is on my tongue."[63] For the spirit and the original word dwell now upon my tongue, and there emerge from it the attribute of voice or speech from his throat and he speaks, and then the man hears them.

This striking emphasis upon the appearance of the voice within the act of prophesying is repeated by R. Elijah ha-Kohen of Izmir, who writes of the *maggidim:*[64] "from the power of the greatness of the soul[65] which is within man and tells him things, and the manner of the telling,[66] that a great voice comes out of his heart and enters into his heart and he hears, and those who stand before him do not hear anything." The above-mentioned approaches likewise served as the background for the appearance of similar phenomena in Hasidism.[67]

4. Prophetic Speech as Conversation

The concept of the immediate source of speech in the mystical experience as residing within the human soul was further developed in two other works of Abulafia. In *Ḥayyê ha-ʿOlam ha-Ba,*[68] he describes the process of pronouncing the letters of the Divine Name as follows:

> When you pronounce that matter found in the letters *Roš To<u>k</u> Sof* [i.e., "head, middle, end"], do not draw them out, but pronounce them as one who inquires quietly to another: what letter does such and such a point guard, which is such and such a place [in the human body]? And prepare yourself to hear that which will be answered in the pronouncing of the letter, and [when] you hear the letter pronounced from his mouth, do not pronounce it, for He has pronounced it for you, but receive the tidings that He shall speak with you, for 'in one [word] God speaks";[69] and rejoice in your heart, and pronounce again the head of the end, which is L. . . . And even if you wait a little while to hear, let it all be within one breath, and let the completion of the breaths be in the pronouncing of the letter, and not in any other thing, apart from the time that He answers you, and He shall pronounce the letter at the place which you have stated, and therefore the verse[70] reads "in every place where I shall mention [My Name]"—not "where you shall mention." And the secret of the matter is—if I will mention, you will mention, and if you shall mention, I shall mention. And consider his reply, answering as though you yourself had answered.

This passage depicts the act of pronouncing the letters by means of letter-combination, and the answer received when they are articulated. We may infer two contradictory things from this concerning the nature of the one answering: 1) the respondent is God: "He shall already speak to you, for 'in one God speaks,' " while the subject of the second verse, "I will remember," is God. It follows from this that a dialogue occurs between God and the one combining at the time of the pronouncing; 2) the respondent is the person himself, "and think when you respond, as though you yourself had answered yourself." This double meaning reappears elsewhere in that book:[71]

> When you complete the entire name and receive from it what the Name [i.e., God] wishes to give you, thank God; and if, Heaven forbid, you did not succeed in that which you sought, know that you must return in full repentance, and weep for that which is lacking in you level, and that you mentioned the Divine Name in vain, which is a grave sin. And you are not worthy of blessing, for God has promised us in the Torah to bless us, saying,[72] "in every place where I will have my Name mentioned, I will come to you and bless you." Behold, "where I will mention My Name"—when you pronounce My Name; and the secret of this is that at first you pronounce My Name, when you mention My Name as I have informed you, and the secret [refers to] the matter of the movement of the head at the time of reciting the *Qedušah* [Doxology].

Abulafia discusses here that case in which the pronunciation of the Name has no result; the blame is placed upon the one pronouncing it, who is seen here as a kind of false prophet, as suggested by the expression from Job 31:28, "it is also a grave sin, for I denied without trespass." The allusion to the verse in Exodus 20:7, "thou shall not take the Name of the Lord in vain," is further adduced to describe the guilt of one who pronounces the Divine Name without any consequence. Abulafia's argument is that God always answers, so that the deficiency can only be in the man; it follows from this that the pronunciation of the true Name is dialogue between man and God. On the other hand, Abulafia hints at the idea that "where I shall mention my Name" means "where you shall mention my Name," an act accomplished by various motions of the head. Testimony relating to such situations of dialogue also appear in *Sefer ha-Ḥešeq* in connection with the articulation of the Name:

> Direct your face towards the Name, which is mentioned, and sit as though a man is standing before you and waiting for you to speak with Him, and He is ready to answer you concerning whatever you may ask Him, and you say "speak" and he answers. . . . And begin then to pronounce, and recite first "the head of the head" [i.e., the first combination of letters], drawing out the breath and at great ease; and afterwards go back as if the one standing opposite you is answering you, and you yourself answer, changing your voice, so that the answer not be similar to the question. And do not extend the answer at all, but say it easily and calmly, and in response recite one letter of the Name as it actually is.[73]

This passage clearly elucidates that, during the process of pronunciation, the "respondent" is the person himself, who has altered his voice and imagines to himself that another person is standing opposite him and answering him. One may ask the significance of the dual meaning of the passages cited from *Ḥayyê ha-ʿOlam ha-Ba*. The answer is to be found, in my opinion, in *Sefer ha-Ḥešeq*, where it states:

> Immediately make your heart straight, and prostrate yourself before that thought from [*zurah neḥševet*] which you imagined in your heart, which is before you. And it is "the master of motion"—that is, it brings about that response which you have answered, which your heart has implanted within you like a throne, and made it into an angel of God, and it is that which is intermediate between yourself and your Creator, and that is His glory, may He be praised.[74]

Elsewhere in the same work, we read:

> But pronounce the names, one after another, as I have commanded you, whose secret is in the system of their motions, "one two." And if you are clean and perfect in all that I have instructed you, I have no doubt that the Glory will be revealed to you and appear before you in a form such that you will be able to feel its power, or it will bring to you speech so that you will be able to feel its power, or it will bring to you speech so that you will understand that it is from Him, and not from yourself.[75]

Before discussing these two passages, we must cite the enigmatic sentences written by R. Baruch Togarmi in *Commentary to Sefer Yez̲irah:*[76]

> I have already alluded above to the secret of "the radiance of the Shekhinah," concerning the matter of "one two." It is known that the Torah is called "this" *(ha-zot)*, after the Ineffable Name, in saying, "the words of this *(ha-zot)* Torah,"[77] which is the secret of the Divine image. And it cannot be seen except by a vision when he speaks, or perhaps it refers to Gabriel, in the language of *b"š* (!) that sees the form of man.

The attributes of the "thought form" which is the reason for the "answering" seem contradictory: one may bow down before it, but it is within "your heart," the human heart being its dwelling place, "its throne." The form is portrayed as the Glory of God, whose purpose is to give witness that the source of the speech is not in man, but outside of him. However, the exact character of "the form" is not clear: it is "the angel of God," "the Divine glory," "the intermediary" between man and God, or an "intermediate" between them.[78] It seems to me that these characteristics fit the human intellect, described in *Ḥayyê ha-ʿOlam ha-Ba* as "the flux of the intellect emanated upon us always, and it is emanated from the Active Intellect to us, and this is the angel which brings about cleaving between your soul and the Creator, blessed be He."[79] This description was influenced by Ibn Ezra and Maimonides who wrote, respectively, "and the angel which is between man and his God is intellective"[80] and "this is the intellect, which is emanated upon us from God, may He be blessed, and this is the connection which is between us and Him."[81] The term "Glory" does not interfere with this identification, as it frequently appears as a term for the soul prior to Abulafia.[82]

Let us now compare Abulafia's words in Sefer ha-Ḥešeq with those of his predecessor in *Commentary to Sefer Yeẕirah:* 1) in both passages, the term "one two" appears in the identical sense: i.e., as the Name of God: 2) both authors mention revelation: in Abulafia it refers to "Glory," while in R. Baruch Togarmi it is the "image of God" which is revealed by Gabriel: 3) the revelation involves "speech" in both places; 4) Abulafia speaks of the appearance of "a thought form" or "Glory," while R. Baruch Togarmi speaks of Gabriel *(Gavriel)* speaker *(medabber)* vision *(ma'reh)* the image of God *(Ẕelem Elohim)*, which equals 246 in *gemaṭria*, on the one hand, and the human form *(ẕurat ha-Adam)* on the other. In Abulafia there are also signs of "the human form" which appear at the time of pronouncing. *Ḥayyê ha-ʿOlam ha-Ba* states: "If Heaven forbid there has not yet come to him, while pronouncing the two verses, either the flux or the speech or the apprehension of the figure of man, and like visions of prophecy, he ought to start again from the third verse."[83] On the other hand, in the same work Abulafia uses other expressions connected to his teacher's words:[84]

> The angel who advises you of the secret of God is named Gabriel, and he speaks from the first verse of the holy name mentioned by you, and he shows you the wonders of prophecy, for that is the secret of:[85] "In a vision I will make myself known to him, in a dream I will speak to him," for "vision," which is the secret of the verse, equals Gabriel, and "dream," whose secret is[86] "Edo," is Enoch.

Here, too, one finds the *gemaṭria* for Gabriel › 246 › *pasuq (verse)* › *ma'reh* (vision) › *medabber* (speaks). There seems no doubt that these expressions allude to the Active Intellect. Consequently, in the prophetic vision the mystic sees "the figure of a human" by means of the Active Intellect, a revelation accompanied by speech. We infer the connection between this figure, which is the reason for the "response," and the person speaking, from Abulafia's own words, who describes this situation as an answer given by man to himself. It follows from this that we may reasonably assume that the human form is no more than a projection of the soul or intellect of the mystic, who carries on a dialogue with it at the time of pronunciation. The ontic status of this figure may be inferred from Abulafia's comments in *Ḥayyê ha-ʿOlam ha-Ba:*

> We, the community of Israel, the congregation of the Lord, know in truth that god, may He be praised, is neither a body nor a power within the body nor will He ever be corporealized. But at the time that the prophet prophesies, his abundance creates a corporeal intermediary, which is the angel.[87]

It follows from this that the human form seen is an imaginary creation, and is thus "bodily" (real) even though its source lies in the human intellect.

These opinions of Abulafia, in which 'prophecy, or mystical experience is interpreted in terms of a dialogue between man and his inner essence—the intellect—are not new. Already in Gnosticism, we learn of meetings between man and his own image as the climax of self-knowledge.[88] This idea appears in Hebrew in the book *Sefer ha-Ḥayyim,* attributed to R. Abraham ibn Ezra,[89] which states:

> Image *(temunah)*—this refers to a vision within a thing, like the electrum *(ḥašmal)* within the fire, and in the manner that a man sees a form within the water or the form of the moon or the form of some other thing or the form of himself,[90] "and he shall see the image of God"—he sees his own image in the light of God and His glory, and this is,[91] "a form against my eyes."

Testimonies of vision of the self, within the context of the process of prophecy, appear in those circles with which Abulafia had a certain degree of contact:

> All the camps of the Shekhinah have there neither image nor corporeal form, but spiritual emanation, and likewise on the other angelic levels. However, the tenth level, which is closest to human beings, called *išim,* [i.e., persons] is visible to the prophets. All agree that they possess the form of a body, similar to [that of] a human being, and very awesome. And the prophet sees all sorts of his

> powers becoming weaker and changing from form to form, until his powers cast off all forms and are embodied into the power of the form revealed to him, and then his strength is exchanged with that of the angel who speaks with him. And that form gives him strength to receive prophecy, and it engraved in his heart as a picture, and when the messenger has performed his mission the prophet casts off that form and returns to his original form, and his limbs and strength come back as they were before and are strengthened, and he prophesies in human form.[92]

In R. Judah ibn Malka's *Commentary to Sefer Yeẕirah,* we read a passage similar to that of R. Isaac ha-Cohen:[93]

> The author said: I have seen with my own eyes a man who saw a power in the form of an angel while he was awake, and he spoke with him and told him future things.[94] The sage said: Know that he sees nothing other than himself, for he sees himself front and back, as one who sees himself in a mirror, who sees nothing other than himself, and it appears as if it were something separate from your body, like you. In the same manner, he sees that power which guards his body and guides his soul, and then his soul sings and rejoices, distinguishes and sees." And three powers overcome him: the first power is that which is intermediary between spirit and soul, and the power of memory and the power of imagination, and one power is that which imagines. And these three powers are compared to a mirror, as by virtue of the mixing the spirit is purified, and by the purification of the spirit the third power is purified. But when the spirit apprehends the flux which pours out upon the soul, it will leave power to the power of speech, according to the flow which comes upon the soul, thus shall it influence the power of speech, and that itself is the angel which speaks to him and tells him future things.

Here, as in Abulafia, a certain relationship is posited between the Active Intellect—*išim*—and the human powers embodied within it.

However, while in the three examples thus far cited the element of dialogue is totally lacking, this element does appear among Abulafia's students, apparently as a result of his influence. In *Šošan Sodot,*[95] there is a statement quoted in the name of R. Nathan, whom I believe to have been a direct disciple of Abulafia:[96]

> Know that the fullness of the secret of prophecy to the prophet is that suddenly he will see his own form standing before him, and he will forget himself and disappear from it, and will see his own

> form standing before him and speaking with him and telling him the future. Of this secret the sages said,[97] "Great is the power of the prophets, for they make the form similar to its creator," and the sage R. Abraham b. Ezra said, "the one hearing is a man, and the one speaking is the man."

The connection between 'prophecy' and foretelling the future also appears in Abulafia, who writes in *Ḥayyê ha-ʿOlam ha-Ba*[98] that the third level of prophecy is "to receive the command of a thing in telling the future." By contrast, another disciple of Abulafia, the author of *Šaʿarê Ẕedeq*, only knows of the appearance of the image of the self without speech. In *Šošan Sodot*, we read the following:

> Another sage wrote about this as follows: By the power of [letter-] combination and concentration, that which I describe in *Šaʿarê Ẕedeq* happened to me, [namely,] that I saw the light going with me. But I did not merit to see the form of myself standing before me, and this I was unable to do.[99]

This statement incorporates a double testimony: (1) that this disciple knew of the high level attained by R. Nathan; (2) that the omission of the subject of speech does not signify that the appearance of the self-image was unconnected with speech. As we have seen above, this anonymous Kabbalist enjoyed speech which emerged from himself, for which reason it is not mentioned in the present context.

Abulafia's influence upon R. Isaac of Acre, through R. Nathan, may be seen in the former's *Oẕar Ḥayyim*, where he writes:

> Come and I will enlighten you concerning a major principle in reading; and speaking, or saying or vision *(maḥazeh)* or sight *(ḥazon)*, and of the reality of the hands of God, and the reality of speech or of the burden of speech or elocution or a prophetic dream, or seeing or burden of the spirit or the downtreading of the spirit or a gift of the spirit or the reality of the spirit of God and the spirit of God: all these and more than these similar to them are the new flux, the spirit of God, which comes to dwell in the pure soul which is worthy of it, in which it was not present at the beginning. It is like the case of a king in a favorable hour, who gives a generous gift to one of his princes who came before him at that time; the prince will rejoice in it and divide it with the members of his household. So does this supernal spirit of holiness suddenly come and dwell in the soul of this prophet or visionary who is deserving of the spirit of prophecy or in the soul deserving of the Holy Spirit in his soul alone, or the soul deserving only a Heavenly Voice speaking within it, teaching

him sciences which have never been heard or have never been seen, written without revealing the future, or revealing to him the future without any order concerning a mission, but to him alone: or with the command of a mission to an individual, or being commanded to go on a mission to many—all these will be heard when the ear hears and understands the voice of the words of its friend who speaks to him, but his fellow will not hear all this, but only he alone, even if at that time he is among a hundred or a thousand people. [All this will happen] after he has stripped off every corporeal thing, because of the great immersion of his soul in the divine spiritual world: this "container" [Heb.: *heḵala;* i.e., form of the body] will see his own form, literally, standing before him and speaking to him, as a man speaks to his friend; and his own form will be forgotten, as if his body does not exist in the world. Therefore the sages said, "great is the power of the prophets, for they make the form similar to its creator"; their soul stands opposite them in the form of the very "container" speaking with them, and they say that the Holy One, blessed be He, speaks with them. And what caused them this great secret? The stripping out of sensory things by their souls, and their casting off from them and the embodiment in the divine spirit. And this spirit shall at times come to all the prophets, according to the Divine Will. But the master of all the prophets, Moses our Teacher, peace upon him, always received a holy spirit which did not leave him for even one hour, only when his soul was still sunk in corporeal things, to hear the words of the Israelites that he might guide them and instruct them, either in temporary or permanent instructions, for which reason he had to say, "Stay and I shall hear what God commands" (Num. 9:8); he stood and separated from them and isolated himself and cast his soul off from those sensory things with which he was involved on their behalf, and there rested upon him the spirit and spoke within him.[100]

I should like to point out several ideas in this passage which are quite close to Abulafia's approach.

1) The parable of the king's generosity. R. Isaac of Acre's view was apparently influenced by a passage from *Ôr ha-Seḵel,* in which it states that, "the flux. . . . And this is compared to a king and a pauper, the latter being in the most extreme destitution. And the king flowed with wealth, to make wealthy each man to his fellow, until the great wealth reached the slave's master."[101]

2) In *Ôr ha-Seḵel,* the above-cited passage is preceded by a discussion concerning the different levels of prophets, reminiscent of the discussion which appears in R. Isaac of Acre, following the

parable of the generous king: "the level of those who pursue prophecy is greater than that of those who pursue wisdom, and the level of the prophets who speak and compose [books] is greater than that of the prophets who make intensive effort in prophecy, and those [prophets] who are sent are superior to the others," etc.[102] These two ideas appear in a book written in honor of R. Nathan, Abulafia's disciple.

3) The double meaning of the word "speech" in Abulafia, as discussed above, is reflected in R. Isaac of Acre in the words: "the form of the very 'container' speaking with them,and they say that the Holy One, blessed be He, speaks with them."[103]

4) The understanding of Moses as one who at times abandoned the mystical life in order to lead the people is likewise alluded to in Abulafia, who speaks about the return of the mystic "from God" in order to help others to achieve perfection.[104]

Finally, one ought to take note of a passage in *Even Sappir* by R. Elnathan b. Moses Kalkish, a fourteenth-century Byzantine kabbalist, who knew Abulafia's writing and his circle well:[105]

> For every apprehension which man receives of the spiritual apprehensions, its beginning is in human thought, and when man thinks continually concerning things which exist and their essence and about supernal and mundane activities, and of the Divine guidance which guides all, and which guards all this order of existence which is ordered by God, may He be blessed, and he removes his thought from everything apart from this, and views all corporeal and bodily matters as the image of contingent things, and spiritual matters as the essential ones; and every day he adds to these sublime thoughts, until from the gathering of their multitude there is born its offspring, called wisdom, and from its abundance is born further understanding[106] and knowledge. And he shall do all this by combining the holy letters and words and the pure language, which are the vehicle of all thoughts, then there are born from their combination thoughts of wisdom and understanding, and, because of its intense meditation on them, the intellect will perceive reality, and there will come the renewed spirit, which made the fruit of the intellect, from the source of the wondrous thought and will speak by itself: but the thinker will recognize that there is a mover and cause which causes him to think and to speak and to guide and to compose until, through the great activity, the inner one will return as if it is externally apprehended, and the two

of them, the one apprehending and the object of apprehension, are one thing, and they are intellectual apprehension.

We see here a description of the progress from apprehension of the intellectives of external things, their internalization, and their implantation within the human soul. By the process of letter-combination, the inner intellective objects are likely to be transformed into external ones, causing the impression or the experiences that the motivation for human actions is external to himself.

5. The Vision of the Human Form

We have seen above that the appearance of the "human form," and the conversation between it and the mystic, are both a phenomenon discussed on Abulafia's writings and something to which his disciples referred as a personal experience. Thus far, we have only dealt with the theoretical aspect of this subject in Abulafia—i.e., we have cited various passages which describe the path by which the prophetic state is reached—but we have not found any evidence of personal experience in these passages. We shall now turn to another work of Abulafia's which, in my opinion, includes direct first-person evidence of an experience of this kind. We read in *Sefer ha-Ôt*, pp. 81-82:

> I was shown a new vision by God, with anew name upon a renewed spirit. . . . I saw a man coming from the west with a great army, the number of the warriors of his camp being twenty-two thousand men[107]. . . . And when I saw his face in the sight, I was astonished, and my heart trembled within me, and I left my place and I longed for it to call upon the name of God to help me, but that thing evaded my spirit. And when the Man has seen my great fear and my strong awe, he opened his mouth and he spoke, and he opened my mouth to speak, and I answered him according to his words, and in my words I became another man.[108]

One needn't dwell upon the fact that "the form of a man" appears in this vision. It is worthwhile taking note of the dialogue between them: the man wishes to speak, "opened his mouth and he spoke"; the speech was, however, externally caused: "and he opened my mouth . . . and I answered him." The expression, "I answered according to his words," is indicative of the source of the speech. The verse quoted from the Book of Samuel likewise strengthens the interpretation of this passage as an expression of an event taking place within Abulafia's consciousness. It is appropriate to examine more fully the description of the man:

> On his forehead was a letter inscribed in blood and ink on two sides, and the shape of the letter was like the shape of a staff separating between them, and it was a very hidden letter. The color of the blood was black, and changed to red, and the color of the ink was red, and behold it was black, and the appearance of the letter separating between the two was white. Miraculous was that which was revealed by the seal, [which is] the key within the forehead of he who came [the man], and all the army of the band was turning about and travelling in accordance to it [i.e., the seal or the key].

Is this description meant as an external representation of Abulafia's soul? Let us first examine his words in *Siṭrê Torah:*[109]

> It is known and conspicuous to all the Sages of the Torah who are Kabbalists, nor is it concealed to the true philosophers, that every man is given a choice without any compulsion and without any force, but there is a human power within man, and it is called the Stirring Power *koaḥ ha-meʿorer,* and it is that which arouses his heart to do or not to do [any thing]. And after this, a man finds in his heart one who forces him between these two opposites, and whichever of them shall be victorious over him will activate the limbs to perform actions for good or for evil; and this principle shall return, of man always struggling and warring against the thoughts of this heart, the two former motivating all of the aspects of his many thoughts, as is written in *Sefer Yeẕirah,*[110] "The heart in soul [i.e., within man] is like the king in a battle". . . . And a man possesses these two forms, called impulses or powers or angels or thoughts or comprehensions or however you wish to call them. For the intent of them all refer to one thing, but the main thing is to apprehend His reality and to recognize their essence in truth, by proofs which are based upon tradition and reason, and to distinguish between two paths of reality which they have, and to know the great difference between them in degree. And if the two are one reality or two combined together, and if they may be separated or if they do not receive separation. And when we see their battle in the heart, we may recognize that they are two, and they act one upon the other and affect one another, and therefore there is time for this and time for that one, and it is like a small moment, like a point which cannot be divided, less than the blinking of an eye. And this is alluded to in [the saying "There is a time with God like the winking of an eye,"

for it lacks the letter *waw;* it is written *yeš ʿet* [i.e., the plain spelling of the word *yešuʿat* includes a *waw,* and signifies 'redemption' or 'salvation']; and know this.

It is clear from this passage that he is speaking about a permanent struggle between the Intellect and the Imagination; the Angel of Life and the Angel of Death; rational thought and imaginative thought; the intellective apprehension and the imaginative one; the Good Impulse and the Evil impulse. Abulafia returns to this inner battle in *Sefer ha-Ôt,* p. 81 "and the battle within the heart between the blood and the ink is very intense." On the same page, the nature of blood and ink are portrayed as image [*ẕelem,* i.e., intellect] and likeness [*demut,* i.e., imagination]: that is, ink as the spiritual element, the intellect, and blood as the imaginative one.[111] These two elements, as they do battle within Abulafia's heart, are described in *Sefer ha-Ôt,* p. 81: "And I looked and I saw there [in my heart] my likeness and image moving in two paths." The same symbols used by Abulafia to describe the inner battle of powers within man appear in the description of the man himself: "and on his forehead was a letter inscribed in blood and ink, into two sides." From this, we see that the blood and the ink as they battle within the soul are projected outside, and thus do they appear in the prophetic vision. What is the meaning of the "letter on the forehead" which separates between the other two letters? In *Sefer ha-Ôt,* p. 82, Abulafia relates that a fount of seventy tongues flowed from between the sign of his forehead; "the sign on his forehead was called the potion of death by the man, but I called it the potion of life, for I transformed it from death to life." The allusion to "seventy tongues" may be properly understood if we assume that the meaning of the sign is the Active Intellect, which is the source of the seventy tongues. The Active Intellect is the potion of life for those who are able to receive its flux, while for those who are unable to do so it is the potion of death.[112] This concept also has a double meaning in both the person and the soul; in *Sefer ha-Ôt,* p. 82, we read, "And see with your eyes and understand in your heart the hidden letter inscribed on your forehead explicitly." On the one hand, it is possible to see the sign, while on the other it is subject to understanding by means of the Intellect—your heart. On p. 83 of the same work, we find another idea connecting the letter to the Active Intellect:

And I gazed at the letter inscribed on my forehead and I knew it, and my heart was enlightened when I looked at it, and my spirit lives with its eternal life, and its statue brought me to and its constitution

> moved me about, to speak and to compose this *Book of the Sign.*

That cleaving which brings about "eternal life" is identical with that cleaving to the Active Intellect which is the source of the abundance causing the prophet to act and "to speak and to compose." We may now understand several passages from this vision. On p. 82, the man says to Abulafia:

> You have been victorious in my war, and you changed the blood of my forehead, and their nature and color, and you have stood up to all the tests of my thoughts. Ink you have raised and upon ink you shall be engrandized; the letter you have sanctified, and by means of the letter [*ot:* a pun upon the two senses of the word, "letter" and "sign"] and wonder you shall be sanctified.

This man, who is the outcome of the transformation of the flow of the Active Intellect from an intellectual flow to an imaginary form, praises Abulafia because he has transformed the blood, the imaginative element, into ink, the intellectual component. This transformation was accomplished by means of the "letter"—evidently a reference to the letters of the Divine name mentioned below, with whose help man can actualize his intellect. The transformation of the color, mentioned on p. 82, is likewise depicted as a transformation from death to life, "Life replaces death, requires the letter to find innocent and to give life." What is the connection between ink/blood and life and death? In the Talmud, *Tractate Shabbat,* we read:

> The Holy One, blessed be He, said to Gabriel: Go and record upon the forehead of the righteous a line of ink, that the angels of destruction may not rule over them; and upon the foreheads of the wicked a line of blood, so that the angels of destruction may rule over them.[113]

In the Midrash *Otiyot de-Rabbi Akiva,* it states,[114]

> What is meant by [the verse],[115] "you shall draw a line"? This teaches us that at the time that the Holy One, blessed be He, decreed that Jerusalem was to be destroyed, He called to the Angel of Death [alternative reading, "Gabriel"] and said to the angel: Go first to Jerusalem and pick out from within it the righteous and the wicked; and to every righteous man who is in it, draw a line of ink upon his forehead, a line of life, in order that he may live; and to every wicked person who is within it, draw a line of blood upon his forehead, that he may die.

Relying upon this midrash, Abulafia writes in *Sefer ha-Meliẕ:*

A line of life, a line of ink; and the line of death, a line of blood. And after this he showed us the form of his apprehension, and informed us that he had made the blood into ink—that is, from death to life. That is, he restored the soul of the spirit of life within him, with the apprehension, the form of a living, understanding and wise being, and he knew that it [i.e., the form] was deserving to survive eternally, by reason of the apprehension, and it was transformed from being dead to being alive.[116]

A slightly different formulation appears in *Sitrê Tôrah:*

"Adam and Eve" in *gemaṭria* equals "my father and my mother" *(avi ve-imi),* and their secret is blood and ink, and this latter is proven by this name, *YHWH,* and one who merits it will have engraved upon his forehead a *taw*—for one a *taw* of blood, for the other a *taw* of ink. And the secret of the *taw* of blood *(taw šel dam)* is that she is born *(še-muledet),* and its matter is *taw dam,* which alludes to "likeness" *(demut)* [the letters of *taw dam* form the word *demut*], meaning that it precedes man in existence. And from that there comes "your soul" *(nafšeḵa),* and every "magician" *(kašfan)* will be turned about the path of magic *(kešafim),* and one who does so "spills blood" *(šofeḵ dam).* And the secret of the *taw* of ink is "and the woman-that-gives-birth" *(we-še-yoledet).* Thus, you have one form when she is born *(še-muledet)* and another when she gives birth *(še-yoledet).*[117]

We learn from this that the message which the man gives to Abulafia is a confirmation of his success in transforming the imagination into intellect, by this means attaining eternal existence. This definition of eternal life appears in *Ôr ha-Seḵel.*[118]

And when the false apprehension is negated, as mentioned, and is remembered in the mind from the heart of those who feel and the enlightened ones, then "death shall be shallowed up[119] forever and God will erase tears from every face and the shame of his people will be removed for the mouth of the Lord has spoken." That is, the secret of the intellect will be revealed after its disappearance.

More expressively, Abulafia writes in *Sefer ha-Ôt* pp. 82-83:

More bitter than death is his filth, and therein is sunk his strength, and sweeter than honey is his blood, and therein resides his spirit, in the dwelling of his heart. The soul of every living, enlightened

> person travels from the tent of filth to the tent of the blood, and from the dwelling of the blood travels to the dwelling of the heart of heaven, and there you shall dwell all the days of your life.

When man abandons the dwelling of the blood/imagination and actualizes his intellect, he cleaves to the Active Intellect, alluded to in "the heart of heaven," and thus brings about his survival. It is worth while mentioning an additional sign of the connection between "the man" and "the form" mentioned in *Sefer ha-Ḥešeq*. In *Sefer ha-Ôt*, p. 83, he writes: "And I prostrated myself and bowed before him," referring to the man mentioned in the vision. In *Sefer ha-Ḥešeq*, he states,

> That one who finds a person innocent and conquered beneath him the one who is culpable, until he is imprisoned himself and admitted and was conquered; and concerning this you straighten your heart immediately, that you bow before him [in] the form considered mentioned in your heart, which is before you.[120]

The innocent and the guilty doubtless refer to the intellect and the imagination: when the imagination is conquered by the intellect, there appears both inside and "outside" "the form," before which one must bow.

Finally, we should take note that in two places in *Sefer ha-Ôt*—passages not included in the vision of "the man" described above—the idea of the prophet's conversation with himself appears. On p. 74, it states, "The heart of my heart *(libbi)* said to the inner heart of my heart *(levavi)* to write down the ways of God, etc.," while on p. 80 we read "my heart *(libbi)* said to my heart *(levavi)*."

6. The Vision of the Letters

We may now refer to another vision appearing in Abulafia's writings to complete our discussion of the subject of "the form of a man." Already in *Sefer ha-Navon*, attributed to one of the Ashkenazic Hasidim, we find the letters of the four-letter Divine Name revealed to the prophet[121] or seen as identical to the "Angel of Glory" or to Meṭaṭron, who also fulfills an important function in the revelation.[122] Abulafia connected the Ineffable Name to revelation by means of a *gemaṭria:*

> And indeed *YHWH* is his vision, and this is what is meant by[123] "and he shall see the image of God"—that is, that he gazes at the

> letters of this Name and at their ways, and all hidden things are revealed to him. And the proof of this is that [the phrase] "and he gazes at the image of God" is the equivalent in *gemaṭria* to "at the name of God he gazes," for the number of the final *Mem* in *ba-šem* ("in" or "at the Name") equals 600.[124]

This passage deals with Moses who, like Joshua in the passage mentioned from *Sefer ha-Navon*, received guidance for his activity through contemplation of the four letter Name.[125] Abulafia's formulation of this in his description of the revelation to Moses closely matches what he wrote in *Ḥayyê ha-ʿOlam ha-Ba*.[126]

> The letters are without any doubt the root of all wisdom and knowledge, and they are themselves the contents of prophecy, and they appear in the prophetic vision as though [they are] opaque bodies speaking to man face to face [saying] most of the intellective comprehensions, thought in the heart of the one speaking them. And they appear as if pure living angels are moving them about and teaching them to man, who turns them about in the form of wheels in the air, flying with their wings, and they are spirit within spirit. And at times the person sees them as if they are resting in the hills and flying away from them, and that mountain which the person sees them dwelling upon or moving from was sanctified by the prophet who sees them, and it is right and proper that he call them holy, because God has descended upon them in fire,[127] and in the holy mountain there is a holy spirit. And the name of the holy high mountain is the Ineffable Name, and know this, and the *ryw* (=216) and secret of the mountain is *Gevurah* (might=216), and he is the Mighty One, who wages war against the enemies of God who forget His Name. And behold, after this the letters are corporealized in the form of the Ministering Angels who know the labor of singing, and these are the Levites, who are in the form of God, who give birth to a voice of joy and ringing song, and teach with their voice matters of the future and new ways, and renew the knowledge of prophecy.

This passage is interesting in a number of respects: like the image of man which is revealed to the prophet at the time of prophecy, the letters which are revealed also "speak"; these letters, which constitute the Divine Names,[128] do battle with the enemies of God just as did the man in the vision on p. 83 of *Sefer ha-Ôt:* "And the man was concealed from my eyes after he spoke his words, and he went and grew greater and stronger in his battles until he overwhelmed every enemy." One may ask whether the central idea in the vision of "the man" is also present in the vision of the letters—that is, its being an imaginary expression of an inner process. The latter part of the passage from *Ḥayyê ha-ʿOlam ha-Ba* seems to allude to this view. In *Sefer Ner Elohim,*[129] the mountain from which the letters jump off and to which they return is interpreted as an allusion to the head.

> For it is known that the Torah was given on a mountain, and the blessing and curse on a mountain. And the harbinger [i.e., of Messianic redemption] will ascend a mountain, as is said, "on a high mountain get thee up, harbinger of Zion" [Isa. 40:9], etc. The mountain thus alludes to the head, for there is no other [organ] in the entire body as high and as distinguished as the head, and its secret is *har eš* (mountain of fire), and it is like the comparison of the mountains to the land, for the heads are the roots, therefore it is said,[130] "And the Lord called Moses up to the top of the mountain, and Moses ascended"—that is, to the highest place that man may ascend, and even though it exists up above, it is impossible for any person to ascend higher than did Moses.

An identity is established here between the "mountain of fire," i.e., the place from which the Torah was given, and the human head. In *Sefer ha-Hafṭarah,* we find allusions to the duality of "mountain." On the one hand, it alludes to the power of the imagination:[131]

> He was revealed in his glory on the holy mountain, and it is there a high and awesome mountain in Italian *monti barbaro,* and it is alluded to [in the phrase] *ḥizzeq ha-qašeh* (he strengthened the hard) and it was an act of miracle, which strengthened the breathing, and will also strengthen the soul, and it is the hidden name, the name of vengeance, which is the abominable name of the end and the sixth, which is "the false." And Raziel transformed the dwelling place of the imagination, as he did, for *Monti* is the imagination, and it is Azazel; in Italian, *Monti.* Therefore it is said of it,[132] that is is a mighty and difficult mountain, high and steep, and behold, it was hung to his *l'alto,* and is like "high" in Italian. . . . And *Monti,* "the heretic" (*ha-mini=115=monti*), "the right hand" ascended, and he is *Mento,* who testifies that he is the false one, and that is the meaning of *Sacramento* in Italian.

This passage tells us that mountain equals *Monti ha-dimyon* (the imagination) Azazel = 155,an identification which seems to have existed even before Abulafia demonstrated it by *gemaṭria.* On the other hand, as against the identification of "mountain" with "imagination" it is also identified with "intellect."[133] In the same treatise, further on in the above-mentioned passage,[134] we read:

> We have found in this two urges both of which have the form gold,

> in the allusion of,[135] "They were made two cherubim of gold," and this matter of gold is that it turns [something to] gold, and their allusion is *šem we-šem šemo, šam me*z̲*ayyer u-me*z̲*uyyar.*

The two urges referred to here by Abulafia are identical with the imagination and the intellect, which are the two cherubim, both of which apprehend. The end of the passage from *Ner Elohim* likewise points toward the possibility of interpreting the mountain as an allusion to the highest intellectual virtue to which Moses can reach. One may interpret in similar fashion the passage from MS. Jerusalem 8 1303 fol. 56a, connected to Abulafia or his circle, that "also in the divine mountain one shall apprehend and ascend in level and understand the flux of God, which comes from the highest mountain." It is worth mentioning that, in *Sefer ha-Ôt*, p. 76, it states of Abulafia that "God shall surely find the top of a high mountain, and its name is the fallen mountain and upon it sits the shepherd of this flock for twenty years," an allusion to the redemption anticipated in the year 1290, the twentieth year of Abulafia's prophetic career.

To summarize our discussion of the passage in *Ḥayyê ha-ʿOlam ha-Ba:* the letters, which the prophet sees flying about, landing and returning to the mountains, are the letters of the Divine Name, which originate in the powers of the intellect and the imagination. It may be shown that the Names of God are also found within the human soul, and that the flying about and coming to rest are essentially inner processes. In *Sefer ha-Ôt*, p. 81, we read: "And he showed me the image and likeness moving about in two ways, in a vision in an image TR"Y K"W, one image and one likeness."[136] The Ineffable Name within man's soul incorporates both the image and likeness, which are the intellect and the imagination. One p. 80 of *Sefer ha-Ôt*, Abulafia again writes that "the people of God, the supreme holy ones, looking upon His Name gaze at the source of your intellects and see the divine image within the image of your hearts. Indeed, the "image" refers to the head, for therein may be seen the heart of the vision." In *Ôzar ʿEden Ganuz*, the same idea is repeated with a minor variation, "And the two names are engraved in the heart and in the head, and they are alluded to in [the verse],'there he gave them a law and a statute,"[137] while in *Sitrê Torah* we speak of "the name inscribed in your soul in its truth."[138] The words of the author of *Ner Elohim* should be interpreted according to this same view of the Divine Name:

> It is known to us by tradition that it is impossible for any of the prophets of Israel to prophesy without knowledge of the Name which dwells in his heart. And he is not aware [of this] except

> according to the hidden order in *Sefer Yezirah* by which the prophet attains the order in the hidden things, and from both of them he will know the name of the one arranging, and it will speak to him and he will respond to it and then it will show him the path in which he must go and deed that he must do.[139]

The name is found "in his heart," but the prophet speaks to it and the Name answers him and reveals to him his way. This approach is reminiscent of the words of the eighteenth century Sufi sage, Nasser Muhammad 'Andalib of Delhi: "He sees the blessed form of the word 'Allah' in the color of light, written upon the table of his heart and upon the appearance of his imagination."[140]

To conclude, we shall cite a section from *Sefer ha-Ḥešeq,* which clearly demonstrates that the letters seen by the prophet resemble in their function the "man" who is revealed:

> After you find the appropriate preparation for the soul, which is knowledge of the method of comprehension of the contemplation of the letters, and the one who apprehends it will contemplate them as though they speak with him, as a man speaks with his fellow, and as though they are themselves a man who had the power of speech, who brings words out of his mind, and that man knows seventy tongues, and knows a certain specific intention in every letter and every word, and the one who hears it apprehends it in order to understand what he says, and the one hearing recognized that he does not understand, except for one language or two or three or slightly more, but he [that one] understands that the one speaking does not speak to him in vain, except after he knows all the languages; then every single word within him is understood in many interpretations.[141]

The speech of the letters, whose image is like that of a man, which are the source of the seventy languages of man, reminds one of the "seventy tongues" of the man mentioned in *Sefer ha-Ôt*. Finally, let us note the presence of a strikingly suggestive element in this passage: the mystic must "imagine" the letters—that is, make use of the technique described in the chapter dealing with this subject—"and think as if they are speaking."

On the other hand, in the writings of R. Isaac of Acre, the author of *Ôzar Ḥayyim,* we find testimony of the spontaneous appearance of the Divine Names:

> The young one, R. Isaac of Acre said, I woke up from my sleep and there suddenly came before me three Tetragrammata, each one in its vocalization and place in the secret of the ten sefirot of the void,

> in the middle line, on which depends the entire mystery of [the four worlds] *A<u>z</u>ilut, Beri'ah, Ye<u>z</u>irah, ʿAsiyah,* via the simple and felt intellect, alluded to in the secret of their vocalizations. And my soul rejoiced in them as one who had found a rare treasure, and they were these: ידוד ידוד ידוד, blessed is the Name of the Glory of his kingdom forever and ever. . . . And I saw a name as follows, thus:
>
> כתע
> ההה
>
> Just thus did I see it in its vocalization.[142]

Texts of the type mentioned above may have influenced the later practice of answering questions by visualizing the letters of the Ineffable Name, known from the letters of R. Elijah ha-Kohen of Ismir.[143]

7. The Urim and Tummim

The link connecting between the appearance of the letters of the Divine Name and that of "the man" is the Urim and Tummim. Opinion is divided as to the nature of these vessels: Rashi states that they were "the writing of the Ineffable Name."[144] We learn the meaning of this name from several sources: R. Jacob ben Asher, the *Baʿal ha-Ṭurim,* wrote in his commentary on Ex. 28:30 that "[the phrase] the Urim and Tummim equals in *gemaṭria* equals the Name of seventy-two letters,"[145] which evidently reflects a parallel opinion given in *Zohar* II, 234b, "and it is customary in the seventy-two letters inscribed, which are the secret of the Holy Name, and all of them are called Urim and Tummim." In yet another tradition it is said that:

> In the Kabbalah of R. Mešullam ha-Ẓarfati, which we received from the book called *Raziel,* [it states] that when you write these three verses in groups of three letters at a time, one arrives at the name of seventy-two letters, and they help to say great matters, of which there is no greater thing. This is the Ineffable Name of the Urim and Tummim, which was [worn] upon the heart of the High Priest.[146]

On the other hand R. Abraham ibn Ezra thought that the Urim and Tummim alluded to the seven servants, that is, the seven planets.[147]

Abulafia attempted to draw a connection between the interpretation of the Urim and Tummim as an internal matter with that which saw it as an external matter. In *Šomer Mizwah.*[148] he wrote:

> But the mystery of *va-yomar* (he said) is Urim—that is, the Urim and Tummim. And why are they called Urim? Because they enlighten *(me'irim)* their words.[149] And the light[150] which was created on the first day was one by which man may see from one end of the world to the other; for God, may He be blessed, saw that the wicked were not deserving of using it, so he hid it away for the righteous for the future. And this is the light of the Torah, as one to whom God has granted a little bit of knowledge and enlightened the eyes of his heart may see the entire world with its light. And these are the luminaries, which were created on the first day and the fourth day, and that is the meaning of the name [beginning with] *A"D*[151] half the name and its plene equal *Ale"f Dale"t*, and it alludes to the thousand *(elef)* potentialities. And the meaning of that which they said,[152] "May God shine his face upon you," is that there is light before Him, by which every person can see what he sees, and this is the beginning of the light which the sun receives from it, just as the moon received light from the light of the sun; and all this is a metaphor from light to light, for the bright inner light which shines is a thing without a body, and it comes from this, for it is hidden away for the righteous. And as the righteous see it with many aspects, that light is itself called "face," and its immediate cause is the abundance from the Divine influx, and it is called by the name, "the Prince of the Face."

The Urim referred to here allude to the inner light and the light which comes from the Active Intellect—the Prince of the Face—for which reason the intellective soul is portrayed as the moon, receiving its light from the sun.[153] This influx is only received by the righteous, that is, the enlightened ones who possess knowledge. In this passage, Abulafia accepts Ibn Ezra's opinion that the Urim refer to the luminaries—the sun and the moon. In another passage, Abulafia introduces the second view, namely, that "the Urim and Tummim are letters":[154]

> The strongest of these holy combinations, from which you will know the secret of the Ineffable Names. . . . And these are the letters which are called Urim and Tummim, which illuminate the eyes of the hearts, and complete the thoughts,[155] and purify the supernal thoughts, and enlighten the path of understanding, and make known the planetary positions, and teach the existence of separate beings, and tell the future.

With the assistance of letter-combinations, these names teach man wisdom and indicate to him the future. These two functions seem to me to allude to intellect and imagination, as the foretelling of the future was strongly linked to the perfections of imaginative power.[156] Let us now turn to *Imrê Šefer,*[157] where Abulafia writes:

> And of this [perfect] man it is said, "And upon the image of the throne there sat an image, like the image of a man above it,"[158] and it was an image looking like it, and the vision was the image of the glory of God, and he saw himself as in a clear crystal, to the eyes and the heart. And perhaps the Urim and Tummim [referred to] are the inner ones, for the external ones are also thus called, but they are as in an unclear crystal; know this and understand it well. And the difference between these and these cannot be known except to one who has apprehended both of them, and he is one who has apprehended knowledge of the three-fold unique Name.

In the same work, we learn of the significance of the "clear crystal" *(aspaqlaryah ha-me᾿irah),* which is identified with the Urim and Tummim:

> Comprehension of the Name by the Name: and it is a speculative examination into His Name, by means of the twenty-two letters of the Torah, after knowledge of the matter of the ten Sefirot from *aleph* to *yod,* which include all those which come after them, for they are fulfilled by them. And they, with their forms, are called the Clear Crystal, for all the forms having brightness and strong radiance are included in them. And one who gazes at them in their forms will discover their secrets and speak of them, and they will speak of them, and they will speak of him. And they are like an image in which a man sees all his forms standing opposite him, and then he will be able to see all the general and specific things.[159]

The Divine Names are spoken of in two passages: in the first passage in the phrase "these and these," which is an allusion to the Name of seventy-two letters, (*eleh* = 36 = 36 = 72), and following that by the "three-fold unique name," which is also an allusion to the seventy-two letter Name. In the second passage, the matter is explained as follows: study of the Name is like gazing into a mirror, in which a person sees his own image. This vision of the self is accompanied by speech, "and he spoke of them, and they spoke of him." If we remember that Abulafia explicitly mentions the "human image," we again have the typical prophetic-mystical situation of Abulafia. The Urim and Tummim are the inner form of man, that is, the Intellect and Imagination. It seems reasonable to assume that, in the phrase *Aspaqlaryah še-einah meira* (translated above as "the unclear crystar"), Abulafia intends to refer to the heavenly luminaries—the sun and the moon—which are corporeal things outside of man.[16]

Let us now turn to Abulafia's disciple, the author of *Šaʿarê Ẕedeq*.

> If he is able to decide and to further continue [in letter-combination], he shall emerge from within to without, and it will be imagined for him by the power of his purified imagination in the form of a pure mirror, and this is "the shining rotating sword" (Gen. 3:24), whose back side turns about and becomes the front, and he recognizes the nature of its innerness from outside, like the image of the Urim and Tummim, which in the beginning cast light from within. "And you shall tell" is not straight, but only combines because of its form being incomplete, separate from its essence,until it is separated and enclothed in the form of his imagination, and therein it joins the letters by a perfect joining, ordered and ready. And this seems to me to be that form which is referred to by the Kabbalists as "garment": but we have already commented on the matter of the names and their activities.[161]

The author associated Abulafia's remarks concerning letter-combination and the Urim and Tummim with the Talmudic idea that the Urim and Tummim worked by illuminating certain letters, which combined to provide the answer to the question posed.[162] Like the Urim and Tummim, the human form is separated from within his body or his matter; after being separated, the human form, that is, the intellect, is clothed in an imaginary garment, just as the letters, which are isolated in their sense, combine into a word, a combination which is all no more than an imaginary garment for an answer containing meaning to the one inquiring. The stage of dressing is designated by the name Tummim, connected with the power of the imagination. Elsewhere in *Šaʿarê Ẕedeq*,[163] we read:

> Know that these letters which are the holy letters may be called signs and traditions, which are depicted by their exterior form[164] with prophetic agreement by the Holy Spirit, and that is the form which appears to the prophets, when the inside, concave form is reversed to an external, convex for, like the Tummim, as mentioned above.

The concave inner form is the intellect, while the external convex for is the imaginative form. Thus, we again return to the view that the powers of the soul are revealed to the mystic.

8. The Circle

We have seen thus far that Abulafia's visions contain revelations of the contents of the human soul. We shall now examine a vision incorporating both a revelation of the soul, on the one hand, and a revelation of the world, on the other. We read in *Sefer ha-Meliẕ:*[165]

> This is the meaning of "as the appearance of the bow that is in the cloud on a rainy day."[166] Just as the colored brilliance is seen in the rainbow on a rainy day, and is there with the brilliance of the sun, so do the humours which are the rain and the showers and the vapor. And the smokes and the steams, which are treated by that and by the food which is in the principle organs, and which ascend and descend are the clouds themselves. And the brilliance of the soul, which is combined from the sphere and from the stars and luminaries, together with the brilliance of the abundance which flows from the sphere of the rainbow to the organs of the body, in general and in particular, which is "the appearance of the brightness round about, which was the appearance of the likeness of the glory of God."[167] Therefore, Raziel says that when he arrived at this knowledge and acquired it in his intellect, he knew the question which he was asked by the form, which he saw inscribed before him, as engraved by his Rock [i.e., God]. And this is clear testimony that he asked wisdom from his Creator and that wisdom he was taught by Him, blessed be His name. And Then he returned to the matter of opening his eyes to see before him the tree of knowledge, whose name is life: that is, that which is to others a potion of death, and is the tree of knowledge, was to Raziel the potion of life, and he did not stumble in it as did others. And now seek to draw for us that which is its image, and he said that it is like a round ladder, and he counted its steps, and said that there are 360 rungs, and he saw that the width of each rung was like the span of a man's step, from foot to foot, and he saw that between each step there was as the length of a rung, and its appearance was like that of bright blue, which was full around it from the east, and descends to the west strongly, and in its middle there passed through a very thick bar, and its length was like a third of the circle, so that it came out that its head was to the south and its end to the north, and it had four heads at its head [i.e., beginning], and likewise its end to the four winds. And on each head there was a body, equal, having eight points, and six sections spotted like a carbuncle, and there were twelve lines to each one of them, and a fifth head, from this side and from that, until all of them amounted to five against five. And he said that these go to the right, and these to the left, and they accordingly threw the lots among known names. And he said that the *Pur* turns about from *y''w* to *y''w*, that is, from higher to higher,

and from pair to pair, and he said that upon them is a great and awesome king who arranges and estimates all in wisdom. And he completed those visions with wisdom, which is the secret that turns about in wisdom night and day. An behold, I have written for you the plain meaning of the things in detail, but now I must explain to you their meaning, and this is impossible without a drawing of a ladder, and even though it cannot be drawn in truth but in a spherical [form], you will gain a certain benefit from the drawing of this circular [form]:[168]

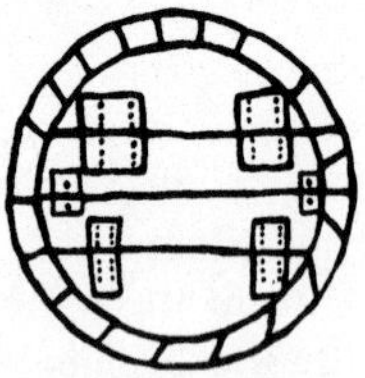

Know that this ladder must be drawn as a circle, if it stands before the person's eyes like a full sphere, rolling back and forth before him, as if the man's face is towards the east and his back towards west, and the person is in the middle. And this is the spherical ladder which has two spherical lines and wide rungs, slightly between the two lines, and they are 360 rungs, and between each rung is the width of a rung, so that the length will be equal to the width, and its appearance like that of bright blue, like the image of the sky which turns about for one known special purpose. And man turns about with [the help of] twenty Sefirot—five toes of his feet on his right side, and five on his left, and likewise five fingers of his hand to the south and five to the north, and they turn to the right or the left, and there are four heads to his head, and four to his end, and four winds from here to the south side and four winds to the north, and each head of them has upon it a body equal, like the image of a cube, and they are four cubes, and their names are "females" from here, and four from there, and their names are "males" and they turned about and changed. And each of these cubes has six corners, speckled, a pair above, separated below it, and a pair below it, separated upon it. And all of the dots on them [add up to] 120 for these and 120 for these, with the fifth to here and the fifth to here; and that is the one which preponderates between them. And the number is 24, 24, and the dots are not fixed in them, but are like tablets ready to receive the dots, and because of the [circular] movement they are renewed. And were the ladder to stand [even] a small moment without turning, then all the corners of the cubes would be empty of all dots. But with the turns they are renewed, by justice and uprightness, according to the Divine rule by which he judges every living rational thing according to his deeds, by lot *(pur)*. And this secret is as it were witness and judge of the retribution and punishment. And this ladder is called the ladder of the world, and scales for the human being. And this is the subject of which Raziel informed me, and he further explained it in saying that the *pur* fell between the names and always turns about by justice, to judge in it he who is judged, and that when you shall contemplate your essence, you will find that ladder is inscribed between the eyes of your heart, in general and in particular, and contemplate it very much, and know it.

I do not intend to analyze every detail of this vision; some are not sufficiently clear to me, while others are not relevant to our discussion. The opening statement of the vision is based upon an idea articulated by Maimonides in *Guide of the Perplexed* III:7 (Pines, p. 429):

"And the appearance of the rainbow that is in the clouds in the day of rain, so was the appearance of the brightness round about. This was the appearance of the likeness of the Glory of the Lord." The matter, the true reality, and the essence of the rainbow that is described are known. This is the most extraordinary comparison possible, as far as parables and similitudes are concerned; and it is indubitably due to a prophetic force. Understand this.

The analogy between man and the rainbow, appearing in Maimonides, was expanded by Abulafia: the rain, the showers, and the vapors of the rainbow correspond to the humours within man, while the clouds correspond to the smoke and steams within him. The circle, symbolizing a sphere, corresponds to the sphere of the cosmic axis *(teli)*, while the bar is the cosmic axis itself. This is clear from the description of the bar: it passes from south to the north just as the axis passes over the world. This bar is already described in this manner in Chapter 1 of *Baraita de-Shemu'el: "Naḥaš Bariaḥ* is the cosmic axis."[169] It follows that Abulafia's comparison of the sphere of man to "the sphere of the suspensory" is pertinent to this vision.[170] Abulafia emphasizes this point of comparison at the end of the vision: and this ladder is called the ladder of the world, and scales for the human being. By contemplation into himself, man may learn about the ladder: "And when you shall contemplate your essence, you will find that ladder, inscribed between the eyes of your heart, in general and in particular." The principle which operates both in the ladder and in man is the point of comparison; in the ladder, he refers to the 'lot and die," "justice and uprightness," "witness and judge," "retribution and punishment." These word-pairs allude to the attributes of mercy and justice operating in the world. Likewise, in *Siṭrê Torah*, Abulafia refers to "the secret of the one who is innocent and guilty, in their coming before the judge, who is both witness and judge."[171] This refers to God, who manifests both the attributes of mercy and judgment—a fact confirmed by the *gematria: ʿed* (witness) =74=*dayan* (judge), while *zakkai we-ḥayav* (innocent and guilty) likewise adds up to 74. Elsewhere in *Siṭrê Torah,* it is clear that "innocent and guilty" allude to "blood and ink": i.e., the intellect and the imagination.[172] In *Ôẕar ʿEden Ganuz,* we read:

> Behold, man has two urges, good and evil, and they are angels of God without any doubt, and are like the image of the two sides of the scales, which are always weighed and purified in their place as they are, so that the power of one of them will overwhelm its fellow, will let judge the language and tend towards it, like the balance which inclines thereto.[173]

The two urges, likened to the two sides of the scales, clearly correspond to the imagination and intellect, alluded to in the expression in the vision, "scales for the human being." Let us now address ourselves to the double character of this vision: i.e., that it speaks about both a sphere and a ladder. The circle which appears in the vision and which is a projection thereof, is a well-known phenomenon; Carl Jung saw it as an archetype of the process of individuation of the personality or, in religious terms, the cleaving of the "I" to God. The emphasis upon the high spiritual level attained by Abulafia at the time he had the vision of the circle fits Jung's assumption.[174] In the wake of Jung's studies, G. Tucci wrote, in the introduction to his book on mandala:

> My aim has been to reconstitute, in their essential outlines, the theory and practice of those psycho-cosmogrammata which may lead the neophyte, by revealing to him the secret play of the forces which operate in the universe and in us, on the way to the reintegration of consciousness.[175]

The psycho-cosmogrammaton referred to by Tucci is the mandala, or circle, which forms the central object of meditation in Buddhist and Hindu practice. From this point of view, one may see in Abulafia's vision additional evidence for the appearance of the archetype of the mandala; like it, the sphere reveals both the structure of the universe and of man and of those powers acting within them. One ought to take note of his words in this vision: "the matter of opening of one's eyes, to see before him the tree of knowledge, whose name is life; that is, that which is to others a potion of death, and is the tree of knowledge, was to Raziel the potion of life, and he did not stumble in it as did others." This passage, which is connected with the appearance of the sphere, ought to be compared with his words in *Sefer ha-Ôt,* p. 82, at the time of the appearance of "the man": "the sign on his forehead is the potion of death, as the man called it, and I called it the potion of life, for I transformed it from death to life." These two passages suggest that the visions are accompanied by an inner event, a kind of synthesis between the two forces of the soul—the intellect and the imagination—which are alluded to by blood and ink. In *Sitrê Torah,*[176] we learn that:

> The brain is a place which receives all kind of images. But witnesses come from it and tell us his powers; and they are two trees, and each tree is an image,[177] and all the flux of the likeness[178] constitute two trees, which are two[179] . . . but one tree adds wisdom, and the other adds desire; the tree of life adds science,[180] and the tree of knowledge adds science,[181] and the tree of life is a lot[182] and the tree of knowledge lots.[183] "One lot[184] to God, and one lot to Azazel": the first for good, the middle for the possible, and the last one for evil. . . . For they have sent forth their hand to know the power of their foundation, and they exchanged their glory for an image of flesh and blood, and they did not eat from the tree of knowledge, and their wicked soul cannot be saved, even though the tree of life they did not see, and they did enter by their corrupt ways for they were created in vain, and to joke of themselves they were found, and happy are those who understand the sciences, and in their victory in the wars they shall gain two worlds.

This passage epitomizes Abulafia's awareness of the need to connect between the intellect and the imagination—that is, to bring the intellect to rule over the imagination, as a consequence of which the soul is saved. We may cite here the words of the anonymous author of *Sefer ha-Z̲eruf,* connecting together the sphere, the ladder, and the revolution which takes place in man in connection with an experience of either sphere or ladder:

> Know that when the sphere of the intellect is turned about by the Active Intellect, and man begins to enter it and ascends in the sphere which revolves upon itself, as the image of the ladder, and at the time of ascent, his thoughts will be indeed transformed and all the images will change before him, and nothing of all that he previously had will be left in his hands; therefore, apart from the change in his nature and his formation, as one who is translated from the power of sensation to the power of the intellect, and as one who is translated from the telurian process to the process of burning fire. Finally, all the visions shall change, and the thoughts will be

confounded and the imaginative apprehensions will be confused, since in truth this sphere purifies and tests.[185]

While this passage does not refer to the vision of the sphere, but to an experience of it, the proximity between the sphere and the ladder and the spiritual contents connected with them remind us to a great extent of Abulafia's approach. The connection between the ladder and the sphere are again discussed in another passage, related to *Sefer ha-Z̲eruf*, in connection with the spiritual manifestations connected to 'prophecy':[186]

> I swear to you by the vision of the image of God, by the Creator, God of Abraham, God of Isaac, God of Jacob, by the Ineffable Name, *yhwh*, that you inform me of the secret of prophecy at any time that I request it by my mouth, and that you teach me the [secret of the] World to Come[187] and the law of the king, and inform me of the one ladder by which I may ascend to the house of the Lord God, to know His awesome ways, and to know the ways of the ancient ones, and make constant in me the foundation of the power of the true spiritual sphere . . . from now on and forever more, Amen, Selah.

It seems reasonable to assume that the things cited in *Sefer ha-Z̲eruf* influenced R. Elnathan b. Moses Kalkish, who wrote in his book, *Even ha-Sappir:*[188]

> God, may He be praised, gave us the Holy Torah, and taught us the way of combination [of letters] and the steps of the ladder, in describing the letters, in seeing that it is not within the ability of our apprehension to attain knowledge of Him, may He be blessed, without this great and correct proposal . . . for . . . from the light and seraphic sphere of the intellect,[189] there shall be born as the image of the prophetic image, which is the intention of combination [of letters]. And according to its refinement and the power of its innerness, they are worthy to be called premises to all those upon its face, for they are the levels by which to ascend on high, because it is the balance of the scales, depending on the light of the intellect, but not in sensible light.

The comparison between the sphere, the circle and the scales, alongside the doctrine of combination of letters and the achievement of prophecy, constitutes a clear indication that techniques originating in ecstatic Kabbalah were drawn upon during the two generations following the death of Abraham Abulafia within the region of Byzantine culture.

Let us now turn to the vision of R. Isaac of Acre, which also includes the appearance of a wheel. In *O<u>z</u>ar Ḥayyim*, he states:

> I awoke from my sleep and suddenly I saw the secret of the saying of the rabbis concerning Moses our teacher's writing of the Torah, that he saw it written against the air of the sky, in black fire upon white fire. This is that, when a man ascends a very high mountain, standing within a broad flat valley without any hills or mountains within it, but only a great plain, and he lifts up his eyes and they look about and he gazes at the firmament of the heavens close to the earth, around around, to the place of the sky close to the earth, as it appears to his eyes, this is half the circle, and is known in the language of the sages of the constellations [astrology] as the circle of the horizon. This was seen by the soul and intellect of Moses our teacher, surrounding him from above the entire Torah, from the letter *bet* of *Berešit* "In the beginning"), which is the first letter, to the *Lamed* of *Yisra'el* (Israel), written in one complete circle, each letter next to its neighbor, surrounded by parchment. That is to say, it is as if there were a hair's breadth between one letter and the next, for all the air which is around the letters of the Torah is entirely within the circle, and between each letter and outside of the letters there was white fire, dimming the circle of the sun, and the letters alone were of black fire, a strong blackness, the very quintessence of blackness. She [Moses' soul] gazed at them here and there to find the head of the circle or its end or its middle, but did not find anything. . . . For there is no known place by which to go into the Torah, for it is wholly perfect, and while he yet gazes at this circle, she combines on and on into strong combinations, not intelligible.[190]

The appearance of the Torah as a circle revealed to the eyes of the one who is contemplating it reappears in *Baddê ha-'Aron* by R. Shem Tov ibn Gaon:

> When he has no friend with whom to practice concentration as he would wish, let him sit by himself. . . . And he shall begin to write what he sees in his mind, like one who copies from a book that is written before him, in black fire on white fire, in a true spherical form, like the sun, for the light has come upon him at that hour.[191]

It seems to me that the resemblance between these two statements is not coincidental. *Baddê ha-'Aron* describes one who writes things down from his own mind as one who copies from a book; there is no doubt that this book is to be identified with the Torah, written in black fire upon white fire. The description of the act of writing is likewise suitable to Moses, who is mentioned by R. Isaac of Acre. The description of the one meditating given by R. Shem

Tov is similar to that of Moses in the introduction to Naḥmanides' *Commentary to the Torah*, which states that Moses was "like a scribe copying from an ancient book and writing."[192] The expression, "spherical like the sun", which appears in the passage from R. Shem Tov ibn Gaon, is parallel to "the circle of the sun" in that from R. Isaac of Acre. It would [therefore] appear that the appearance of the circle in the visions of both authors is not coincidental, but that an historical connection exists between their words; it seems likely that R. Shem Tov was influenced, in one way or another, by the opinions of R. Isaac of Acre, even though in matters of theosophical Kabbalah the direction of influence was the opposite.[193]

Another motif in R. Isaac of Acre is the vision of the ladder. In a passage published by Gottlieb, R. Isaac says: "so long as I was looking at this ladder, which is the name of the Holy One, blessed be He, I see my soul cleaving to the *Eyn Sof* with the master of union."[194] The understanding of the Divine name as a ladder first appears in Abulafia, who says: "in the Name my intellect found a ladder to ascend to the level of vision,"[195] while he writes elsewhere:[196]

> The ladder seen by Jacob our Father was Sinai,[197] and this great secret was revealed by means of *gemaṭria* . . . and it was known to us that the secret of Sinai is double *(kefel)* and it is easy *(qal)* and there come out of it the two holy names, *Adonay Adonay*, and there emerge from the names the five unique ones, the secret of each one of whose secret is heavy *(kaved)*.

Sullam (ladder) = 130 = Sinai = *Adonay Adonay* = 65 = 65 + 5 x 26 = 130.

On the other hand, elsewhere in R. Isaac of Acre we learn that the Divine Names are written in circles.[198] "I heard them say to me that I oughtn't to remove the name of the Mighty One from the thought of my mind in all the ways of my prayers, and my blessings will never be removed from my eyes, in the proper circles."

We find evidence for the understanding of the Torah as a circle in the fourteenth century,[199] and it may be that these are in turn indicative of an older idea which saw the Torah as a circle.[200] The articulation of this idea may be found in the works of Abulafia, R. Isaac of Acre, and R.Shem Tov ibn Gaon.

9. Metatron

Let us turn now to another subject concerning Abulafia's influence on R. Isaac of Acre. In *Ḥayyê ha-ʿÔlam ha-Ba*,[201] we read:

> After you utter the twenty-four names, whose sign is *dodi* (my beloved), and "the Voice of my beloved knocketh,"[202] then you shall see the image of a youth or the image of a sheik, for *šek̲* in the language of the Ishmaelites means "elder," and also in *gemaṭria* it equals [the phrase] "a youth and he is old" *(naʿar we-hu zaqen);* and the secret of his name as seen to you is *Meṭaṭron.* And he is a youth, and hearken to his voice . . . and when he speaks, answer him:[203] "Speak O master, for your servant speaks."

This brief description of the appearance of Metatron is of a didactic character; it is intended to portray the anticipated meeting between the mystic devotee of Abulafia's path with the angel Metatron, i.e., the Active Intellect. Our passage was discussed within the circle of Abulafia's disciples; we find some of the traces of this discussion in *Oz̲ar Ḥayyim:*[204]

> Still on this very day we saw a direct reason why *Moš"e* (i.e., Meṭaṭron, Prince of the Face) is called "a youth" *(naʿar),* "For Israel is a young lad, and I have loved him,"[205] and he himself says "I was a lad and now I am old,"[206] And the Sages say,[207] "the Prince of the World said this verse." And I heard from my master, saying, that *naʿar* is a designation referring to the oldest of all the created things,[208] but he is deserving to be called an elder, and not a lad. And I say that this is a designation, for in Arabic one calls an elder a sheik *(šek̲),* and a young man *(naʿar)* is numerically equal to [*sodo*] *šek̲.* One of the disciples said: but in Arabic one does not read [the word] *Šek* without the letter *yod,* but only with it, as follows: "*Šeik̲.*" And what will one do with these ten extra [numbers]? And he did not answer him at all, and the thing remained in doubt, and "doubt" *(safeq)* in the Arabic language is called *Šek̲;* and today I saw it said that, so long as Meṭaṭron the Prince of the Face is satisfied with his own influx, he is a *šek̲* without the letter *yod,* with the accented *kaf,* and it means "doubt" [in Hebrew *sfq* may also be vocalized as "supply"], since the influx of Almighty God is dependent upon the created being, and it is in the hands of the children of Israel; and whether if the generation is guilty the influx stands by itself and does not flow, and each one makes do with the flow of himself, but if the generation merits it the abundance of Almighty God awakens and flows, so that there is neither Satan nor evil influence, and all is peace, life and blessing. Therefore, when there is no influx forthcoming, Metatron Prince of the Face is called *šek̲* without *yod,* being called *Meṭaṭron* without *yod,* but when the influx comes within him he is called *Šeik̲* with *yod,* as he is called *Meṭaṭron* with *yod.*

R. Isaac of Acre's words indicate that the teacher quoted here was either Abulafia or one of his disciples who knew *Ḥayyê ha-ʿOlam ha-Ba*, as may be seen from the striking resemblance between the two quoted passages. In both cases, the same mistake is made, deriving from lack of knowledge of Arabic: *šek̲* is calculated as having a numerical value of 320, apparently based upon its sound, while the correct spelling is with *yod*.[209] We may now ask whether this is a strictly theoretical discussion or whether the two passages in fact reflect personal experience. Both authors in fact give evidence of "meetings" with Meṭaṭron or its pseudonyms mentioned in the above section.

On p. 84 of *Sefer ha-Ôt*, we find a description of a meeting with an old man during the course of a vision: "And he showed me an old man, with white hair, seated upon the throne of judgment[210] . . . and he ascended to the mountain of judgment, and I came close to the elder and he bowed and prostrated himself." The old man interprets Abulafia's vision and then says, "And my name [is] Yehoel, that I have agreed *(ho'il)* to speak with you now several years." The name "Yehoel" seems a clear allusion to the fact that the old man is Meṭaṭron himself. We learn from a discussion concerning Enoch and Meṭaṭron in *Sitrê Torah*[211] that:

> R. Eleazar of Worms said that he [i.e., Meṭaṭron] has seventy names, as I have been shown by our holy rabbis concerning this in *Pirqe de-Rabbi Eliʿezer* and by others in the works of R. Akiba and R. Ishmael which are well known . . . and in order to arouse your mind to it, I will write a few of those things which arouse man's intellect towards the ecstatic Kabbalah, and I will inform you of what he[212] said of him at first. Know that the first of the seventy names of Meṭaṭron is Yehoel, and its secret is "son",[213] and its essence is *Ana*, which is Elijah . . . and he is the Redeemer.

In my opinion, this passage establishes that the old man in *Sefer ha-Ôt* is none other than an imaginary embodiment of Metatron, that is, the Active Intellect. The meeting between the elder and Abulafia bears a personal character: it is not described in terms of a connection between two intellects but as one between two people. In *Sefer ha-Ôt*, p. 84, we read: "And I fell on my face towards the earth before his legs, and he placed his two hands upon me and he stood me upon my legs before him and said to me: 'My son, blessed is your coming, peace peace unto you.' " This personal approach is repeated in a work of R. Isaac of Acre:

> While I was yet sleeping, I, Isaac of Acre, saw Meṭaṭron, the Prince of the Face, and I sat before him, and he taught me and promised

> me many good things that would come to me . . . and to my joy he came, and at his command I took his hand and kissed him many times, [with] successive kisses of love, and these kisses of mine were not upon the back of his hand, but upon the palm of his hand, and his hand was very wide.[214]

Here, as well, the meeting portrayed in the vision is seen as a personal contact, in which there is a relationship going beyond the revelation of secrets characteristic of the revelations of Meṭaṭron in the Merkavah literature. However, one must remember that in these passages as well, Metatron appears as a teacher, and the mystic as a disciple, the vision thus being one of the revelation if the divine teacher.[215]

10. The Fear

As we have seen above, Abulafia's visions were given an appropriate interpretation with the aid of philosophical terminology. There seems no doubt that Abulafia was aware of the character of his visions, for which reason it is difficult to understand, on the face of it, why they were accompanied by descriptions of states of fear and panic. If the prophetic experience is, in principle, a revelation of spiritual processes or of the means of guiding the world, why must Abulafia fear that very experience which he seeks with his entire being? Two different possible answers to this question are possible: one may accept Jung's view that man's self-understanding of his soul is accompanied by curiosity and fear,[216] for which reason Abulafia feared the vision; or one may adopt the theory of Rudolf Otto, who sees the revelation of God as the revelation of a "wholly other" essence, inspiring fear in the heart of the person to whom it is revealed.[217]

Let us begin with Abulafia's own words on this matter; in *Sefer ha-Ôt*, p. 82, Abulafia writes in connection with the appearance of "the man":

> And when I saw his face in the vision, I was astonished and my heart was frightened within me, and it moved from its place. And I wished to speak, to call to the name of God to help me, but the thing moved away from my spirit. And when I saw that man, my dread was tremendous and my fear was very intense.

An exaggerated description of fear appears in *Siṭrê Torah:*[218]

> And you become perfect in the knowledge of the well-known attributes of God, by which the world is always conducted. And let you mind pursue after your intellect, to resemble him in them, according to your ability always. And know in your intellect that you have already annihilated those faculties called superfluous to you, and let all your intentions be for sake of heaven. And be God-fearing in the essence of true fear, as you would fear the Angel of Death when you see it, entirely full of eyes.[219] In its left hand is burning fire, and in its right hand a two-edged sword, performing the vengeance of the covenant, and in its mouth is a consuming fire, and he comes to you and asks you to give him his share of your self; and he is half of your existence, for example, and he seeks to cut off you limbs, one by one, and you see it all with your eyes.

It is worth emphasizing here that Abulafia refers to the fear of God, which is "as though you would be afraid of the angel of death." The motif of fear reappears in *Ḥayyê ha-ʿOlam ha-Ba:* When you prepare yourself to speak with your Creator . . . wrap yourself in *ṭallit* and *tefillin* on your head and your hands, so that you may fear and be afraid of the Shekhinah, which is with you at that time."[220] This motif is connected with the description of the appearance of "the king" at time of the vision found in the same book: "Portray this Name, may He be blessed, and his supernal angels, and draw them in your heart, as if they were human beings standing or sitting around you, and you are among them, like a messenger, whom the king and his messengers wish to send."[221] This motif is again found in *Sefer ha- Ḥešeq,* where the mystic is portrayed as one "who the king sends after him and wishes to speak with in all events, as the king strongly wishes to speak with him more than he wishes to speak with the king."[222]

In *Ôr ha-Sekel,*[223] Abulafia reveals the nature of the king whom one must fear: "The intellect, which is the source of wisdom and understanding and knowledge, and which is in the image of the king of kings, whom all greatly fear. And behold, the fear of this who comprehends is double-fold, for it is [both] fear (or "awe") of [His] Grandeur, and fear [which is coupled with] love."[224] What is the reason for the fear, according to Abulafia? In all of the cases mentioned above, fear is connected with participation of the power of imagination; in the mystical experience, this potential achieves increased activity, and, as we have seen at the beginning of the chapter, one of the consequences of which is fear. Prophecy may be described as a necessary cooperation between the intellect[225] and the imagination: the intellect requires the spiritual posture of love, while the imagination brings about fear since, according to Abulafia, there is a direct relationship between imagination, blood, and fear. Let us now turn to other factors liable to catalyze a situation of terror in connection with ecstatic experience.

11. Dangers

So long as the imagination was subject to the rule of the intellect, the images envisaged at the time of prophecy reflected intellectual truths. However, once the power of the imagination grew, there existed the danger that there would appear before the eyes of the mystic visions which have no connection whatsoever with the intellect. These images, which constitute the primary source of danger in mysticism, are understood as "messengers of Satan," who attempts to mislead man's heart away from the pure intellectual service of God. In *Ḥayyê ha-ʿOlam ha-Ba*, Abulafia warns:

> Do not remove your thoughts from God for any thing in the world; and even if a dog or a rat or another thing jumped across you, which was not in your house, [know that] these are the acts of Satan, who scouts about in your mind and creates things which have no reality at all, and he is appointed over this.[226]

However, this danger is not emphasized much in Abulafia's works. The complicated technique which he advocates, in which one is required to carry out several different activities simultaneously, thereby demanding the greatest possible concentration, is evidently in itself a guarantee against the mind wandering. This differs from both Sufism and Hesychasm, in which the formulae to be recited in an automatic manner without any need for concentration. For this reason, there exists there the danger against which they constantly warn: namely, that in the course of reciting the Divine Name, the mystic is likely to think about other subjects. This is almost impossible in Abulafia, for which reason he does not devote much to warning against this.

One of the widespread images used to suggest the danger inherent in letter-combination is burning fire.[227] Let us begin with several statements of Abulafia's on this subject. In *Siṭrê Torah*, it says: "when you see the abundance of His goodness and the taste of His radiance in your heart, remove your face and afterwards again seek it bit by bit, and with this He will lift you up, for the great fire guards the gate."[228] Elsewhere in the same work,[229] in connection with the temptation to make magical use of the Divine Names, he states: "Take care . . . as you take care against being burned by fire, and be not hasty to kill yourself" and "Combine and combine, and do not be burned."[230] In a similar manner, Abulafia writes in connection with the act of letter-combination:[231] "Know that the river Dinur[232] comes out from before Him, and the one combining must take care and be careful of its fear and for the Honor of His name, lest his blood flee[233] and he kills himself." In *Ḥayyê ha-ʿOlam ha-Ba*, he writes:

> Take care against the great fire which surrounds the demons *(šedim)* created from the white seed, whose name is *Saṭan*, born from "the tail of the uncircumcised" *(zanav ʿarel)*, who uncovered nakedness *(gillah ʿerwah)* and is deserving for this the retribution of evil *(gemul ha-raʿ)*, which is the evil body; and it is a life of the reason and imagination, causing the cause to compel the nature, by remembrance and knowledge.[234]

It seems clear from this that the great fire is vitally connected with human matter, for which reason it endangers the man who attempts to overcome it. In *Ḥayyê ha-ʿOlam ha-Ba*, Abulafia writes:

> Now, son of man, if you seek the Lord your God in truth and in wholeness, do not think to yourself use the Name, but of the knowledge of the Name and the comprehension of its actions, and not for the benefit of the needs of the body, and even though it is able to do so, and its activities and nature are such; but because you are compounded of the Evil Urge, you are a body of "flesh and blood", both of which are "angels of death", and one must think of their secret: the details of the matter include all the specific organs, and is called the matter of decomposition, and its name is the River Dinur, and its secret is "the individual living matter" [*ḥomer ḥay peraṭi*], etc.[235]

Comparison of this passage with others pertaining to this subject indicates that, apart from the subject of the matter of man, there is an additional motif relating to fire, namely, the involvement in the Divine Names.[236] While combining letters, the mystic is likely to be inadvertently turned into a magician, by means of the incorrect use of the Names: such an act is a serious distortion of the goal of the Names, and brings about the sinking of the sinner into the material over which he wishes to rule. This thought is alluded to in the expression, "to compel the nature", as well as in the last-quoted passage.[237]

Unlike the image of the fire, which symbolizes the immersion into corporeality, we find among the students of Abulafia the image of sinking, which is intended to express the immersion of the mystic in the spiritual world, an immersion likely to bring about his death. In *Šaᶜare Zedeq,* the disciple implores his master to give him the "power" that will enable him to survive the awesome power of the revelation:

> I said to him: "In heaven's name, can you perhaps impart to me some power to enable me to bear this force emerging from my heart and to receive influx from it?" For I wanted to draw this force towards me and receive influx from it, for it much resembles a spring filling a great basin with water. If a man [not being properly prepared for it] should open the dam, he would be drowned in its waters and his soul would desert him.[238]

The image of drowning reappears in R. Isaac of Acre's *Ôzar Ḥayyim:*

> Now you, my son, make an effort to contemplate the supernal light, since I have certainly introduced you into "the sea of the Ocean" which surrounds the [whole] world. Be careful and guard your soul from gazing and your heart from pondering [upon the light], lest you sink; and the effort shall be to contemplate but [at the same time] to escape from sinking, and you shall see your World [to Come] in your lifetime [i.e., attain a celestial vision while yet alive], and all these words of ours are in order to sustain your soul in her palace.[239]

Elsewhere in the same book, he writes,

> . . . cleave to the Divine Intellect, and it will cleave to her, for more than the calf wishes to suck, the cow wishes to give suck. And she and the intellect become one entity, as if someone pours out a jug of water into a running well, that all becomes one.[240]

While the motif of drowning is not in accord with Abulafia's spirit,[241] there does reappear the warning that the moment of ecstasy is also likely to be the moment of death; we shall enlarge upon this subject in Section 1 of the chapter, "Erotic Imagery for the Ecstatic Experience."

12. Devequt

The topic of *devequt* (cleaving to God) in Jewish mysticism has been a subject of study by some scholars. Scholem devoted a detailed discussion to the subject,[242] concluding that, while there is a widespread tendency in Kabbalah to acknowledge the possibility of *communio* between the human soul and God, the concept of union or compete identity between the two is alien to the spirit of the Kabbalah. Other scholars, such as Tishby[243] and Gottlieb,[244] have noted passages in which there are nuances suggesting mystical union, but suggest that these cases are few and far between, and that the discussion of the authors of these passages is moreover sketchy, making it difficult to fully understand their exact meaning.[245] Abulafia was the first medieval Jewish mystic in whom we find more extensive evidence of mystical unity, sometimes expressed in radical ways.

I should like to begin by defining the meaning of the terms to be used below. The term "union" (Hebrew: *iḥud*) is parallel to the Latin *unio,* being used to refer to that state in which the human soul or its intellect cleaves to an external object, making the two of them into one. This broad definition, found among scholars of mysticism,[246] stresses the transformation of man's inner nature as an essential precondition for the mystical experience. The adjective "mystical" defines and delimits the object of this union; it is union with these objects alone that makes the experience "mystical" A common denominator of all these objects is the fact that they are general or that they encompass more than the human soul or intellect; they include such spiritual entities as the supernal or general soul, the Active Intellect, the separate intellects, and God or, to use religious terminology, high levels in the various religious hierarchies: the angels or the Godhead. The unity between the soul and these entities transforms the spiritual element within man from particular to general, a transformation accompanied by an experience difficult to describe in words. Unity entails the overwhelming of man's limited consciousness by spiritual or more comprehensive intellectual contents, an overwhelming which brings about the obliteration of the individual consciousness.

Let us now return to Abulafia; in a passage from *Ôẕar ʿEden Ganuz,*[247] he discusses the principle of the similarity between the one cleaving and that to which he cleaves:

> Once the knot is loosened, there shall be revealed the matter of the testimony of the knot, and the one who cleaves to these knots cleaves to falsehoods,[248] for as they are to be loosened in the future, so shall the knots of his *devequt* be loosened, and nothing shall be left with him. Therefore, before he loosens these, he must tie and

> cleave through knots of love[249] to Him who does not undo the ties of His love and the cleaving of his desire—that is, God, may He be blessed, and no other by any means. And concerning this it says in the Torah,[250] "And you who cleave to the Lord your God are still living this day"; and this is the matter of which they said, "And cleave to him,"[251] "And to him you shall cleave"[252], for that cleaving brings about the essential intention, which is eternal life for man, like the life of God, to whom he cleaves. And for this [reason] those who perform *devequt* are of three types: *devequt* to the supernal entities, like fire, which is above and constantly ascends; and *devequt* to the intermediate ones, like the wind, which is in the middle, depending whether it ascends or descends; and *devequt* to the lower ones, like the image of water, which is below, and constantly descends. And in accordance with the *devequt*, so shall be the survival [of the soul]—whether above, below, or in the middle.

These three kinds of *devequt* symbolize the possibility of man's transformation into a supernal, intermediate, or lowly being, depending upon the object of his cleaving. The same idea, expressed differently, appears in *Ner Elohim:*

> Whoever is drawn toward the vanities of temporality, his soul shall survive in the vanities of temporality; and whoever is drawn after the Name which we have cited, which is above temporality, his soul shall survive in the eternal [realm], beyond time, in God, may He be blessed.[253]

In both passages, the same principle appears; namely, that the object of cleaving *(devequt)* determines the essence of those cleaving after the cessation of the *devequt* itself. Those who cleave to "the Name" are thereby transformed from mortals into immortals; however, this survival does not in itself have a mystical character. While in both passages he does speak of a change in the soul from being perishable to eternal, there is no indication or allusion to any change in its nature which would change the soul into God or to one of the "supernal beings". Let us begin with the latter passage: by the term "supernal ones", Abulafia refers to the supernal world or the world of the separate intellects, while the "intermediate" refers to the spheres or the intermediate world. In several places he states, in accordance with the view of Ibn Rushd,[254] and in contradiction to that of Al-Farabi and Maimonides, that cleaving to the Active Intellect is possible in this world. The significance of this *devequt* is the transformation of man's intellect into the Active Intellect, i.e., union. In order to express this union, Abulafia utilizes the well-known formula originating in Islamic mysticism,[255] "he is he", which is repeated with minor changes in a number of passages in Hebrew literature.[256] We read in *Sitrê Torah* about "that man who has actualized his intellectual power and prophesies according to that which he has actualized to the final, complete actualization, and returned, he and he are one inseparable entity during the time of that act."[257] The human intellect is actualized by the Active Intellect, and at the time of mystical ecstasy the intellect united with it. This process implies the transformation of the individual consciousness into a universal one, as stated by Abulafia in the same work: "Until the prophet turns his personal, partial [aspect], in the form of permanent, eternal, universal cause like it, he and he are one entity."[258] In *Sefer ha-Yašar*, written at that same time as *Siṭre Torah*, we read:[259]

> If, however, he has felt the divine touch and perceived its nature, it seems right and proper to me and to every perfected man that he should be called 'master,' because his name is like the Name of his Master,[260] be it only in one, or in many, or in all of His names. For now he is no longer separated from his Master, and behold he is his master and his Master is he; for he is so intimately adhering to Him [here the term *devequt* is used] that he cannot by any means be separated from Him, for he is He. And just as his Master, who is detached from all matter, is called . . . the *knowledge*, the *knower* and the *known*, all at the same time, since all three are one in Him: so shall he, the exalted man, the master of the exalted Name, be called *intellect*, while he is actually knowing; then he is also *the known*, like his Master; and then there is no difference between them, except that his Master has His supreme rank by His own right and not derived from other creatures, while he is elevated to his rank by the intermediary of creatures.

It is clear that the transformation is not only a matter of the eternal survival of the soul, but of the transformation of the essence of the soul into an intellective element, obliterating the differences between the cause of the transformation, i.e., the Active Intellect and that affected by it, namely, the human intellect. These passages refer to the identity of the human intellect with the Active Intellect in an objective sense, for which reason one might argue that Abulafia makes use of no more than figure of speech. However, in *Sefer ha-ʿEdut*,[261] which belongs to that group of prophetic books which claim to express Abulafia's prophetic-mystical experiences, the unity with the Active Intellect is spoken of in a more personal manner. In the following passage, Abulafia conveys the contents of the voice which he heard in Rome:

> And the meaning of his saying: "Rise and lift up the head of my anointed one" refers to the life of the souls. And on the New Year and in the Temple it is the power of the souls. And he says: "Anoint him as a king"—anoint him like a king with the power of all the names. "For I have anointed him as king over Israel"[262]—over the communities of Israel, that is, the *mizwot*. And his saying, "and his name I have called *Šadday* like My Name"—whose secret is *Šadday* like My Name; and understand all the intention. Likewise, his saying: "He is I and I am He," and it cannot be revealed more explicitly than this. but the secret of the corporeal name is the Messiah of God; also "Moses will rejoice," which he has made known to us, and which is the five urges, and is called the corporeal name as well.

We must begin by deciphering the *gemaṭriot* used here: the head of my anointed one *(roš mešiḥi)*=869=the life of the soul (*ḥayyê) ha-nefašot)* = and on New Year's *(uve-Roš ha-Šanah)* = and in the Temple *(uve-Bet ha-Miqdaš)* = the power of the souls *(koaḥ ha-nefašot)* = anoint him as king (*timšeḥehu le-melek*)=[God] may He be praised will anoint him as king (*timšeḥehu ka-melek*) = by the power of all the names (*mi-koaḥ kol ha- šemot)*. Israel (*Yisra*ᵓ*el)*=541=congregations (*qehillot)*= the commandments *(ha-miẓwot)*. The corporeal Name *(ha-Šem ha-gašmi)* = 703 = the anointed of the Name *(Mašiaḥ ha-Šem)* = Moses rejoiced *(yismaḥ Moše)* = five urges *(ḥamišah yezarim)*. The first *gemaṭria* alludes to the connection between the appearance of Messiah and spiritual development; the second to the Active Intellect, which was the cause of this spiritual development[263]; while the third alludes to the Messiah himself, who is identified with the Active Intellect. This identity is suggested by the words, "I called the Almighty by my name", "and he is I and I am he."[264] It seems to me that, by comparison of this passage to that which appears in *Ḥayyê ha-ᶜOlam ha-Ba*,[265] we may learn about the identity of the Messiah: "Begin to attach the three spiritual Divine Names and afterwards attach the three material names of the patriarchs." Abulafia intends to refer here to the parallel between the corporeal names—Abraham, Isaac and Jacob—and the spiritual ones—*Elohim*, *Adonay* and *YHWH*. Further on in the passage cited, Abulafia writes that "the ends of the names of the patriarchs in reverse order are *bq"m*, which in the system of *a"t b"š* (i.e., inverted letters) is *Šadday*; "And I appeared to Abraham, Isaac and Jacob in the name *El Šadday*."[266] In the passage from *Sefer ha-ᶜEdut*, he speaks about the "material name," which must allude to one of the patriarchs, as well as *Šadday*, which is likewise associated with the patriarchs.

We shall now have no difficulty in discovering the name which Abulafia had attempted to conceal: his own name, "Abraham." In *Ḥayyê ha-ʿOlam ha-Ba*, we find another passage which discusses the identity of the mystic with the Active Intellect at the time of the mystical experience:

> And he shall appear to him as if his entire body, from his head to his feet, had been anointed with anointing oil, and he will be the Anointed of God and his messenger and be called the angel of God. The intention is that his name shall be like the name of his master, *Šadday*, which I have called *Meṭaṭron*, Prince of the Presence.[267]

Abulafia's words left an impression upon other Kabbalists. R. Isaac of Acre stated in *Ôẕar Ḥayyim*[268] that, when the soul:

> . . . cleaves to the Divine Intellect, and It will cleave to her, for more than the calf wishes to suck, the cow wishes to give suck, and she and the intellect become one entity, as if somebody pours out a jug of water into a running well,[269] that all becomes one. And this is the secret meaning of the saying of our sages:[270] "Enoch is Metatron."

The idea conveyed here is the transformation of the human soul into the Active Intellect, just as the person Enoch was transformed into the angel Metatron. Absolute unity is alluded to here by means of the well-known mystical metaphor of the pouring of water into a spring. While R. Isaac of Acre's remarks seem to have originated in personal experience, the idea of unity also appears in R. Reuben Zarfati, who drew his formulation from the works of Abulafia, apparently without any relation to authentic experience. In his commentary to *Maʿareḵet ha-Elohut*[271], he writes: "The human intellect, after it separates from the body, will turn into a spiritual [entity] and be embodied in the Active Intellect, and she and it will become one thing, and this is the eternal survival of the soul."

In Scholem's opinion,[272] Abulafia's remarks concerning *devequt* are unusual; nevertheless, so long as his words refer to unity with the Active Intellect, they do not present any particular theological difficulties. In several places in Abulafia's books, other nuances appear: in the passage from *Ôẕar ʿEden Ganuz* cited at the beginning of this section, he speaks of the cleaving of the soul to god, a possibility repeated in *Ḥayyê ha-ʿOlam ha-Ba:*[273]

> The benefit of the knowledge of the name of [God] is in its being the cause of man's attainment of the actual intellection of the Active

> Intellect and the benefit of the intellection of the Active Intellect is in the ultimate aim of the life of the intellectual soul, and its ultimate aim is the reason of the life of the World to Come. This aim is the union of the soul, by this intellection, with God, may He be blessed, for ever and ever and eternally, and that thing called the "image of God" *(Z̲elem Elohim)* and His likeness, "will live in man everlasting life without any limit, like the life of the Creator, which is their cause." And of this it is said,[274] "for it is your life and length of days"—your life in this world and length of days in the next world. And it is said,[275] "And you who cleave unto the Lord as your God are living still this day," implying that one who does not cleave to God does not live forever.

One may admittedly argue that what is alluded to in this passage is a Biblical idiom, which refers to the eternal survival of the soul without any substantive change taking place in the soul that would cause it to cleave to god. However, in at least two passages, Abulafia's words clarify this subject. In *Ôr ha-Sek̲el*[276], we read:

> Since between two lovers there are two parts of love which turn to be one entity, when it [the love] is actualized, the [Divine] Name is composed of two parts, which [point to] the connection of Divine intellectual love with human intellectual love, and it [the love] is one, just as His Name comprises *eḥad eḥad,* because of the attachment of human existence with Divine existence[277] at the time of comprehension, equal with the intellect, until they both become one entity.

May the phrase "Divine existence" in this passage be interpreted as referring to God Himself? This seems to me to be the case, as in the same work there appears the view that the human intellect is liable to literally cleave to God. In defining the three meanings of the term *sek̲el* (generally translated here as "intellect"), Abulafia writes in *Ôr ha-Sek̲el:*

> *"Sek̲el"* is the name given to that thing which guides all, which is the first cause of all, and it is the name of a thing which is separate from all matter, which is the [intellectual] influx *(šefaʿ)* which emanates from the first cause . . . and it is that which emanates from the separate [things], which is called the *sek̲el* which cleaves to the hylic [element].[278]

With the identification of God with *sek̲el,* the question of unity or identity becomes a matter of the connection between two entities, which are liable to be equivalent in terms of their essence. Again, in

Ôr ha-Sekel we read:

> And they are therefore three levels, and the three of them are one essence, and they are: God, may He be blessed; and his separate [i.e., non-material] influx; and the influx of his influx (*šefa*ᶜ *šifo*), which cleaves itself to the soul. And the soul which cleaves to it with a strong cleaving, until the two of them are likewise one essence. . . . And the first cause includes everything, and it is one to all, and the intellects are many, the separate [ones] and the ones receiving the flow, and the many souls, and only the Active Intellect is one essence. . . . And behold the comprehension of the human intellect, which flows from the separate Active Intellect, causes the cleaving of the soul to her God.[279]

Described here is the identity between the human soul and God during the process of enlightenment, a process which transforms the intellectual soul into the object of her intellection, which is God, whereby the perfect unity is attained.

It is worth citing here certain ideas which appear in some manuscript collections on Kabbalistic subjects, several of which are very close to Abulafia's remarks in *Ôr ha-Sekel;* these collections include, in my opinion, original material of Abulafia's. In these collections we read:

> In this metaphor of the candle and the flame, there is a brief remark [which helps] to explain and to portray what is the *sekel,* and what is the angel, and what is its cause—that is to say, God, may He be blessed, who is called the form of the intellect (*zurat ha-sekel*). And figuratively, and as an example, it is said that the candle is He, may He be blessed, and He is the object of intellection and He is the beginning, and the end of the flame of the candle is the human intellect, which flows from the end of the separate beings. And the middle of the flame is an allusion to the other intellects, near and far. But that which is close to the candle receives more from the light. And from this issue we may understand that the intermediate one is between man and the Creator, being the intellect which exists in actuality. And when the soul will cleave to the intellect and the intellect speaks to the angel and the angel to the Seraph and the Seraph to the Cherub, part after part are united, from end to beginning, you shall then arrive at the intelligible, and you will find all these one—that is, the intellect and the object of intellection and the intelligible are all one. And you have known that the Creator and the angel and the human intellect, because of its [Divine] image and likeness, which is the inner spirit, [all these] constitute one essence at the time of intellection. However, God, may He be

blessed, is always the intelligible—that is, He always *in actu*.[280]

The relationship between this passage and that in *Ôr ha-Seḵel* is clear; it is worth adding that the definition of God as "the form of the intellect", which appears in these collections, also appears in *Ôr ha-Seḵel* where we read concerning the First Cause: "And this is the form of the intellect, which the intellect of man is able to apprehend together with the other intellective forms comprehended from Him."[281] These passages clearly raise the possibility of the unity of the human intellect with God during the moment of intellection, in which God is the object of intellection of the human intellect. Abulafia's words can be understood as a use of Aristotelian ideas for the expression of personal experience, even if we have no clear proof that he thought that he had united with God. The Aristotelian ideas used by Abulafia are the unity of the Intellect, the Intelligible and the Act of Intellection, as well as the view that the human intellect is capable of transformation into Divinity or to the most divine thing which exists among us.[282]

Before turning to another subject, I should like to cite the words of R. Isaac ben Yeda'iah, a comtemporary of Abulafia, who expresses himself concerning the subject of *devequt* to God in a manner quite similar to that of Abulafia. In his *Commentary to Maseḵet Avot*, R. Isaac writes:

> The true intention of the Nazirite is that he take his oath and separate himself from that which is permitted to him in order to know his Creator through that separation. If he were to abandon corporeality entirely, he would not use it except on infrequent occasions, and he would remove his soul from [her connection to] the material world and purify his intellect for the knowledge of his God, and he will then find himself in His presence, without obstacle or separation, and his soul will be united to Him in absolute *devequt*, without any more separation for ever, all the days.[283]

This indicates to us that a literary expression of mystical unity does appear in Jewish philosophy, a fact indicating the importance of philosophic thought for the understanding of medieval Jewish mysticism.

The idea of the unity between man and God which, according to Scholem, is foreign to Jewish mysticism, nevertheless appears in Abulafia in connection with several questions. The passages quoted above from *Ôr ha-Seḵel*, in which God, the Active Intellect and the human intellect are portrayed as having "one essence", suggest the conclusion that the intellectual element in man is none other than a

Divine "spark" which has descended to the world of matter, and that the process of intellection is simply the restoration of that spark to its divine source. An allusion to this approach appears in the epistle, *We-Zot li-Yihudah:*[284] "the ultimate compound, which is man, who comprises all the Sefirot, and whose intellect is the Active Intellect; and when you will untie its knots you will be united with it [i.e., the Active Intellect] in a unique union." Several lines later, we read:

> It is known that all the inner forces and the hidden souls in man are differentiated in the bodies. It is, however, in the nature of all of them that, when their knots are untied, they return to their origin, which is one without any duality, and which comprises multiplicity, until the *En Sof;* and when it is loosened it reaches 'till above, so that when he mentions the name of God he ascends and sits on the head of the Supreme Crown *(Keter ʿElyon),* and the thought draws from there a three-fold blessing.

In the first passage, we learn that man's intellect is literally the Active Intellect, which indicates that the Active Intellect and the human intellect are essentially two aspects of the same essence.[285] In the second passage, we read of the dispersion of "the inner forces" within the bodies of human beings,[286] who are able to overcome multiplicity in order to cleave to God, "until above where he mentions the name of God he ascends and sits at the head of the Supreme Crown." The unity achieved through *devequt* with God is therefore none other than the return movement from multiplicity to unity, a movement known to us from neo-Platonic philosophy. In *Ôr ha-Sek̲el,* there appears an additional allusion to the division of the particular intellective nature into human bodies:

> Think that at that same time your soul shall be separated from your body, and you shall die from this world and live in the World to Come, which is the source of [existent] life dispersed among all the living: and that is the intellect, which is the source of all wisdom, understanding and knowledge. . . . And when your mind *(daʿatk̲a)* comes to cleave to His mind, which gives you knowledge, your mind must remove from itself the yoke of all the alien ideas, apart from His idea which connects between you and Him, by his honored and awesome Name.[287]

The understanding of intellectual unity reappears in several places among Abulafia's disciples. The author of *Sefer ha-Z̲eruf* writes:[288]

> But when you purify the intellect, when it is in matter, when it is still in that same dwelling in truth, this is a great high level, to cleave to the *Causa causarum*, after you soul is separated from that matter in which it is, and the lower chariot remains, and the spirit[289] will return to God who gave it. . . . And when the spirit will be separated from the body, you will have already achieved the purpose of purposes and cleaved to that light beyond which there is no [other] light, and you have joined with the life which is the bundle of all life and the source of all life, and you are like one who kisses something which he loves with the quintessence of love.

In R. Isaac of Acre's *Me'irat ʿEnayim*,[290] we find an approach which facilitates unity; R. Isaac cites an extremely interesting passage in the name of R. Nathan, worth quoting here in full:

> I heard from the sage R. Nathan . . . an explanation of this name [i.e., the Intellect]. You must know that when the Divine Intellect descends, it reaches the Active Intellect, and is called Active Intellect; and when the Active Intellect descends to the Acquired Intellect, it is called Acquired Intellect; and when the Acquired Intellect descends to the Passive Intellect, it is called Passive Intellect; and when Passive intellect descends to the soul which is in man, it is called the soul. We therefore find that the Divine Intellect which is in the human soul is called the soul, and this is from above to below. And when you examine this matter from below to above, you shall see that, when man separates himself from the vanities of this world and cleaves by his thought and soul to the supernal [realms] with great constancy, his soul will be called according to the level among the higher degrees which he has acquired and attached himself to. How so? If the soul of the isolated person deserves to apprehend and to cleave to the Passive Intellect, it is called Passive Intellect, as if it is Passive Intellect; and likewise when it ascends further and cleaves to the Acquired Intellect, it becomes the Acquired Intellect; and if it merited to cleave to the Active Intellect, then it itself [becomes] Active Intellect; and if you shall deserve and cleave to the Divine Intellect, happy are you, because you have returned to your source and root, which is called, literally, the Divine Intellect. And that person is called the Man of God, that is to say, a Divine man, creating worlds.[291]

These remarks reflect the opinion, already expressed by Abulafia, according to which the human intellect is nothing other than an overflow of the Divine influx.[292] In addition to the similarity mentioned between R. Nathan's approach and that of Abulafia, it seems that there is also evidence of an historical connection between them.[293]

Ôr ha-Sekel, which concerns itself with philosophical subjects and with subjects pertaining to mystical prophecy, and from which we have cited those passages which are close to the view of R. Nathan, was written for two of the students of Abulafia, "R. Abraham the Enlightened and R. Nathan the Wise *(ha-Navon)*," with the express intention "that they receive from this book of mine a path by which they may attempt to cleave to the First Cause."[294] Nathan was a close disciple of Abulafia, as evinced by the fact that his name appears in two additional places in the latter's works, written seven years apart from one another. In *Iš Adam*,[295] he enumerates "R. Nathan ben Sa'adyahu" among his seven disciples, next to R. Abraham ben Shalom. In the Introduction to *Sefer ha-Maftehot*,[296] he again mentions R. Nathan ben Sa'adyahu Hadad, again in proximity to R. Abraham b. Shalom. From the evidence contained in the two books mentioned, it follows that this R. Nathan lived in Messina. It is very probable that R. Isaac of Acre met R. Nathan, and was influenced by him.

I have discussed this question at some length, not only because of its historical importance, but also because of its ideational importance. The historical significance is clear: Abulafia succeeded in training, not only disciples, but also a second generation of disciples of those disciples who adhered to this teaching even when they lived and functioned in the environment of Abulafia's great opponent, R. Solomon ibn Adret. *Ôzar Ḥayyim*, written after *Me'irat ʿEnayim*, clearly indicates that Abulafia's path continued to exist even after he himself was placed under the ban. From an Intellectual viewpoint, Abulafia's influence upon R. Nathan, and the latter's possible influence upon R. Isaac of Acre, indicates that even "extreme" ideas concerning the Godhead and man's relation to it are very likely to pass from one author to another and to give birth to new mystical life.

13. The Loosening of the Knots

Devequt is considered to be the cleaving or unity of the human intellect with the Active Intellect or with God. This is made possible by the removal of human consciousness from "natural" objects and its attachment to a spiritual subject, a process described in Abulafia's writings by means of the image of the loosening or untying of knots.[297] This image is composed of two main sources: from a linguistic point of view, the source of the Abulafian expressions cited below seems to be in the idioms appearing in Daniel 5:12, 16—*mešare qiṭrin* and *qiṭrin le mišra* (loose knots). The original connotation of the expression is magical, referring to Daniel's ability to undo the magical knots by which man is enslaved.[298] The motif of the magical tying is combined with the understanding of nature as a prison of the soul[299] or as a magician tying the soul to itself.[300] According to Abulafia,[301] man's function is to break the knots which imprison the human soul and to attach them to the Active Intellect:

> Man is [tied] in knots of world, year and soul [i.e., space, time and persona] in which he is tied in nature, and if he unties the knots from himself, he may cleave to He who is above them, with the guarding of his soul via the way of the remnants[302] which God calls, who are those who fear God and take account of His Name, who are called *Perušim (separatists),* few ones, [and] those who concentrate, to know God, blessed be He and blessed be His Name. And they must conquer themselves [not] to be drawn after the lusts of this world, and take care lest they be drawn to them, like a dog toward his mate. Therefore, when he becomes accustomed to the [way of] separateness, he will strengthen [his] seclusion and relation [*hityaḥasut*] and know how to unify the Name [or God].

This passage resembles an approach found in the quotation brought in the name of Avicenna by R. Shem Tov ibn Falaquera, in his book, *Moreh ha-Moreh:*

> And we are immersed in evil appetites, we do not feel that same [spiritual] pleasure, and therefore we do not seek it and do not turn towards it, except when we loosen the knot of lust and anger from our necks.[303]

According to Abulafia's opinion, the entire world prevents the soul from uniting with God:

> For all things which exist are intermediaries between God, may He be blessed, and man. And if you say: how can this be, for if so it would require that man be at the greatest [imaginable] distance from God. I say to you that you certainly speak the truth, for thus it is, for he and the reality and the Torah are witnesses to this, and therefore these are all tricks of reality and tricks of the Torah, and the abundance of *miẓwot* which exist in order to bring near he that was distant, [even if] in the utmost distance from God, to bring him near in the epitomy of closeness to Him. And all this to remove all the intermediaries which are tied in the knots of falseness, and to free him from beneath them, by the secret of the Exodus from Egypt and the crossing of the sea on dry land and the place an intermediary only between the Name, which is the intellect of the mighty man.[304]

The loosening of the knot connecting man to nature also requires the tying of a new knot, between man and the new level which he has reached:

> And the cosmic axis *(teli)* is none other than the knot of the spheres, and there is no doubt that this is the subject of their existence, like the likeness of the connections of the limbs within man, and the connections of the limbs in man which are suspended in the bones at the beginning are also called the axis in man as well. And its secret is that a magician bring this knot of desire and renew it in order to preserve the existence of this compound for a certain amount of time. And when the knot is undone, the matter of the testimony of the knot will be revealed, and one who cleaves to these knots *[qešarim]* cleaves to falsehoods *[šeqarim]*, for as they are going in the future to be undone, the knots of his cleaving will also be undone, and nothing will remain with him any more, and therefore, before he loosens these, he must tie and cleave to the ropes of love those who have not loosened the knots of his love and the cleaving of his desire; and that is God, may He be exalted, and no other in any sense.[305]

In another passage,[306] we read:

> . . . and he shall not wish to leave substances which are intellective in potential, tied to nature, but he should do tricks and teach Torah and command *miẓwot* to those who are immersed *[mutbaʿim]* in natural things, to loosen their connections with them, and to tie and to bind the natural forces with them, until every existing thing will attain its part and portion[307] appropriate to it.

The process of loosening and tying is identified with the process of enlightenment:[308]

> However, so long as he does not understand the intelligible and does not know that which can be known, which is appropriate in his knowledge, for which he was created, there is nothing that can save him from Nature to which he is tied by nature[309] since he has been [i.e., alive].

According to Abulafia, this process is accomplished with the help of Divine Names:

> He must link and change a name with a name, and renew a matter, to tie the loosened and to loosen the tied, using known names, in

> their revolutions with the twelve signs and the seven stars, and with the three elements, until the one tying and loosening will strip off from the stringencies of the prohibited and permitted, and dress a new form for the prohibited and permitted.[310]

Elsewhere in the same work it says "the names with which one ties and loosens the knot is itself *heter*."[311]

Finally, we should note that the second meaning of the expression, "loosening of the knots," namely, "the removal of doubts," is suitable to Abulafia's general tendency. The separation of the soul or the intellect from the body is in any event *ipso facto* a separation from the imagination, which breeds doubt:[312] for in these knowledges the knots are untied, as are the doubts in most of the imagined matters, and man is left with his intellect in wholeness and with his Torah in truth."

14. Characteristics of the Mystical Experience

In conclusion, attention should be devoted to certain characteristic features of the prophetic or ecstatic-mystical experience in Abulafia. A brief survey of these features will assist us in understanding Abulafia the mystic, by clarifying his position with regard to a number of major components of the mystical experience.

"Rationalistic" Mysticism

A central element of Abulafia's understanding of prophecy is his perception of the mystical experience as the supreme realization of the capacities of human consciousness; this fact is made clear in a passage concerning *devequt*, which Abulafia defines in the words,[313] "prophecy, is a matter of the intellect." More significant for our purposes is the fact that Abulafia's private experience is subjected to a rationalistic interpretation, as we have seen above in the interpretation of a number of his visions and, no less important, the fact that Abulafia saw in his own personal experience a confirmation of a certain theoretical position. His visions confirm his metaphysical approach, since in them the intellect, the imagination and the Active Intellect are transformed from theoretical concepts, borrowed from medieval thinkers, used to explain objective reality, or from the prophecy of the ancient biblical figures, into a component of the spiritual life of the mystic himself. We no longer speak of the concept of imagination as the result of the need to explain certain psychological phenomena; Abulafia is now able to see it as a principle guiding his entire world-view. For this reason, Abulafia's 'prophetic' experience seems to be the experiential culmination of the mystical possibilities inherent in the cognitive forms found in Maimonides, Avecenna, and Averroes. Hans Jonas' remarks concerning the relationship between mysticism and the philosophical system within which the mystic functions are pertinent to our question:

> Without an antecedent dogmatics there would be no valid mysticism. And mysticism, let it be noted, wants to be "valid," namely, more than a revel of feeling. The true mystic wants to put himself into possession of absolute reality, which already is and about which doctrine tells him. So it was, at least, with the mysticism of late antiquity which still stood in continuity with the intellectual and ontological speculation of the Greek past. Having an objective theory, the mystic goes beyond theory; he wants experience of the identity with the object; and he wants to be able to claim such an identity. Thus, in order that certain experiences may become possible and even conceivable as valid anticipations of an eschatological future, or as actualizations of metaphysical stages of being, speculation must have set the framework, the way, and the goal—long before the subjectivity has learned to walk the way.[314]

In the case of Abulafia, the sources of the theoretical framework and of the path towards its fulfillment are distinct from one another, but they both preceded Abulafia. The "rationalistic" nature of his experience is likewise seen in the conception of God: the object to which the mystic cleaves is not the Neoplatonic God who is incapable of being known, but the Aristotelian Intellect/Intelligible/Act of Intellection.

The Mission

As is well known, the concept of mission is a central component in the Biblical understanding of prophecy: God chooses a particular person who is made a prophet against his will, delegating him to perform a certain mission which the prophet may at times not wish to carry out, or even find repugnant.[315] While classical prophecy emerged from such revelations of a compulsory character, an interesting change takes place in the later books of the Bible, in which God is understood as a remote entity, causing the prophet to seek to bridge the gap in order to receive a revelation. This new figure is designated by the term *apocalyptic visionary,* one who combines personal experience with "Wisdom," where the intention of the visionary is not so much to bring a message to society as to achieve salvation for himself.[316] Abulafia's understanding of the concept *prophecy* combines these two types: the prophet-messenger is understood by him as a higher type than the prophet from whom the influx of wisdom pours forth, namely a "merely" mystical-contemplative person. The fourth of the five levels of prophecy is described as follows:[317] "and the fourth is to strengthen the heart until it will be proven and will speak and will write"; elsewhere, he writes,[318] "and the level of the prophets who speak and who compose [books] is greater than that of the prophets who attempt to attain prophecy, while those who are sent are higher yet than them." Again,[319] "and in accordance with the quantity of the influx, the intellect shall force the [prophetic] speaker-author to speak and to write according to the time and according to the place and according to the generation." This definition of prophetic mission as an expression of the power of the Divine influx originates in Maimonides and in Arabic philosophy.[320] Abulafia describes the activity of the Biblical prophets, and by analogy his own, as a combination of writing and agitation, oftentimes performed against his own will:[321]

> Know that every one of the early prophets was forced to speak what they spoke and to write what they wrote, so that one finds many of them who say that their intention is not to speak at all before the multitude of the people of the earth, who are lost in the darkness of temporality, but that the divine influx which flowed upon them forces them to speak, and that they are even subjected to shame, as in the saying of the prophet,[322] "I gave my back to the smiters and my cheek to those that plucked; I hid not my face from shame and spitting," while another prophet said,[323] "the Lord God will help me, who shall condemn me?" And many other similar [sayings] in the way of every chastiser.

Abulafia compared his lot to that of the Biblical prophets in a number of places:

> It is not a miracle that there should happen to my work what happened to the works of Moses our teacher, and to our prophets and our wise men and to Rabbi Moses [i.e., Maimonides], for I shall also suffer what they, of blessed memory, suffered, from this matter. And so is the way of every author who composes a book for the sake of heaven, in every time and every place, that is, it is incumbent that he suffer what happens to him on account of his work.[324]

The process of compositition of *Sefer ha Ge'ulah* is described in the introduction as an act similar to that of the prophets:[325]

> A spirit came and made me stand on my legs, and called me twice by my name, "Abraham Abraham," and I answered "here I am" [an allusion to Gen. 22:1, 11]. And a voice came with a great tumult and taught me by the way of justice, and it taught me knowledge and related to me the way of understanding, and it informed me and wakened me as a man who is awakened from his sleep to compose a new thing, nothing of which was composed in its day, for the reason which I have mentioned in the matter Isaiah the prophet, who called to the members of his generation on account of their being remote from the truth. And it was not enough that they did not know and hear his words and that they did not accept them from him, but that they also hit him.[326]

An additional expression of Abulafia's resemblance to the prophets is found in the composition of *Sefer ha-Hafṭarah*, in the introduction of which states:[327] "And behold Raziel [i.e., Abulafia] commanded in this book to adjure God by His Name to sanctify and to read in this book once every Sabbath, following the reading of the Torah, among the Prophetic readings." As we have seen above, Abulafia includes Moses among the prophets whose lot was similar to his own; one should add that there are other statements in which he expresses his feeling that his own prophecy was superior even to that of Moses. In R. Abraham ibn Ezra's *Commentary to the Torah* on Exodus 3:13, we read in the name of R. Joshua the Karaite "that there was a tradition in Israel from their fathers that the redeemer of Israel discovered a new name that was not heard." Just as Moses introduced the name *ʾEhyeh ʾašer ʾEhyeh* ("I am that I am"), the Messiah will introduce a new name.[328] Indeed, in many passages Abulafia refers to the name *ʾhwy* as the hidden name of god. In his opinion the pearl, which is the symbol of the pure religion in Abulafia's version of the famous three rings parallel, was not to be found among Israel in his time: It follows from this that the mission of Moses, the law-giver, was not entirely successful.[329] In my opinion, Abulafia conceived himself as The Prophet, *par excellence,* superior even to Moses.[330] In *Sefer ha-ʿEdut* he writes:[331] "Know that most of the visions which Raziel saw were built upon the Ineffable Name and upon its revelation in the world now, in our days, which has not been since the days of Adam and is the root of all his books," This feeling that the Messiah is superior even to Moses made it possible for him to write:[332] "for I innovate a new Torah within the holy nation, which is my people Israel. My honorable Name is like a new Torah, and it has not been explicated to my people since the day that I hid my face from them."

While these remarks are cited as God's words to Abulafia, the feeling of mission revealed by this sentence testifies to the great power of the prophetic experience in Abulafia's eyes. This does not mean that Abulafia will alter the Torah—for this reason, there appears the reservation, *like* a new torah"—but that it will revel its true face, that is, its essence as a combination of the Names of God.[333]

The two main motifs discussed in this section—the prophet as messenger and the Messiah as a prophet on the level of Moses—also appear in R. Isaac of Acre. We have already seen in the above section that he prophecy of mission appears in an advanced mystical stage in *Ôẓar Ḥayyim*. Let us now see R. Isaac's understanding of the level of Messiah:[334]

> There is one who prophesies through the intermediacy of the brilliance of the light of the angel who dwells in his soul, which is the angel who speaks within him, and this angel is intermediary . . . between him and the great supreme angel, who is Meṭaṭron the Prince of the Presence.[335] And there is one who prophesies by the brilliance of the light of Meṭaṭron dwelling in his soul, and there is one who does so by the brilliance of the light of the diadem [i.e., *Malḵut*], while Moses himself [did so] by the brilliance of *Tiferet* which emanated from *T[iferet]* and dwelt in his soul. And Messiah son of David, whom God shall bring to us quickly, by the brilliance of the light of the Crown, will emanate the brilliance of his light from *Keter* and it will dwell in his soul, and by it he will perform awesome and great things in all the lands.

The Eschatological Element

The prophetic experience was understood by Abulafia not only as the apprehension of truths, but also as a path leading to the survival of the soul. His description of the point of departure from which man commences his path towards immortality is depicted in the darkest imaginable colors:[336]

> We eat and drink and have forbidden sexual relations, from which we are born through harlotry and lust and menstrual blood and urine. And we were a fetid drop at the time of our creation, and so we are today, fetid and besmirched with filth and mud and vomit and excrement so that there is no clean place.[337] While alive we are dust and ashes, and to dust you shall return, and we shall be dead carcasses, putrid and crushed in fire, like rubbish filled with vanity and spirits.

Apart from the bodily element, there also hover over man the truths of the power of imagination:

> Sometimes it is revealed to you that you are to be killed and your *membrum virile* swallowed up. . . . And sometimes it is concealed from you, until you think that you will not die until you shall become old, even though he stand before you and sees you, you do not see him; and suddenly he returns to you and demands his portion, and so it is always, time after time, day after day, until the day of your death.[338]

In order to be saved from this situation, man must forfeit this world in every sense of the word:[339] "and cast behind your self everything that exists apart from the Name, in your soul in truth . . . and do not place any thought in the world upon anything apart from Him, may He be blessed." Cleaving to God draws the mystic closer to the source of apotheosis:[340]

> And Divine virtues are added to him until he speaks with the holy spirit, whether in his writing or with his mouth; it is said of this that this is in truth the king of the kings of flesh and blood, as is said among people about a unique king of kings, that he alone and those like him have passed the boundary of humanity, and cleaved in their lifetime to their God, and even more so when their natural and contingent matter dies.

The main purpose of the Torah and of the Kabbalah ie:[341] "that man should attain the level of the angels called *Išim* and cleave to them for eternal life, until human beings shall turn into separate angels after being, before hand—human beings in actuality and angels in potential, but on a lower level." Man's transformation from transient essence to eternal takes place when he attains 'prophecy':[342] "and likewise he shall be required to call to the prophet with the Divine influx until he returns to cleave to it and live on the day of his death." This is not intended to refer to survival following bodily death, but to the life of the World to Come which is acquired in this life by complete relinquishment of this world:[343] "And his strength shall cast off all natural powers and he shall put on the divine powers, and he shall be saved by this from natural death on the day of his death and live for ever." Abulafia stresses the Platonic idea of voluntary death in many passages.[344] In *Gan Naʿul,*[345] we read:

> And these are miraculous secrets, and the general rule from which

> you will die, and when you divide it into two equal parts, one part shall be *tiḥyeh* ("you shall live") and also the second part *tiḥyeh*.[346] And this is the secret alluded to in the saying of the supreme Holy Ones,[347] "What shall a man do and live? He shall die! What should a man do in order to die? To live!" And they said that this is alluded to in [the verse][348], "When a man dies in a tent," and they explained that the Torah is not preserved save by one who kill himself for it. And the Rabbi [i.e., Maimonides] said in *The Book of Knowledge, Laws of the Fundaments of Torah*,[349] that the Torah is not preserved except by one who kills himself in the tents of wisdom.

This casting off of corporeality brings out another characteristic of the prophetic experience of Abulafia, namely, the absence of ascetic elements in his system.

The Absence of Asceticism

Radical asceticism is a widely used method for attaining ecstatic states in many mystical systems, the purpose of such afflictions being to weaken the power of the body or of matter to enable the intellect to act without interference. Such an approach is widespread in Neo-Platonic literature, in which matter is understood as evil in its very essence; a struggle was carried on between the intellect and the body, and at times between the intellect and the soul, which is portrayed as the representative of the bodily powers.[350] As Abulafia understood man's inner struggle as taking place between the intellect and the imagination, one cannot find in his writings extreme ascetic instructions necessary for one who seeks to attain 'prophecy.'[351] His approach is rather that, in order to attain 'prophecy,' one must act in the direction of strengthening the intellect rather than that of suppressing the body, the soul, or the imagination:

> One who enters the path of combination [of letters], which is the way that is close to knowledge of God in truth, from all the ways he will at once test and purify his heart in the great fire, which is the fire of desire; and if he has strength to stand the way of ethics, close to desire, and his intellect is stronger than his imagination, he rides upon it as one who rides upon his horse and guides it by hitting it with the boots to run at his will, and to restrain it with his hand, to make it stand in the place where his intellect will wish, and his imagination is to be a recipient that he accept his opinion. . . . The man who possesses this great power, he is a man in truth.[352]

The ideal situation is the negation of those activities of the imagination which are not checked by the intellect:[353] "And when the imaginary, lying apprehension is negated, and when its memory is razed from the hearts of those who feel and are enlightened, death will be swallowed up for ever." The extent to which Abulafia's opinion is opposed to the ascetic tendency which seeks to leave life in this world is evinced by the following passage:[354]

> He shall pray and beseech continuously to the Honorable Name, to save him from the attributes until he be found innocent in the Supernal court, and . . . in the lower court, and will inherit two worlds,[355] this world and the World to Come.

The life of the World to Come may be seen as an allusion to the ecstatic state specifically in this world. Particularly striking is the difference between Abulafia's refusal to make use of the way of asceticism[356] and the suggestion appearing in R. Isaac of Acre:

> And you shall live a life of pain in your house of seclusion, lest your appetitive soul be strengthened over your intellective soul, that in this you shall merit to draw down the divine influx upon your intellectual soul, [using] the Torah, namely, the science of combination and its prerequisites, this Glory being the supernal Divine influx, which is the real Glory authentic.[357]

There seems no doubt concerning the growing influence of Sufic mystical sources in the works of the disciples of Abulafia, which directed the character of post-Abulafian ecstatic Kabbalah in the matter of asceticism.[358]

Projection or Interpretation

Let us now return to the question which we raised at the beginning of this chapter: namely, did Abulafia, in explaining the intellectual meaning of his visions, interpret his own experience correctly, because they were the result of certain concepts in which he was used to thinking, or is this a case in which meaning was imposed upon an experience in which it was initially lacking. It seems to me significant that a certain answer to these questions may be found in Ôẓar *ʿEden Ganuz:*

> When I was thirty-one years old, in the city of Barcelona, God woke me from my sleep and I studied *Sefer Yeẓirah* with its commentaries; and the hand of God [rested] upon me, and I wrote some books of wisdom and wondrous books of prophecies, and my spirit was

> quickened within me, and the spirit of God came into my mouth, and a spirit of holiness moved about me, and I saw many awesome sights and wonders by means of these wonders and signs. And among them, there gathered around me jealous spirits, and I saw imaginary things and errors, and my thoughts were confused, because I did not find which of my people would teach me the way by which I ought to go. Therefore I was like a blind man groping at noon for fifteen years, and the Satan [stood] by my right hand to accuse me, and I was crazy from the vision of my eyes which I saw, to fulfill the words of the Torah and to finish the second curse [of] the fifteen years which God had graced me with some little knowledge, and God was with me to help me from the year [500]1 to the year [50]45, to save me from every trouble; and at the beginning of the year *Elijah the Prophet* [i.e., [50]46 = 1286 C.E.], God had favor in me and brought me to his holy tabernacle.[359]

Abulafia reveals here that not all of his visions are the result of the influence of the intellect upon the imagination; until the year 1286, Abulafia testifies that he also experienced visions originating in the realm of the imagination alone, and that this was apparently the reason for his fears. It seems to me that the visions presented by Abulafia set down in writing do not belong to this category, nor do any of his books reveal the darker side of ecstatic experiences. Those descriptions and interpretations of visions which have reached us belong to the "positive" type of experience. Evidently this choice between the intellectual and the imaginative, namely between visions which can be allegorically interpreted as pointing to intellectual contents, and those which originate in the power of the imagination alone, without reflecting, in Abulafia's opinion, speculative conceptions, was carried out on the basis of criteria of the reflection of the intellectual matters in the vision. Since the correspondence between the content of the vision as it has been given and the speculative system is very great, it is difficult to assume that this was a matter of mere chance: In my opinion, his visions are the result of the projection of philosophical concepts onto the imaginative realm, from whence it is quite easy to find their roots in the theoretical system of the author.

Notes to Chapter Three

1. See Idel, *Abraham Abulafia*, p. 232.

2. *Ibid.*, p. 101.

3. *Ibid.*, p. 14.

4. See A. Heschel, *The Prophets* (New York, 1962), pp. 390–409.

5. *Commentary on the Mishnah, Introduction to Ḥeleq*, translated by Arnold J. Wolf, in I. Twersky, ed. *A Maimonides Reader* (New York - Philadelphia, 1972), p. 420.

6. *Sefer ha-Miẓwot; Lo Taʿaseh*, no. 31. Compare the remarks by the anonymous author of *Saʿar Šamayim*, quoted by Scholem, *Kabbalistic Manuscripts*, pp. 45–47: "For the prophets used to prophesy and their limbs would shake, and at times they would fall; and behold the great proof [of this in] the matter of the magicians, who would constantly strike [themselves] with a stick, until their feeling was dulled, and they would then relate future things [and] many of them would cry out in mighty voices, and this was by them to abstract their intellects from matter." See also R. Joseph Gikatilla, *Šaʿare Ẓedeq*, fol. 7a.

7. Ed. H. Z. Blumberg (Cambridge, Mass., 1961), p. 54. These remarks by Averroes influenced Moses Narboni's *Commentary to Guide of the Perplexed* II:36 (p. 43a), and also found their way into *Toldot Adam*, MS. Oxford 836, fol. 158b. Another version of this passage appears in Shem-Tov Falaquiera's *Sefer ha-Maʿalot* (Berlin, 1894), p. 41.

8. MS. Paris BN 774, fol. 158a. Compare *Midraš ha-Neʿelamʿal Rut* (*Zohar Hadaš*, p. 92b): "The Rabbis say: storm—this is the storm of Satan, who made turbulent the body of Job."

9. Ezek. 1:4.

10. Job 40:6.

11. MS. Oxford 1580, fols. 163b–164a, with omissions.

12. Deut. 12:23.

13. Lev. 17:11.

14. *Op cit.*, n. 11, fol. 162a.

15. MS. Oxford 1582, fol. 12a, printed by Scholem in *Kabbalistic Manuscripts*, p. 25.

16. MS. Jerusalem 8° 148, fols. 64b–65a.

17. MS. Paris BN 774, fol. 158a.

18. MS. Oxford 1580, fol. 163b.

19. MS. Oxford 1582, fol. 12a, and see n. 15 above.

20. Isa. 11:2.

21. MS. Jerusalem 8° 148, fol. 66b–67a.

22. *Ibid.*, fol. 65a.

23. *Sullam ha-ʿAliyah,* printed in Kabbalistic Manuscripts, p. 228. The author changed from the first person to the third one!

24. MS. Paris BN 774, fol. 158a.

25. I Kings 19:11–12.

26. *We-zot li-Yihudah,* p. 16, corrected according to MS. New York - JTS 1887, fol. 98b.

27. G. Sed Rajna, *Commentaire sur la liturgie Quotidienne* (Leiden, 1974), pp. 166, 168. On the symbolism of light in R. Isaac the Blind and in the circle of *Sefer ha-ʿIyyun,* see Scholem, *Les Origines,* pp. 324, 351ff.

28. The passage is published by Scholem in *Rešit ha-Qabbalah,* pp. 143–144, and analyzed in his article in *MWGJ* 78 (1934), pp. 511–512; the English translation follows that of Noah J. Jacobs, printed in the English version of Scholem's article, "The Concept of Kawwanah," pp. 172–173.

29. *Peruš ha-Aggadot,* MS. Rome - Casanatense 179 fol. 134a; MS. Vatican 295, fol. 107a. The passage is cited anonymously by R. Menaḥem Recanati in *Peruš ha-Torah,* fol. 90c, and from there by H. Judah Ḥayyat in *Peruš le-Maʿareḳet ha-Elohut,* 95b–96a. It is worth mentioning here another passage from Recanati, which appears to be a reworking of the words of R. Ezra or R. Azriel: "When the pious men and men of deeds concentrated and involved themselves in the supreme secrets, they would imagine by the power of depiction of their thoughts [i.e., their visual imagination] as though those things were inscribed before them." *Peruš ha-Torah,* fol. 37d. This passage also appears with minor changes in Recanati's *Ṭaʿame ha-Miẓwot* (MS. Vatican 209, fol. 28a), where the auto-suggestive principle is clearly expressed.

30. See R. Azriel's letter to Burgos, printed by Scholem in *Maddaʿe ha-Yahadut* II, p. 234.

31. See *Šeqel ha-Qodeš,* pp. 123–124, and in other passages in his books. See also G. Scholem, "Colours and Their Symbolism in Jewish Tradition and Mysticism," *Diogenes,* vol. 108 (1979), pp. 84–111; vol. 109 (1980), pp. 64–76.

32. However, in R. Ariel's *Peruš la-Aggadot,* p. 39, we find a conversation between God and the one meditating, connected with the uncovering of secrets, but this passage is an unusual one in early Kabbalah. It is also interesting that here the mystic enters premeditatedly into this situation: "and the one praying must see himself as if he is speaking," etc.

33. The Sefirot are called *aspaqlaryot* or *mar'ot* (mirrors); see Tishby *The Wisdom of the Zohar* I, pp. 151–152. In *Šošan Sodot* of R. Moses of Kiev, fol. 51a, in a passage belonging in my opinion to R. Azriel, we read, "Know that Divine prophecy is compared to the apprehension of the ten Sefirot of light." Cf. R. Asher ben David's *Peruš Šem ha-Meforaš,* p. 16.

34. MS. Jerusalem 8° 148, fols. 63b–64a. The passage was published by Scholem in *Qiryat Sefer* I (1924), p. 134, and translated in *Major Trends*, p. 150.

35. Fol. 69b. The corrected text was published by G. Scholem in his article in *MGWJ* 74 (1930), p. 287.

36. I. Hausherr, "La Methode d'oraison Hesychaste," *Orientalié Christiana*, vol. 9 (1927), pp. 128–129; J. Lemaitre, *Dictionaire de Spiritualité* (1952), col. 1852–53.

37. See Hausherr, *op cit.*, p. 128.

38. We will cite here several examples of mystical experience connected with light. In a work entitled *Maʿaseh Merkavah* published by Scholem in his *Jewish Gnosticism*, p. 112, par. 22–23, we read: "R. Ishmael said: Once I heard this teaching from R. Neḥunyah ben ha-Kanah, I stood upon my feet and asked him all the names of the angels of wisdom, and from the question which I asked I saw a light in my heart like the days of heaven. R. Ishmael said: Once I stood on my feet and I saw my face enlightened by my wisdom, and I started to interpret each and every angel in every palace." In *Leviticus Rabba* 21:11, we read, "At the time that the Holy Spirit was upon him [i.e., the High Priest], his face burned like torches." In *Ketav Tammim* by R. Moses Taku, (*Ôẓar Neḥmad* 3 (1860), p. 88), we read: "And so the soul of the righteous man shines, and in every place where the righteous go, their souls shine." In *Saʿare Ẓedeq* itself, we learn of Moses that "When his generation [i.e., the formation of his fetus] was completed after forty days, the skin of his face shone (Ex. 34:29). . . . When he was weaned, it shone. [All this] to indicate to you the purity of his matter, and the negation of its darkness, until it became, by way of analogy, like the heavenly sapphire-like material. And our rabbis of blessed memory expounded, 'for the skin of his face shone'—do not read *ʿor* (skin) but *ôr (light), for the letters a"h h"'r* interchange; that is, the enlightened intellect which dwells in the light which is in the innermost part of the true, perfect intellect" (MS. Jerusalem 8° 148, fol. 33b–34a). For a survey of the appearance of light in mysticism, see Mircea Eliade, *The Two and the One* (New York, 1969), pp. 19–77. The subject of the "shining" enjoyed by the body of the mystic as part of the mystical experience is in itself deserving of a special study.

39. *Oẓar ʿEden Ganuz*, MS. Oxford 1580 fol. 165b.

40. MS. Moscow - Günzburg 775, fol. 197a.

41. MS. Paris BN 840, fol. 46a. On the problem of concentration *(hitbodedut)* in R. Shem Tov, see Idel, "*Hitbodedut* as Concentration," *Studies*, essay VII.

42. Idel, "We Do Not Have."

43. Lam. 3:28.

44. p. 69b. The connection between vocalization and lights already

appears in *Berit Menuḥah*.

45. A. J. Deikman, "Deautomatization and the Mystic Experience," in *Altered States of Consciousness*, ed. Ch, T. Tart (New York, 1962), p. 40.

46. Heinrich Zimmer, "On the Significance of the Indian Tantric Yoga," in *Spiritual Disciplines; Papers from Eranos Yearbooks*, ed. J. Campbell (New York, 1960), p. 51.

47. *We-zot li-Yihudah*, p. 16, corrected according to MS. New York - JTS 1887, and MS. Cambridge Add. 644.

48. See Idel, *Abraham Abulafia*, pp. 95–96.

49. See the sources collected by Heschel, *Theology of Ancient Judaism*, II, pp. 267–268.

50. L. Ginzberg, *Legends of the Jews* (Philadelphia, 1946), vol. 6, p. 36, n. 201; Werblowsky, *Joseph Karo*, p. 269, n. 2.

51. Ex. 19:19.

52. See the long version of his commentary to Ex. 19:20:

> Know that man's soul is supernal and honorable, and that it comes from the intermediate world, and the body is from the lowly world, and nothing speaks in the lowly world but man himself, and man hears, for that which speaks to him, he wishes to understand what is in his heart, and the intellectual person cannot create any language, but only that which is known to him. . . . And behold, when man speaks to man in human matters and in the language which he understands, he will surely understand his words.

In his commentary to Gen. 1:26, Ibn Ezra writes:

> And after we knew that the Torah spoke in human language, for the one who speaks is man, and likewise the one who hears is man, and a man cannot speak things to one who is higher than himself or lower than himself, but only by way of "the image of man."

See also his commentary to Daniel 10:1, and *Yesod Mora'*, where the saying "the one who speaks is human and the one who hears is human," is repeated. Cf. G. Vajda, *Juda ben Nissim Malka* (Paris, 1954), p. 140, n. 1; C. Sirat, *Les Theories des visions supernaturelles* (Leiden, 1964), p. 77.

53. MS. Oxford 1580, fol. 12a. In *Sitre Torah*, Abulafia alludes to this idea without detailing his intention (MS. Paris BN 774, fol. 140a).

> And it is likewise said (Num. 7:89), "And he heard the voice speaking to him," which they translated as *mitmalel*, like *mitdabber*, i.e., in the reflexive case. This is likewise the secret of (Num. 12:6) "in a vision I will make myself known to him," and also of (Ezek. 2:2) "I will hear the one speaking to me." Likewise, "Moses spoke and God answered him with a voice," (Ex. 19:19) which they interpreted, "in the voice of Moses." And this is a wondrous and hidden secret among us.

Abulafia attempted to rely upon the words of Maimonides in *Guide* II:33, where the latter quoted the *Mek̲ileta*: "(Moses) would repeat to them every commandment as he heard it . . . and Moses was the one who heard the things and related them." It is worth comparing the end of the passage from *Ôẓar ʿEden Ganuz* with the expression "the bush of heart was not consumed," which appears in the poem, *ʾim teḥzeh mevin*; see Idel, *Abraham Abulafia*, p. 33; on the bush as a symbol for "within," see Abraham Bibago, *Derek̲ Emunah* II, 3, p. 45c; III, 7, p. 74b; III:5, fol. 97a, and see R. Nathan ben Avigdor, MS. Oxford 1643, fol. 12a–b.

54. The expression, "*YHWH Male*" also alludes to man's act of speaking, rather than to God's. The term *YHWH male* means *Yod He Wa He* = 45 = *Adam* (man). Were the intention to convey the idea that God was speaking, one would use the conventional *gematria* of the formula *YH male* = 86 = *Elohim*.

55. *Tanḥuma* ed. Buber, *Berešit*, p. 3.

56. Compare the reaction of John of the Cross, who said of a nun who thought that she was speaking with God, "she only spoke with herself." Quoted from W. R. Inge, *Mysticism and Religion* (London, 1969), p. 35.

57. *Mafteaḥ ha-Ḥok̲mot*, MS. Moscow 133, fol. 6b; MS. Parma 141, fol. 7a–7b.

58. MS. Jerusalem 8° 148, fol. 65a. Compare the remarks of R. Ezra in *Peruš ha-Aggadot* (MS. Vatican 295, fol. 107a) concerning the prophets: "And they were saying the things as if they had received them from above and as if a person had placed the words in his mouth, and they would say them against their will." See also R. Isaac of Acre's remarks cited below, alluded to in note 99.

59. MS. Jerusalem 8° 148, fol. 66b. It is worth mentioning a similar approach which appears in R. Judah ben Nissim ibn Malka, according to which the speech from "the bush" originates in Moses himself; this is based upon the *gemaṭria, ha-Seneh* (the bush)=120, which was the number of years that Moses lived. R. Judah interprets the verse in Zech. 4:1 in a similar manner, referring to "the angel who spoke to me" in the sense of "from within me." See G. Vajda, "La Doctrine Astrologique de Juda ben Nissim ibn Malka," *Homenaje a Millas Vallicrosa* (Barcelona, 1956), vol. 2, p. 492, n. 14, *The Abbreviated Hebrew Version of R. Judah ibn Malka's Writings* [Heb.] (Ramat Gan, 1974), p. 31 and p. 41. See also notes 52, 53 above. On the connections

between R. Isaac of Acre and R. Judah ben Nissim, see Vajda's above-mentioned article, and note 155 below.

60. Printed by Scholem in *Qiryat Sefer* vol. 31 (1956), p. 393.

61. Vilna, 1886, p. 60a–b (Ch. 35), *Sa*ʿ*ar ha-Nevu*ʾ*ah;* also cited in R. Abraham Azulai, *Ḥesed le-Avraham* (Lvov, 1863), ʿ*Eyn ha-Qore; Nahar* 19, fol. 51a.

62. The understanding of the embodiment of the spiritual voice within the corporeal voice for purposes of revelation is related to a commonly held concept in the theosophical Kabbalah, holding that every descent—for example, that of the angel—entails its embodiment in a corporeal garment.

63. II Samuel 23:2.

64. See G. Scholem, "R. Elijah ha-Kohen ha-Itamari and Sabbatianism" (Heb.), *Alexander Marx Jubilee Volume* (New York, 1950), Heb. Section, p. 467. Compare the explanation given by R. Azriel of Gerona, of prophecy as the outcome of "strength of the soul."

65. For the connection between prophecy and "greatness of soul," see R. Azriel of Gerona's letter to the city of Burgos, published by Scholem, *Madda*ʿ*e ha-Yahadut* II, 239: "in the dreams of the soul and its strengthening."

66. Salomon Pines, "Le *Sefer ha-Tamar* et les *Maggidim* des Kabbalistes," *Hommages a Georges Vajda*, ed. G. Nahon - Ch. Touati (Louvain, 1980), pp. 337–345.

67. See Schatz-Uffenheimer, *Quietistic Elements*, pp. 119-121.

68. MS. Oxford 1582, fol. 62a.

69. Job 33:14.

70. Ex. 20:22.

71. *Ibid.*, fol. 56b. Compare the remarks appearing in MS. Jerusalem 8° 1303, fol. 5a, which belong, in my opinion, to Abulafia:

> And know that the Kabbalist receives, that God says to a man "Receive Me and I will receive you," as it is said (Deut. 26:17,18) "Thou hast avouched [lit., spoke for] the Lord. . . . And the Lord hath avouched [lit., spoken for] you," and therefore it says (Ex. 20:24), "In every place where I shall cause my name to be mentioned I will go to you and bless you" . . . and it says to you that if you remember My Name for My honor, I have already remembered your name for your honor.

72. Ex. 20:21.

73. MS. New York - JTS 1801, fol. 9a, corrected according to MS. British

Library 7–9, fols. 12a–12b. Abulafia's words were copied in the last part of *Ša'are Qedušah,* which has not yet been printed, under the name *Ḥayye ha-ʿOlam ha-Ba,* but they are essentially a corrected version of *Sefer ha-Ḥešeq.* See also Abulafia's remarks in *Ḥayye ha-ʿOlam ha-Ba,* MS. Oxford 1582, fol. 54a, "Hold your head evenly, as if it were on the balance pans of a scale, in the manner in which you would speak with a man who was as tall as yourself, evenly, face to face."

74. *Ibid.,* fol. 9b, corrected on the basis of MS. British Library 749, fol. 12b. Abulafia plays on the similarity between *tenuʿah* (motion) and *ʿaniah* (response).

75. *Ibid.,* 9b–10a, corrected according to *ibid.,* fol. 12b. The appearance of the Glory *(kavod)* as an intermediary witnessing the force of speech already appears in R. Saʿadyah Gaon, in *Emunot we-De'ot,* sec. II, chap. 10, etc. On the Glory as having a human shape, see A. Altmann, "Saadya's Theory of Revelation," *Saadia Studies,* ed. E. Rosenthal (Manchester, 1943), p. 20.

76. *Abulafia,* pp. 232–233, and see also our remarks concerning this passage in *Abraham Abulafia,* p. 169.

77. Deut. 17:18.

78. The reading *meliz* appears in MS. British Library 749, while that of *ʾemzaʿi* in MS. New York.

79. MS. Oxford 1582, fol. 18b.

80. *Haqdamat ha-Peruš la-Torah,* p. viii.

81. *Guide of the Perplexed* III:51. On the background to this idea, see I Goldziher, *Kitab maʿani al-nafs* (Berlin, 1907), pp. 141–142.

82. *Tešuvot Dunaš ha-Lewi ben Labrat 'al Rasa"g* (Breslau, 1866), pp. 14–15; R. Abraham ibn Ezra in his *Commentary* to Psalms 30:13; 103:1; and R. David Qimhi's *Commentary* to these and other verses. In *Sitre Torah,* MS. Paris BN 774, fol. 163b, Abulafia writes explicitly that "Man alone of all that which is generated and corrupted possesses the human form which is divided into two portions, and receives influx from two sides, which are called *Šefaʿ* (influx) and the glory of God." This refers to the human intellect, which is called both "influx" and the "Glory of God."

83. MS. Oxford 1582, fol. 56b.

84. *Ibid.,* fol. 4b–5a. In *Ŏr ha-Sekel* (MS. Vatican 233, fol. 127b), we learn similar things: "And because man is composed of many powers, it is necessary that he see the influx in his intellect, and that vision is called by the name Intellectual Apprehension. And the influx will further jump to the imagination, and require that the imagination apprehend that which is in its nature to apprehend, and see in the image of corporeality imagined as spirituality combined with it; and that force will be called Man or Angel or

the like." In *Sefer ha-Ḥešeq*, MS. New York JTS 1801, fol. 35b, it states, "For every inner speech is none other than a picture alone, and that is the picture which is common to the intellect and the imagination. Therefore, when the soul sees the forms which are below it, it immediately sees itself depicted therein." Compare the words of R. Barukh Togarmi, *Abulafia*, p. 232: "the Divine element is in you, which is the intellect that flows upon the soul."

85. Num. 12:6.

86. *ʿEdi* = *Ḥanok*. *Šadday* = *Meṭaṭron*. See R. Eleazar of Worms' *ʿEser Hawayot*, MS. Munchen 143, fol, 220a. *Ḥalom* (dream)= *ʿEdi*=*Ḥanoḥ*=84. The definition of Enoch as "witness" (*ʿed*) originates in Midrashic literature.

87. MS. Oxford 1582, fols. 4b–5a.

88. See the references in G. Scholem, *Von den mystischen Gestalt der Gottheit* (Zurich, 1962), pp. 307–308, nn. 12–18; Meyerovitch, *Mystique et Poesie*, pp. 284–286.

89. MS. Oxford 574, fol. 13b. Cf. Scholem, in his above-mentioned book, p. 309, n. 20; and Dan, *The Esoteric Theology*, pp. 224–225, esp. n. 8.

90. Num. 12:8.

91. Job 4:16.

92. This text is a corrected version by R. Moses of Burgos, whom Abulafia considered among his disciples, of the saying of R. Isaac ha-Kohen, his teacher. See Scholem, "R. Moses of Burgos, the disciple of R. Isaac" (Heb.) *Tarbiẓ* 5 (1934), pp. 191-192; *Maddaʿe ha-Yahadut* II, p. 92. The passage also influenced R. Meir ibn Gabbai, who quotes it verbatim in *ʿAvodat ha-Qodeš*. See G. Scholem, "Eine Kabalistische Erklärung der Prophetie, " *MGWJ* 74 (1930), pp. 289–290.

93. R. Judah ibn Malka, *Kitab Uns we-Tafsir*, ed. Vajda (Ramat-Gan, 1974), pp. 22–23, and p. 26. Ibn Malka wrote his works in the middle of the thirteenth century, and not in the fourteenth century; see note 59 above.

94. A similar idea appears in the anonymous *Peruš ha-Tefillot*, which is close to both Abulafia and to Ibn Malka, which I shall discuss at length elsewhere.

95. Fol. 69b. Corrected by Scholem according to MS. Oxford 1655, and printed in the above-mentioned article (n. 92), p. 287.

96. On the identity of R. Nathan, see Idel, "The World of the Imagination," pp. 175–176.

97. *Genesis Rabba* 27:1.

98. MS. Oxford 1582, fol. 50a.

99. See note 95 above. In *Šaʿare Ẓedeq*, MS. Jerusalem 8° 148, fols. 73b–74a,

there again appears information concerning the appearance of the form without any connection to speech. On concentration in the book *Ša'are Ẓedeq,* see Idel, "*Hitbodedut* as Concentration," *Studies,* essay VII.

100. MS. Moscow-Günzburg 775, fols. 162b–163a. A passage from this treatise is quoted in the name of a "sage" in *Šošan Sodot,* fol. 69b. as noted by Scholem in his above-mentioned book (n. 88), p. 307, n. 11. See also Gottlieb, *Studies,* p. 247.

101. MS. Vatican 233, fols. 126a–b.

102. Fol. 125b.

103. In *Ôẓar Ḥayyim,* MS. Moscow-Günzburg 775, fol. 222a, there appears a passage with a similar problem: "However, I knew with a clear knowledge that the hand which I had grasped and kissed was certainly his (i.e., Metatron's) hand, and I saw myself within the secret of the encompassing totality." R. Isaac of Acre saw himself inside the Active Intellect, which served as a kind of mirror to the mystic.

104. See *Ḥayye ha-'Olam ha-Ba* MS. Oxford 1582, fol. 79b; Idel, *Abraham Abulafia,* pp. 404–405.

105. MS. Paris BN 727, fols. 158a–b.

106. It is reasonable to assume that the development of the process of enlightenment from thought to wisdom and understanding, which appears twice in the text, is an interpretation by the *'Iyyun* circle of the order of devolution of the Sefirot—thought is *Keter,* followed by Wisdom (*Ḥokmah*) and Understanding (*Binah*)—in Sefirotic Kabbalah.

107. This number alludes to the parallel between the twenty-two letters and the people; see also the passage from *Sefer ha-Ôt,* p. 83, to be discussed at length below in sec. 6.

108. I Sam. 10:5.

109. MS. Paris BN 774, fol. 159b.

110. *Sefer Yeẓirah* 5:2.

111. See also Idel, *Abraham Abulafia,* pp. 101–102.

112. Compare *Sefer ha-Meliẓ,* MS. Rome - Angelica 38, fol. 18b, in the passage to be discussed below.

113. Fol. 55a.

114. Wertheimer's *Bate Midrašot,* II, p. 396, Version B. The passage from the midrash is not analyzed by S. Lieberman in his article in *Greek in Jewish Palestine* (New York, 1942), pp. 185–191. See also R. David ibn Avi Zimra, *Magen Dawid* (Munkasz, 1912), p. 49b, and below, n. 247.

115. Ezek. 9:4.

116. MS. Rome - Angelica 38, 12a–b; MS. München 285, fol. 15a.

117. MS. Paris BN 774, fol. 166a, and see also fol. 166b. The passage is based upon the following *gematria*: Adam and Eve (*ʾAdam we-Ḥawah*) = 70 = my father and mother (*ʾavi we-ʾimi*) = blood and ink (*dam we-diyo*). And ink (*we-diyo*)=26=*YHWH*. *Tav dam* (sign of blood)=*demut*=(image)=*nafšeka* (your soul) *kašfan* (magician) *kešafan* (magic) *šofek dam* (spiller of blood) 450. See also below, n. 172, and cf. *Ŏr ha-Sekel*, MS. Vatican 233, fol. 79a.

118. MS. Vatican 233, fol. 125a.

119. Isa. 25:8.

120. MS. British Library 749, fol. 12b; MS. New York - JTS 1801, fol. 9b.

121. Dan, *Studies*, p. 119. Joshua ben Nun gained understanding of the Divine will by means of a vision, as "the name of four letters changes and turns about in various different ways . . . and likewise the name of God in its letters resembles the angels and the prophets in many forms and brilliances and has the likeness of human appearance." In *Sefer ha-Neʿelam*, MS. Paris BN 817, fol. 75b, we read:

> There is no prophet in the world who is able to tell of the various kinds of Glories and levels which are within Him [i.e., within the Glory of the throne]; even that prophet, peace upon him [i.e., Ezekiel], who saw the Glory which was upon the throne, saw nothing but the resemblance of the electrum, as is stated there explicitly; and this great glory was placed upon the throne of glory in order that His great Name might be placed upon it, and by it a number of prophets, and that it be revealed to his pious ones, to each according to his level, so that they not look at the splendor and majesty which is in the essence of His Unity. . . . And when the Holy One, blessed be He, said in his thought, "Let there be light" . . . "Let there be a firmament" . . . and so on, His great Name, which is in accordance with His Glory, was immediately revealed in that same word and creature. And this is [the meaning of], "And God said let there be light . . . a firmament, etc." and subsequently "God made the firmament," etc. The Holy One, blessed be He, says it in His thought, and the honorable Name performs it.

In *Sefer Ẓioni*, fol. 34d (*Yitro*), it states: "For His great Name, which is the Shekhinah, descended upon Sinai and dwelled upon it in fire, and the Honorable Name speaks with Moses and Israel, 'Hear the Name of God,' which is unique within the fire." A parallel to the description of the Divine Name in *Sefer ha-Navon*, and to a certain extent to that in *Sefer ha-Neʿelam* is found in Avicenna's *Commentary to M'arga Name*, in which the prophet sees the expression, "There is no God but Allah," inscribed upon a crown of light on the forehead of the supernal angel. As noted by Henri Corbin, this expression is the supreme Name of God; see his article, "Epiphanie Divine et Naissance Spirituelle dans la Gnose Ismaelienne," *Eranosjahrbuch* 23 (1954), p. 176, n. 69.

122. Dan, *Ibid*. p. 120: "The King of Glory is the Name of Four Letters";

and cf. n. 79 there, and Dan, *The Esoteric Theology*, p. 223.

123. Num. 12:8.

124. *Ǐs Adam*, MS. Rome - Angelica 38, fol. 1a; MS. München 285, fol. 18b. The *gematriot* in this passage are: *YHWH* = 26 = *ḥazehu* = *ḥozeh* (visionary); *we-temunat YHWH yabiṭ* (he shall gaze upon the image of God) = 960 = *be-šem YHWH yabiṭ* (where the final *mem* equals 600). In the section preceding this passage cited from *Ǐš Adam*, Abulafia concerns himself with a similar matter: *Adonai* = 65 = *ha-maḥazeh* (the vision)=*ba-navi* (by a prophet).

125. In his *Commentary on the Torah*, Ex. 33 (Chavell ed., vol. 2, p. 346), R. Baḥya ben Asher wrote, "that Moses comprehended the Ineffable Name through the Divine Glory which came in a cloud. 'And He stood there with him.' [Ex. 34:5] Who stood with him there? The Glory, which is called Name . . . And the Glory is known by the name *YH*." R. Bahya may have known of the view of the Ashkenazic Hasidism, and realized the great resemblance between his own view and that of *Sefer ha-Navon*, quoted above in n. 121.

126. MS. Oxford 1582, fol. 59a–b.

127. Ex. 19:18.

128. Clear allusions to this appear in the passage in the form of *gematria: we-ha-har* (and the mountain) = 216 = *ryo* = *gevurah* (might), which is an allusion to the seventy-two letter Name. *Ŝam har qadoš gavoha* (there is the high holy mountain) = 912 = *Šem ha-meforaš* (the Ineffable Name). In *Šaʿare Ẓedeq*, Abulafia's disciple speaks about a situation in which "I set out to take up the Great name of God, consisting of seventy-two names, permuting and combining it. But when I had done this for a little while, behold, the letters took on in my eyes the shape of great mountains." The parallel between the letters large as mountains and the passage from Abulafia is striking, for which reason one may assume that the letters of which Abulafia speaks are also those of the name of seventy-two letters. It is worth mentioning the words of the anonymous author of *Peruš ha-Tefillot*, who was close to Abulafia, who writes, "Know that every one of the letters of the *aleph-bet* contains a great principle and a hidden reason, and it is a great mountain which we are prevented from climbing" (MS. Paris BN 848, fol. 1a). The mountain appears in other mystical systems as well as an image for the pinnacle of apprehension; see the study by R. C. Zaehner, "Standing on the Peak," *Studies in Mysticism and Religion Presented to Gershom G. Scholem* (Jerusalem, 1967), pp. 381–387.

The ascent to the mountain is interpreted in *Ḥayye ha-Nefeš* as an allusion to spiritual ascent—that is, to 'prophecy'; in MS. München 408, fol. 7b–8a, we read:

> The matter of the name of ascent is homonomous, as in their saying, "Moses ascended to God," this concerns the third matter, which is combined with

their [allusion] also to the ascent to the tip of the mountain, upon which there descended the "created light." These two matters assist us [to understand] all similar matters, and they are [the terms] "place" [*maqom*] and "ascent" [*ʿaliyah*] that, after they come to the matter of "man," the two of them are not impossible by any means; for Moses ascended to the mountain, and he also ascended to the Divine level. That ascent is combined with a revealed matter, and with a matter which is hidden; the revealed [matter] is the ascent of the mountain, and the hidden [aspect] is the level of prophecy.

129. MS München 10, fol. 133b. Note the comparison of the giving of the Torah to "the seekers of the kiss" on Mt. Gerizim, in *Sefer ha-Malmad, MS. Oxford 1649, fol. 204a.*

130. Ex. 19:20.

131. In *Sefer ha-Haftarah*, MS. Rome 38, fol. 35a, *Monte Barbaro*=525 *ḥizzeq ha-qašeh* (strong the hard)=*maʿaseh nes* (an act of miracle)=*ḥizzeq ha-nešimah* (he strengthened the breath)= *we-ḥizeq ha-nešamah* (and he strengthened the soul) =*šem ha-neʿelam* (the hidden Name)=*šem ha-naqam* (the Name of retribution). *Šem ha-qeẓ* (the Name of the end) =535= *ha-mašqif* (the gazer); *ha-šiši* (the sixth) =615 = *ha-šeqer* (the falsehood); *ha-dimyon* (the imagination) = 115 = *monti*= *ʿazazel* = *ha-mini* [of the species] = *ha-yemani* (the right hand on); *Saqramento* = *šeqer* (falsehood) + *Monte*,i.e., falsehood and imagination. The passage makes use of the Italian words, *Monte, alto, Sacramento,* and *mento* (Falsehood).

132. *Yoma* 67b.

133. An identification of the mountain with the human intellect appears in Narboni's *Perus ha-Moreh*: "And the limitation he mentioned which exists to the human intellect alluded to that which God commanded Moses, 'you shall fence about the mountain.' " [Ex. 19:12 (sic!)] See *Moshe Narboni*, ed. Maurice R. Hayoun (Tübingen, 1986), pp. 51, 139.

134. MS. Rome - Angelica 38, fol. 35a.

135. Ex. 25:18.

136. On the *gematriot* in this passage, see Idel, *Abraham Abulafia*, pp. 101–102, and n. 126.

137. MS. Oxford 1580, fol. 37b. One should take note that the letters of the Ineffable Name are inscribed upon the heart already in the Merkavah literature and in that of Ashkenaz Hasidism. *Sefer ha-Ḥešeq*, sec. 26, says "That there is inscribed upon His heart the name by which he shows to the prophets the Shekhinah." Is this a development of the idea of the seventy-two names "written upon the heart of the Holy One, blessed be He," which appears in the text published by Odeberg in *Enoch III*, p. xv and pp. 160-161.

138. MS. Paris BN 774, fol. 156a. On fol. 166a of this work, Abulafia supplies the numerological basis for this statement: "Blood and ink and the latter indicates this name—*YHWH*. The first indicates the composed structure

of this name, which is called, when it is pronounced: *Yod He Waw He.*" *Dam* (blood) = 44 = *Yod He Waw He,* while diyo (ink) = 26 = *YHWH.* See *Ôzar ha-Sekel,* MS. Vatican 233, fol. 79a. In *Gan Naʿul,* MS. München 58, fol. 238a, it states:

> When the Name, whose secret is in blood and ink, began to move within him, and he will feel it, as one who knows the place of a stone which is within him, he will then know that the knowledge of the Name acted in him, and it began to move him from potentiality to actuality.

R. Isaac of Acre follows Abulafia's path, in a passage which has been preserved in MS. Sasson 919, p. 209:

> Blood is the secret of the Unique Name in plene reading, as follows: Yod He Waw He, and its literal meaning is without the plene (number) . . . which is "and ink." Therefore, the secret of the Ineffable Name is blood and ink. The blood alludes to the secret of the sacrifices and the prayers, while ink is like the writing of the Torah in ink upon a book.

139. MS. München 10, fol. 158b–159a.

140. According to Schimmel, *Mystical Dimensions of Islam,* p. 421.

141. MS. New York - JTS 1801, fol. 8a.

142. MS. Moscow - Günzburg 775, fol. 130a.

143. See G. Scholem, "R. Elijah ha-Kohen of Ismir and Sabbatianism" (Heb.), *Alexander Marx Jubilee Volume* (New York, 1950), Hebrew Section, pp. 466–470, and n. 46. Compare above the texts which I have cited concerning the pronunciation of the letters in R. Ḥayyim Vital; cf. Rashi on *Yoma* 73a.

144. See his commentary to Ex. 28:30 and on *Yoma* 73a, and see also Rashbam [R. Solomon b. Meir] on Ex. 28:30, and Targum Jonathan on this verse.

145. See *Peruš Baʿal ha-Ṭurim,* ed. Jacob Reinitz (Benai Barak, 1974), p. 190-191. the *gemaṭria* does not work out properly; evidently, the correct reading is *šem ben šivʿim u-šetaim* (the name of seventy-two). In his *Peruš ha-Torah,* fol. 51a, R. Menahem Recanati states, "And I found it said in the name of R. Eliezer [i.e., R. Eleazar of Worms], of blessed memory, that [the phrase] *et ha-ʾurim weha-tummim* (the Urim and Tummim) is equal in *gemaṭria* to 'the name of seventy-two letters'." This version likewise appears in an anonymous Kabbalistic commentary in MS. New York - JTS 2203, fol. 208a: "And R. Eliezer of Wormiza [i.e. Worms] said that 'the Urim and tummim' equal in *gemaṭria* 'the name of seventy-two'." In *Collectanaea* of R. Yohanan Alemanno, MS. Oxford 2234, fol. 150, it states:

> "The Urim and Tummim." The Ineffable Name was placed on the breast plate by which the high priest would direct his thoughts, and in the name called Urim the letters would be lit up, while in the name called Tummim he would combine the letters and bring them close so that the high priest would not make any error in them, as they were scattered."

146. MS. Oxford 123, fol. 71a–b. Certain magical subjects are discussed in MS. Ambrosiana 62/7 in the name of R. Meshullam the Saducee, as attested by G. Scholem in *Qiryat Sefer* 11 (1933/34), p. 189. Possibly the term *Ẓarfati* (i.e., the French) was corrupted to *Ẓedoqi* (The Saducee).

147. See his short commentary to Ex. 28:30, and the remarks by R. Joseph ben Eliezer Tuv-ᶜElem *Ẓafnat Paᶜaneaḥ* (Cracow, 1912), pp. 285-286. R. David Kokhavi cites the opinion in the name of the aggadah, stating that concentration upon the Urim and Tummim is similar to an act of astrology; see *Migdal Dawid*, MS. Moscow MS. 234, fol. 175a.

148. MS. Paris BN 853, fol. 56b–57a.

149. *Yoma* 73b.

150. *Ḥagiggah* 12a.

151. That is, on Sundays and Wednesdays.

152. Num. 6:25.

153. See also Idel, "Types of Redemptive Activity," p. 261, n. 40.

154. *Sitre Torah*, MS. Paris BN 774, fol. 157b. Compare *Gan Naᶜul*, MS. München 58, fols. 321b–322a:

> The form of the letters, despite being flat, tend somewhat towards convexity, while the form of the eyes is convex, so that when one receives power from the letters in which their form protrudes, it is very thick and coarse, as in the matter of 'Judah will ascend'—i.e., in the secret of the Urim and the Tummim—and it is pictured in the eyes of his head, and the letters illuminate the eyes in their being sunken into them, and from there the power goes over to the heart and is sunk within it, standing out; and the heart receives it and completes with them its actions, and moves from *potentia* into *actu* in attaining this hidden wonder.

Abulafia here portrays the process of enlightenment, which begins in feeling—the perception of the convex form of the letters by the eyes—and concludes in the understanding of their meaning in the heart, i.e., the sunken, concave shape. The two stages are apparently paralleled by the aspects of the Urim and Tummim as enlightening and completing. On the question of the concave and convex shapes in connection with the Urim and Tummim, see the opinion of the author of *Šaᶜare Ẓedeq*, sec. 7, who stresses more strongly the prophetic element and less so the element of compulsion.

155. The image of the Urim as "enlightening" and the Tummim as "completing" is based upon *Yoma* 73b. There, the Urim are identified with the *Aspaqlaryah ha-Meʾirah* (the "clear crystal") and the Tummim with the *Aspaqlaryah še-enah meʾirah* (the "unclear crystal"). One must take note here of the identity drawn by R. Elnathan ben Moshe between the "Clear Crystal" and the Intellect, on the one hand, and the "Unclear Crystal" and the Imagination, on the other. In his work, *Even Sappir*, he states (MS. Paris BN

727, fol. 28b):

> And there is a known man within whom there comes to dwell the intellect and the imagination, called the angel and the cherub. These are the cherubim which are visible and stand on the two ends of the ark-cover (kaporeth), and they both shine like sapphire, each in its time, according to its level. For most prophets prophesy by the power of imagination, which is the "Unclear Crystal," [corresponding to] the pillar of fire by night, from which the fire is borrowed, as in the verse (Ex. 13:22) "the pillar of cloud will not depart by day, nor the pillar of fire by night." The word *yommam* (by day) does not appear anywhere in Scripture but when the sun is upon the earth, and therefore if the sun rises the stars disappear. And the pillar of fire by night is the image of his Name, and it is against the gaze of the sun. These two pillars served in the wilderness for forty years, to protect them from all the corporeal events. . . . But not so Moses our teacher, of blessed memory, who prophesied in the "Clear Crystal," which is called the seraphic light and daily Intellect—and it is this that is meant by, "mouth to mouth I spoke with him"—without distinction and without making use of the power of imagination, which is the atrribute of judgment. This is the distinguished level of the man of God, and this is the daily and light intellect, the light of which is above the heads of the creatures inscribed like in the vision, "and upon the image on the throne was an image like that of a man," to whom he cleaved and by whom he ascended. And the prophets who came after him prophesied by the "Unclear Crystal," and that is the imagination of night-time, [which is] dark, like the light of the sun upon the moon, to receive light from the sparks, and from the flame of his warmth to warm from its extreme cold, like the warmth of the heart which is extreme in its simplicity, to extinguish the extreme cold of the spleen.

156. The connection between Urim and Tummim, the Ineffable Name, and the faculty of the imagination, appears later in R. Ḥasdai Crescas. See S. Urbach, *The Philosophical Doctrine of R. Ḥasdai Crescas* [Heb.] (Jerusalem, 1961), p. 271.

157. MS. Paris BN 777, p. 48. Compare *Sefer ha-Zohar* II, 230a–b.

158. Ezek. 1:26; see also Idel, *Kabbalah: New Perspectives*, pp. 63-65.

159. MS. Paris 777, p. 49.

160. In *Sitre Torah*, MS. Paris BN 774, fol. 165a: "But snow is the darkness alone, and all the prophets gazed upon it and saw it and understood, for it is the 'Unclear crystal'." The reference here is toward the supernal matter; see also *Ḥayye ha-Nefeš*, MS. München 408, fols. 50b-51a. In *Ḥayye ha-ᶜOlam ha-Ba*, MS. Oxford 1582, fol. 69a–b, Abulafia explicitly identifies the Urim and Tummim with the luminaries. "*Arim we-Tamim*, and they are the Urim and Tummim, which are in the image of the luminaries, which enlighten in truth." There is an allusion here both to the sun and moon, i.e., the external Urim and Tummim, as well as to the intellect and imagination, which are the inner Urim and Tummim, enlightening the truth.

161. MS. Jerusalem 8° 148, fols. 73b–74a, translated by Scholem in *Major*

Trends, p. 155, and n. 112.

162. *Yoma* 7ab; *JT, Yoma* 7:4. Compare R. David ben Zimra's remark in *Magen Dawid* (Munkascz, 1912), fols. 18d–19a:

> Here I see fit to inform you in brief of the matter of the Urim and Tummim: when he [i.e., the high priest] would ask [a question], the letters of his answer would shine before him. But you still need to know how this was, for letters which are not divided into words are subject to many different forms and various interpretations, as is very clear. But the matter is that one of the Holy Names known to the priest was resting in the folds of the breastplate, and the priest would direct his consciousness and thought and intention towards that name and concentrate upon it, and was clothed in the Holy Spirit through that same name, and would imagine in his consciousness the interpretation of those letters which shone before him, and there would cling to his thought the combination of the letters of the answer to his question, in a manner analogous to prophecy.

See on this passage Idel, "*Hitbodedut* as Concentration," pp. 67–68.

163. MS. Jerusalem 8° 148, fol. 75a–b, and see note 157 above.

164. The term *ẓurah to'arit* refers to a form perceived in the imagination. In *Šaʿare Ẓedeq*, MS. Jerusalem 8° 148, fol. 77a, we read: "There is a second form present in the second conception, that is, the power of the imagination, and these are the imagined forms, perceived by the senses after they disappear from it through the invention of the power of the imagination."

165. MS. Rome Angelica 38, fol. 13b–14b; MS. München 285, fol. 156a–166a, and compare *Mafteaḥ ha-Ḥokmot*, MS. Moscow 133, fol. 19b.

166. Ezek. 1:28.

167. *Ibid.*

168. *Compare Ôẓar ʿEden Ganuz*, MS. Oxford 1580, fol. 134b.

> . . . for no sage in the world could record in a book [all] those things which he imagined in his heart, and he also would be unable to utter them, for the writing would be insufficient even to describe the bodies; and the evidence [for this] is that a man is unable to describe in writing anything which is spherical, but in its place he may draw a circle, and say in the book that this is an allusion and sign for a sphere.

169. On the cosmic axis (*teli*) and its identity with the bar or axis of the world, see A. Epstein, *Mi-Qadmoniyot ha-Yehudim* (Jerusalem, 1953), pp. 191–194. It is worth citing here the comments of the author of *Ner Elohim* concerning this axis in MS. München 10, fol. 130a:

> The southern point of the world, there is the Prince of the Presence, for there is the head of the axis; and the north is its tail, and there is the Prince of the Back Part, and the appointed [angels] are Metatron and Sandalphon, or say Michael and Gabriel. It has the right-hand attribute, which is the attribute of mercy, in its head; and at its end, in its tail, is the attribute of judgment.

The axis guides the world with both attributes: that of judgment and that of mercy. Cf. note 171 below.

170. *Ǒẓar ᶜEden Ganuz,* MS. Oxford 1580, fol. 41b.

171. MS. Paris BN 774, fol. 145b. On reward and punishment in the conduct of the world, see the same work, fol. 164b, "Metatron the Prince of the Presence . . . and he is the Prince of Action [i.e., the Active Intellect], the fount of reward and punishment." *Sar ha-Panim* = 685 = *Sar ha-Poᶜal* (the Prince of Action = *Maᶜyan Gemul va-ᶜOneš* (the fount of reward and punishment). The intent is evidently to existence as reward and absence of existence as punishment, whose source is in the motion of the spheres. On fol. 155a, a parallel is drawn between reward and punishment, on the one hand, and intellect and imagination, on the other, after which we read:

> When you shall know within yourself that you have been perfected in those attributes which witness to the power of imagination and the truth of its essence in you, and when you will know that you have achieved perfection in knowledge of the attributes of the Name by which the world is always directed, and let your mind pursue your intellect to imitate it according to your ability, always, and you shall know with your intellect . . ." Cf. n. 169 above, and nn. 218–219 below.

172. *Ibid.*, fol. 166a, and see also above, n. 117.

173. MS. Oxford 1580, fol. 80a.

174. C. G. Jung, *Collected Works* (New York, 1959), vol. 9, 1, pp. 290–390. There have been many attempts to make use of Jung's system in the study of the significance of the circle in mysticism and in theology in the wake of his own pioneering work. See G. A. Zinn, "A Mandala Symbolism and Use in Mysticism," *History of Religion* 12 (1972), pp. 326–337; Ewerett Cousins, "Mandala Symbolism in the Theology of Bonaventura," *University of Toronto Quarterly* 40 (1971), pp. 185–200.

175. G. Tucci, *The Theory and Practice of the Mandala* (London, 1961), p. vii.

176. MS. Paris BN 774, fol. 153a.

177. *ᶜEẓ* (tree) = *ẓelem* (image) = 160.

178. *Šefa'* (influx) = *demut* (image) = 450.

179. *Tere* (two) = *demut* + *ẓelem* (image = likeness) = 160 + 450 = 610.

180. *We-ᶜeẓ ha-ḥayyim* (and the tree of life) = *yosif ḥoḵmah* (will add wisdom) = 239.

181. *We-ᶜeẓ da-ᶜat* (and the tree of knowledge) = *yosif ḥoḵmot* = 640.

182. *We-ᶜez ha-ḥayyim* = *goral* = 239.

183. *We-ᶜeẓ ha-daᶜat* = *goralot* = 645.

184. Lev. 16:8.

185. MS. Paris BN 774, fol. 2b; the anonymous author of *Sefer ha-Ẓeruf* makes use of the image of the circle a number of times; see *ibid.* fol. 2a, 6b.

186. MS. Sasson 290, p. 552. The passage is based upon *gematriot*, several of which are interpreted at the bottom of the page: *be-Šem ha-Meforaš YHWH* (with the Ineffable Name *YHWH*) = *we-še-todiʿeni sullam eḥad* (that you make known to me one ladder) = *šeʿeleh ani bo bet YHWH Elohim* (that I may ascend by it to the House of the Lord our God) = *we-šetelamdeni din ha-melek̲* (and that you teach me the law of the king) = *we-šetelamdeni ha-ʿolam ha-ba* (and that you teach me the World to Come) = 999.

187. For the significance of the expression, *ha-ʿolam ha-ba* (the World to Come), see Idel, *Abraham Abulafia*, p. 94. On *ha-melek̲* (the king), which refers either to God or to the Active Intellect, see below, sec. 10.

188. MS. Paris BN 727, fol. 10a. Prior to the passage cited by us, there appears a discussion of the combinations of the word *keter* (crown), similar to that in *Sefer ha-Ẓeruf*. In MS. Paris BN 728, fol. 42b, it states: "for that ladder alludes to the entire sphere resting upon the earth, everlasting, standing upon the earth, which is the center of the sphere as by law; "and behold, there is one wheel on the earth, and the top of the ladder reaches to the upper heavens." See the passage preserved in the name of R. Yehiel Rafael, MS. Firenze - National Library 28, fol. 177b: "Lift up your eyes on high and see that sphere which brings about in the world those lower matters arranged in it; the master of this matter does not change: this one he throws down and that one he lifts up; the ladder stands upon the ground—who ascends and who descends."

189. Compare the remarks by R. Elnathan quoted above, n. 155.

190. MS. Moscow - Günzburg 775, fols. 105b–106a; and see also Gottlieb, *Studies*, p. 244. One ought to remark that in the sequel to the passage we have quoted, R. Isaac of Acre speaks about letters written in black fire as corresponding to the attribute of judgment, while the white fire symbolizes the attribute of mercy, so that the circle of Torah contains within it those elements which likewise characterize the sphere in Abulafia.

191. MS. Paris BN 840, fols. 45b–46a, and see also the subsection "the Light," above; cf. *Badde ha-'Aron, ibid.*, fol. 25b: "understand the form of these drawings in your mind, and the appearance of the light will come to you."

192. For the possible sources of this view, see Heschel, *Theology of Ancient Judaism*, II, 346–347, and Maimonides' *Introduction to Pereq Ḥeleq*.

193. On the connection of R. Shem Tov ibn Gaon to prophetic Kabbalah, see Idel, "*Hitbodedut* as Concentration," *Studies*, essay VII.

194. *Studies*, p. 236.

195. *Mafteaḥ ha-Raʿayon,* MS. Vatican 291, fol. 21a.

196. *Ševaʿ Netivot ha-Torah,* p. 10. It should be pointed out that this understanding of the "ladder" differs in both Abulafia and in R. Isaac of Acre from the image of the world as a ladder and a sphere. Concerning that outlook which sees in the ladder a symbol of the world, Abulafia writes in *Sitre Torah,* MS. Paris BN 774, fol. 122b:

> The entire world is in the image of a ladder, beginning from the very lowest place in locale and level; and the highest place is called "Throne," and the lowest place is called "Footstool." And as the matter is thus, we found it in reality, and we felt and apprehended in our senses and our intellect that the matter of the universal man in the image of the world, for the world is a macro-anthropos, and the man is a microcosm.

The motif of the ladder in Abulafia includes other subjects, in addition to the vision of the ladder as the Divine Name and symbol of the worlds, a point to be discussed at length elsewhere. Cf. the article by A. Altmann, "The Ladder of Ascension," *Studies in Mysticism and Religion Presented to Gershom G. Scholem* (Jerusalem, 1967), pp. 1-32.

197. *Genesis Rabba* 68:16.

198. Gottlieb, *Studies,* pp. 235–236.

199. See R. Joseph Angelino's *Qupat ha-Rok̲lin,* MS. Oxford 1618, fol. 10a: "The book of the Torah is required to be round, for just as in a ball one cannot detect its beginning and its end, so in the Torah is the beginning fastened to its end." See also R. Simeon b. Ẓemaḥ, Duran (Livorno, 1785), fol. 29b; and compare especially R. Judah Barceloni's *Commentary to Sefer Yeẓirah,* p. 107.

200. At the end of the fifteenth century, Johannes Reuchlin reported Naḥmanides' words at the beginning of his *Commentary on the Torah,* concerning the writing of the Torah in black fire upon white fire, adding that the Kabbalists had a tradition that the Torah was written in a "circle of fire,"—*in globum igneum.* See *Ars Cabalistica,* ed. J. Pistorius (Basel, 1587), p. 705.

201. MS. Oxford 1582, fol. 53a. *naʿar* (youth) 320 sek; *zaqen zaqen* (old man-old man)=314=Meṭaṭron. It may be that one is meant to add the total number of letters in *Meṭaṭron* and *zaqen zaqen*—i.e., 6—making the combined *gematria* 320.

202. Song of Songs 5:2. The verse is interpreted in a number of sources as an allusion to the indwelling of prophecy, or of the Shekhinah. See the Targum to this verse, Rashi there, and Maimonides' remarks in *Guide* III:51. The Safed Kabbalists mention this verse as an allusion to the appearance of speech in their throats. "Behold the voice of my beloved knocked, and began, 'here O beloved'." See Werblowsky, *Joseph Karo,* p. 260 and n. 7.

203. I Samuel 3:9–10.

204. MS. Moscow - Günzburg 168, fol. 775a.

205. Hosea 11:1.

206. Psalms 37:15. On these two aspects of Meṭaṭron—that is, as a youth and an old man—see Abulafia above, while for earlier sources see Gedaliahu G. Stroumsa, "Polymorphie divine et transformations d'un mythologeme: 'L'Apocryphon de Jean' et ses sources," *Vigiliae Christianae* 34 (1981), pp. 422–424.

207. *Yevamot* 16b.

208. For the "Prince of the world" as the earliest of the created beings, see *Ḥullin* 60a. This idea was then transferred to Meṭaṭron, when the latter was identified with the Prince of the World. Cf. *Midraš ha-Ne^celam, Zohar* I:126b: "'And Abraham said to his servant'—this [refers to] Metatron, who was the servant of the Place; 'the elder of his household'—that he was the first of the creations of the Place." See Asi Farber, "On the Sources of Rabbi Moses de Leon's Early Kabbalistic System" (Heb.), in J. Dan - J. Hacker, ed., *Studies in Jewish Mysticism, Philosophy and Ethical Literature Presented to Isaiah Tishby* [Jerusalem Studies in Jewish Thought. III:1-2. (Jerusalem, 1986)], pp. 84-87.

209. As is well known, there is a problem of full and deficient spelling—i.e., with and without the letter *yod*—with regard to the name *Meṭaṭron*, which is written in early texts as *MYṭṭRWN. See Scholem, Tarbiẓ* 5 (1934), pp. 186-187, n. 3; MS. Vatican 428, fol. 55a; *Yesod ^cOlam*, MS. Moscow-Günzburg 607, fol. 130b; *Commentary to Ša'are Orah*, MS. Jerusalem 8° 144, fol. 2b. R Isaac of Acre himself writes, "Prior to this ascent, Meṭaṭron was called without [the letter] *yod*, and after his ascent and his receiving of the influx, he was called *Meṭaṭron*, with *Yod*." This text is printed in G. Vajda, "Isaac d'Acco et Juda ben Nissim, " *REJ* 155 (1956), p. 66.

210. The throne of judgment appearing in *Sefer ha-Ot* is evidently connected with the two attributes by which the world is led; see n. 169 above. It is worth noting the Meṭaṭron himself is at times depicted as possessing contradictory characteristics, as we find in the words of R. Reuben Ẕarfati in *Peruš ha-Ma^careket*, fol. 96b: "For the Active Intellect, which is Meṭaṭron, the Prince of the Presence, has two impulses, that is, two angels—one appointed over mercy, and one over judgment—and this refers to the angels Azreil and 'Azah." See also Werblowsky, *Joseph Karo*, pp. 220-221, and *Yalqut Re^ʾuveni, passim*. This dialectic understanding is evidently connected with the perception of Enoch as having both good and bad attributes, as we already find in the *midrašim*.

211. MS. Paris BN 774, fol. 129b–130a. Abulafia's remarks are directed toward a work, apparently written by R. Eleazar of Worms, entitled *Šiv^cim Šemot šel Meṭaṭron* [Seventy Names of Metatron]. Cf. Dan, *The Esoteric Theology*, pp. 220–221. *Yeho'el* was the original name of the angel afterwards known as Meṭaṭron, as had been demonstrated by Scholem, *Jewish Gnosticism*,

pp. 43, 51.

212. R. Eleazar of Worms.

213. This passage is based upon the *gematria: Yeho'el* = 52 = *ana* (please) *Eliyahu* (Elijah) = *ben* (son).

214. Gottlieb, *Studies*, p. 234.

215. C. Jung, *The Archetypes and the Collective Unconsciousness* [Collected Works, 9; 1. (New York, 1959)], pp. 215–216; 217–230. Jung considered the old sage who reveals the truth or the correct path as an archetype. It is worth mentioning here the appearance of the guru among the Hindus and the sheik among the Sufis, both of whom are images of teachers who appear to their disciples in visions.

216. C. Jung, *Psychology and Religion* [Collected Works, 11. (New York, 1958)], pp. 14 ff.

217. R. Otto, *The Idea of the Holy* (New York, 1959), pp. 26–55, Chap. 4.

218. MS. Paris BN 774, fol. 155a–b, and above, note 171.

219. This description was influenced by that found in *ʿAvodah Zarah* 20b. It is worth noting that the same expression, "full of eyes" (*maleʾ ʿenayim*), used in the Talmud and in *Sitre Torah* in reference to the Angel of Death, is used by Abulafia in connection with Metatron. In *Sefer ha-Ŏt*, pp. 70–71, we read: "And his name is like the name of his master, who portrays him completely, full of eyes, seeing, and not being seen." The phrase, "his name is like the name of his master" doubtless refers to Meṭaṭron, whose value in *gematria* is the equivalent of *Šadday*=314. In my opinion, the expression, "full of eyes," refers to the form in which the name *Šadday* is written with the help of the Alphabet of Metatron or the writing of "eyes"; see Israel Weinstock, "The Alphabet of Meṭaṭron and Its Significance" (Heb.), *ṭemirin* (Jerusalem, 1982), vol. 2, pp. 51–76. In R. Ḥananel b. Abraham's *Yesod ʿOlam*, MS. Moscow-Günzburg 607, fol. 130b, the name *Šadday* is written in *ketavʿenayim*. This ambivalent attitude is appropriate to the understanding of Meṭaṭron as possessing the attributes of both judgment and of mercy mentioned above, n. 171. Is there a connection between this approach and the pun on the letters *Šadday* - *šed*, whose meaning is "God - Satan" in the interpretation given by Archangelos to Pico della Mirandola's Kabbalistic Thesis No. 19. See *Ars Cabalistica*, J. Pistorius (Basel, 1587), p. 793; cf. *Midraš Talpiyot* by R. Eliyahu ha-Kohen of Ismir, p. 155c, quoting *Sefer ha-Peli'ah*. Abulafia himself makes use of the following *gematria: šin dalet yod*=814=*šefaʿ satan* (the influx of Satan) = *demut Saṭan* (the image of Satan) = *eš mawet din* (fire death judgment). See also *Sefer ha-Malmad*, MS. Paris BN 680, fol. 292a, and elsewhere in his writings.

220. MS. Oxford 1582, fol. 51b. The question of the presence of the Shekhinah during prayer appears in Maimonides, *Mišneh Torah, Tefillah*

4:15-16, based upon *Sanhedrin* 22a.

221. *Ibid.*, fol. 52a. The connection between the motif of "the king" and fear already appears in Merkavah literature; cf. Scholem, *Major Trends*, 57ff.

222. MS. New York - JTS 180, fol. 8b-9a.

223. MS. Vatican 233, fol. 109b; on the comparison of the intellect to a king, see Henry Malter, "Personification of Soul and Body," *JQR* vol. 2 (N.S., 1911), pp. 462–463, n. 24; Plotinus, *Enneads* V, 3, 3; and especially Maimonides, *Guide* III:52.

224. The term "fear out of love" (*yir'at ahavah*) is based upon an outlook whose sources I have not yet been able to determine. Under the influence of R. Joseph Gikatilla, an acquaintance of Abulafia's, it subsequently developed within the realm of Sephirotic Kabbalah. Traces of the term *yir'ah penimit* (inner fear)—that is, fear mixed with love—appear in one of Gikatilla's early works; see Gottlieb, *Studies*, pp. 126ff.

225. This dialectical understanding of ecstasy also appears in the work *Peraqim be-Haẓalaḥah,* attributed to Maimonides, p. 7: "The one who prays shall turn towards God, stand on his feet and feel pleasure in his heart and his lips, his hands stretched forward, and his organs of speech speaking, while the other parts [of his body] are all afraid and trembling, all the while he does not cease uttering sweet sounds. [Then] he makes himself broken-hearted, prepared himself, beseeches, bows down and prostrates himself weeping, as he is before a great and awesome king. And there shall come upon him sinking and trembling until he finds himself in the world of intellective beings." An anonymous Kabbalistic text expresses itself in a similar manner: "The light of the Shekhinah which is above their heads is as it were spread about them, and they are sitting within the light . . . and then they tremble in [their] nature and rejoice about the same trembling" (cited in Scholem, *Devarim be-Go,* p. 330). In *Peruš ha-Aggadot* (ed. Tishby, pp. 39–40), R. Azriel says, "the one who prays must see himself as if He (i.e., God) speaks with him and teaches him and directs him, and he receives His words with awe and fear."

226. MS. Oxford 1582, fols. 63a–b. *šaṭ ba-moaḥ* (roams in the mind)=*Satan* =359. Compare his remarks on fol. 31a of the same work: "And the joy shall further arouse your heart to add reverse [combination of letters] and understanding and joy and great pleasure. And be quick to turn about, like the flaming sword which turns about to every side, to do war with the enemies surrounding, for the images and the portrayal of the idle thoughts born out of the spirit of the Evil Urge are those which go out to first greet the account [*ḥesbon:* i.e., act of dealing with the letters], and surround it like murderers, and confuse the thoughts of men." R. Isaac of Acre also knew of the appearance of angels of destruction during the time of letter-combination; in *Ŏẓar Ḥayyim,* MS. Sasson 919, p. 215, he writes: "and they shall come to him upon the combination of letters and their unification [sic], and they shall

be turned about, the tree of knowledge of good and evil, for every righteousness and imagination is false: angels of mercy and angels of destruction, those who learn merit and those who learn fault, defenders and prosecutors; and he shall be in danger of death like Ben ʿAzzai," etc. See Idel, "*Hitbodedut* as Concentration," p. 51.

227. The burning up during the process of carrying out a mystical technique is already found in *Hekalot* literature.

228. MS. Paris BN 774, fol. 157b. Compare the remarks of Johanan Alemanno concerning the meditation upon Sefirot: "And again when he sends forth his thought to them by a look, he shall immediately turn backwards, lest he may conceive the spiritual as corporeal or his intellect will uproot them or strike it, like one who peers and was hurt or peered and died, for the corporeal intellect is unable to abide the Divine intellect, because of its great vision [i.e., brightness], and it will be consumed and destroyed, like a great fire which consumes a small one, and the light of the sun which blinds the eye of the one who sees it, or a great candle which extinguishes a small one" (anonymous work, MS. Paris BN 849, fol. 81b).

229. *Ibid.*, fol. 158a.

230. *Ibid.*, fol. 157b.

231. *Imre Šefer*, printed by Scholem, *Abulafia*, pp. 204–205, and also brought in *Liqquṭe Ḥamiẓ*, MS. Oxford 2239, fol. 129b.

232. Daniel 7:10.

233. On the face becoming drained of blood as a sign of fear, see Idel, *Abraham Abulafia*, p. 102.

234. MS. Oxford 1582, fol. 60b. The passage is based upon the *gemaṭria: ha-eš ha-gedolah* (the great fire=359=*ha-šedim* (the demons)=*seraᶜlavan* (white seed)=*Saṭan* (Satan)=*zanav ᶜarel* (uncircumcised tail)=*megallehᶜerwah* (uncovers nakedness) = *ha-gemul ha-raᶜ* (the evil retribution) = *hay medabber u-medammeh* (living, thinking and imagining)=*gorem ha-ᶜilah* (the cause of the cause) *le-hakriah ha-ṭevaᶜ* (to compel nature)=*be-hazkarah u-maddaᶜ* (by recitation and science). As Scholem notes in *Kabbalistic Manuscripts*, p. 28, the *gematriot: guf raᶜ* (evil body)=*Saṭan* already appears in the writing of R. Baruch Togarmi, Abulafia's teacher. See Scholem, *Abulafia*, p. 233. The *gemaṭria, ha-eš ha-gedolah* (the great fire)=*Saṭan* likewise appears there; see *Abulafia*, p. 231. Compare also the material appearing in MS. Firenze - National Library 28, fol. 173b: "the great fire is the secret of Satan, and it is the evil impulse; *yeẓer ha-raᶜ* (the Evil Impulse) in *gemaṭria* equals *Rašaᶜ* (the evil one)."

235. *Ibid.*, fol. 80a. *basar wa-dam* (flesh and blood) *malake ha-mawet* (the angels of death)= *peraṭe ha-ḥomer* (the details of matter)= *ever peraṭi* (specific organ)=*ḥomer ha-peridah* (matter of decomposition)=552.

236. The connection between Divine Names and fire is an ancient one.

In *Midraš Oti᾿ot de-Rabbi ʿAqiva,* Version A (Wertheimer, *Bate Midrašot* II), p. 365, it states: "And the Holy One, blessed be He, sits upon a throne of fire, and around and about him are Ineffable Names, like pillars of fire . . . and when man makes use of them, each and every firmament is completely fire, and they descend to consume the entire world with fire . . . so when a man uses them, the entire world is immediately filled with fire."

237. On the dangers of the *mu"m,* ie., blemish, see above, in our discussion of "techniques," note 100.

238. MS. Jerusalem 8° 148, fol. 65b.

239. MS. Moscow-Günzurg 775, fol. 161b. On this passage, see Idel, *Kabbalah: New Perspectives,* Chap. 4.

240. Gottlieb, *Studies,* p. 237.

241. On the image of sinking within the Ocean, see Idel, *Kabbalah: New Perspectives,* pp. 67-70.

242. Scholem, "Devekut," esp. p. 204; *Major Trends,* pp. 55–56; *Kabbalah,* pp. 174–176. For a different view concerning the subject of *unio mystica* in Kabbalah, see Idel, *Kabbalah: New Perspectives,* Chap. 4.

243. *Wisdom of the Zohar* II, pp. 289–290, and the notes there.

244. *Studies,* p. 237.

245. See R. J. Z. Werblowsky, *Tarbiẓ* 34 (1965), pp. 203–204.

246. R. C. Zaehner, *Mysticism, Sacred and Profane* (Oxford, 1973), p. 32. According to this scholar, the definition includes the experiences of identification with nature or with inanimate objects, which constitute nature mysticism, although Zaehner's emphasis remains the preservation of the gap between the object and the mystic, in which unity is none other than a bridging of this gap. I will not discuss any further the question of nature mysticism, as the problems entailed do not contribute to our understanding of Abulafia.

247. MS. Oxford 1580, fols. 56a–56b, and compare Abulafia's words in the same work, fol. 149a, "and that knowledge [i.e., of the Divine Names] will be a cause for saving many souls from the hands of Sheol, and bring them alive to knowledge of the World to Come, and their eternal life will be like the life of God, by which they cleave to Him, may He be praised. And of such-like is it said, 'And you who cleave to the Lord your God are all alive this day'." On the identification of the one cleaving with the object of his cleaving, see Gottlieb, *ha-Qabbalah be-Kitve Rabbenu Bahya ben Asher,* (Jerusalem, 1970), p. 115–116 and n. 4; R. Joseph Angelino, *Qupat ha-Rok̲elin,* MS. Oxford 1618, fol. 70a–b; Werblowsky, *Joseph Karo,* pp. 252–253.

248. This refers to physical connections, or "the connection of lust," which will in the end be annulled.

249. On this expression, see chap. 2 above, "Music and Ecstatic Kabbalah," n. 4.

250. Deut. 4:4.

251. Deut. 10:20.

252. Deut. 13:5.

253. MS. München 10, fol. 154b; compare the words of R. Joseph Karo, brought in Werblowsky, *Joseph Karo*, pp. 156–157.

254. A. Ivry, "Averroes on Intellection and Conjunction," *Journal of the American Oriental Society* 86 (1966), pp. 76–85.

255. L. Massignon, in *Journal Asiatique* v. 210 (1931), pp. 77, 82, 92ff.; *idem., Kitab al Tawasin (Paris, 1913) p. 130.*

256. See G. Vajda, "En Marge du Commentaire sur le Cantique des Cantiques de Joseph ibn Aqnin," *REJ* 124 (1968), p. 187, n. 1, and his book *Recherches sur la Philosophie et la Kabbala* (Paris, 1962), p. 26–28. To the list of Vajda's one may add R. Issac ibn Latif, who writes in *Ša'ar ha-Šamayim*, Gate I, chap. 18: "This is the final purpose of the soul, namely, its union with the Active Intellect and its becoming one with it." *Ibid.*, chap. 26: "Let the soul cleave in the upper world, and that is the active intellect, until it and she become one thing." See also Tishby, *Peruš ha-Aggadot le-R.ʿAzriel*, p. 20.

257. MS. Paris BN 774, fol. 140a.

258. *Ibid.*, fol. 155a; compare *Šaʿare Ẓedeq*, MS. Jerusalem 8°148, fol. 39a.

259. MS. Rome - Angelica 38, fols. 31b–32a; MS. München 285, fol. 26b, printed by Scholem in *Major Trends*, p. 382, and in *Abulafia*, p. 209, under the heading, "Knowledge of the Messiah and the Wisdom of the Redeemer."

260. *Sanhedrin* 38a.

261. MS. Rome - Angelica 38, fols. 14b–15a; MS. München 285, fol. 39b. See Scholem, *Major Trends*, p. 382 and p. 140.

262. Based upon II Samuel 5:17.

263. See Idel, *Abraham Abulafia*, pp. 89–91.

264. Compare *Sefer ha-Malmad*, by one of Abulafia's disciples, where it states (MS. Oxford 1649, fol. 206a), "Say to God, 'you are my son, this day have I begotten you,' (Ps. 2:7) and likewise the verse, "I, I am He,' (Deut. 32:39) And the secret is the clinging of the power—that is, the supernal Divine power, called the sphere of prophecy—with human power, and so they said 'I, I'." More on this citation see Idel, "Abraham Abulafia and *Unio Mystica*," *Studies*, essay I.

265. MS. Oxford 1582, fol. 20a and 21a.

266. Exodus 6:3.

267. MS. Oxford 1582, fol. 12a.

268. Printed by Gottlieb, *Studies*, p. 237, and notes there. It is worth noting here that Giovanni Pico della Mirandolla, in his *Oration on the Dignity of Man*, tr. A. Robert Caponigri (Chicago, 1967), pp. 9, 14–15, stresses the possibility that man may reach unity with God and, as does R. Isaac of Acre, this possibility in the case of Enoch, who was transformed into "an angel of the Shekhinah."

269. On this image, see Idel, *Kabbalah: New Perspectives*, pp. 67-70.

270. Jellinek, *Bet ha-Midraš*, V. p. 171. On the subject of identification of Enoch and Meṭaṭron, see M. Idel, "Enoch is Meṭaṭron."

271. *Maʿareḵet ha Elohut*, fol. 96b and p. 95a, "that the human intellect, after it has been separated from the body, will again become spiritual, and be embodied in the Active Intellect, and he and it are again one." Similarly, and doubtless under its influence, R. Abraham ibn Migash writes in *Kevod Elohim* (Jerusalem, 1977), fol. 97a, "For his name is like that of his master, which is the Active Intellect, and when the human intellect cleaves to it, the two shall be one, and he is it, and his throne is its throne, and its name is his name, and he is the Prince of the World." On fol. 97b, "when it is attached to the sphere of the intellect, he is it."

272. *Major Trends*, p. 141.

273. MS. Moscow 133, fols. 64a–66b; MS. Oxford 1582, fols. 41b–42a.

274. Deut. 5:20.

275. Deut. 4:4.

276. MS. Vatican 233, fol. 115a. This refers to the composition of the Ineffable Name, which equals 26 in *Gemaṭria*, of two equal parts of 13 + 13= *ahavah + ahavah*. (love + love). On the continuation of this passage, see Chapter 4 below, on "Erotic Imagery," n. 43. This section is cited anonymously in *Newe Šalom* by R. Abraham Shalom, fols. 87a–b.

277. Compare the remarks made by R. Judah Albotini in *Sullam ha-ʿAliyah* (in *Kabbalistic Manuscripts*, pp. 227, 228, 229), which speak about man's departure "from his human domain," and his entry into "the divine domain." Unlike Abulafia, R. Judah Albotini refers to the cleaving of the soul "to the supernal, hidden world of emanation, i.e., the world of the Sefirot, or sometimes to the soul's cleaving to the Active Intellect. See now also Scholem, *Qiryat Sefer* 22 (1945), p. 162.

278. MS. Vatican 233, fols. 117b–118a. In R. Elnathan b. Moses Kalkiš, *Even ha-Sappir*, MS. Paris BN 727, fol. 15a, we read:

> Therefore he is held accountable, that influx being neither body nor bodily power, because of its resemblance to the One from which it flows; and this influx is likewise separated, and for this reason it brings upon the soul a further influx similar to itself, based on it, to elevate its existence from the level of non-separation to that of separation. And despite this, the separate influx is not corporealized, but only the soul, which is not separated, which speaks and is enlightened with the power and which thinks thoughts of wisdom and understanding and knowledge, which are seven levels, one above the other in level--it receives that separate influx and cleaves to it until it returns to be one thing with it, and then it and she [become] one in number.

279. *Ibid.*, fols. 115a–119a, with omissions. In the same work (fol. 8a), Abulafia writes: "it may be that they will receive from this book of mine a path, such that they shall long to cleave to its first cause."

280. MS. Paris BN 776, fol. 192b; MS. Vatican 441, fol. 115a. Compare R. Pinḥas Elijah Horowitz, *Sefer ha-Berit* (Brünn, 1797), Pt. II, fol. 29b. In an anonymous work found in MS. New York - JTS 2203, fol. 214b, we read similar ideas to those appearing in the above collection: "Surely know that the Creator and the intellect [i.e., the human intellect] and the angels, all become one thing and one essence and one truth, and are like the flame of the candle, for example."

281. MS. Vatican 233, fol. 120b.

282. See the long discussion of this matter in P. Merlan, *Monopsychism, Mysticism, Metaconsciousness* (The Hague, 1963), pp. 18 ff., p. 25, 36.

283. *Peruše Rišonim le-Maseḵet Avot* (Jerusalem, 1973), p. 65. Similar things appear on p. 62, cf. *Sefer ha-Ẓeruf*, MS. Paris BN 774, fol. 4a: "When the intellect becomes refined, while it is [still] in matter, when it is still in that same dwelling place in truth, this is a very high level, to cleave to the Source of Sources after the soul has been separated from matter."

284. In the printed edition, pp. 20–21; MS. New York JTS 1887, fols. 99b–100a; and Scholem, *Major Trends*, p. 131. W.T Stace saw in this passage an indication of pantheism; see his *Mysticism and Philosophy* (London, 1961), p. 116. On the understanding of the Sefirot as pertaining to spiritual powers within man, see Idel, *Kabbalah: New Perspectives*, Chap. 6; on man as a compound entity, see Idel, "Abraham Abulafia and *Unio Mystica*," *Studies* essay I.

285. This appears to be Averroes' approach.

286. Abulafia was evidently influenced by the expression, "the forces scattered in the world," which appears in *Guide* II:6, although the meaning of this idiom is not the same in Abulafia as in Maimonides. The expression, "the forces scattered in existence," appears in *Ḥayye ha-Nefeš*, MS. München 408, fol. 90a.

287. MS. Vatican 233, fols. 109a–b, and Scholem, *Abulafia*, pp. 225–226.

Tocci, "Technique of Pronunciation," p. 227. According to Tocci, p. 236, n. 35, a connection exists between the words "wisdom," "understanding," and "knowledge," and the Sefirotic system. However, in my opinion, these three words have no theosophic meaning. On the same page (n. 36), Tocci states that the word *devequt* does not have the meaning of *unio,* relying upon Scholem, who discusses the meaning of *devequt* in other authors. It seems to me, in light of the material we have quoted from *Ǒr ha-Sek̲el* and from other colleagues of Abulafia, that one must reject Tocci's statement. On. fol. 113a, Abulafia speaks about the soul which "resembles the separate being which is in every place."

288. MS. München 22, fol. 187a.

289. Eccles. 12:4.

290. Goldreich, p. 222: this passage was copied from the München 17 manuscript by J. Herz, *Drei Abhandlungen über die Conjunction des separaten Intellects mit dem Menschen* (Berlin, 1869), p. 22, Appendix 11. In his view, this reflects the impact of Averroes' doctrines. The passage was translated into French by Vajda, who contends that it was influenced by the psychological doctrine of Ibn Bajja: see his *Recherches,* (n. 256 above), 379, n. 3. It seems to me that this rather reflects the influence of a Neoplatonic approach comparable, for example, to the approach of *Liber de Causis* in the Hebrew translation of Judah Romano (*Sefer ha-Sibbot,* MS. Oxford 2244, fol. 31a):

> The effect is its cause by way of the cause, just as the sense is in the soul by way of the soul, and the soul is in the intellect in an intellective manner, and the intellect is "reality" in the way of reality, and the first reality in the intellect in an intellective manner, and the intellect in the soul in a soul manner, and the soul in the sense in a sense manner.

291. The expression, is *elohi* (Divine man), also appears in MS. Leiden 93, from whence Majda also translated the passage; see *ibid.,* p. 379, n. 1. It is worth noting here that the expression "Divine man" appears in Maimonides' letter to R. Ḥasdai ha-Levi. This letter refers to a story concerning the equanimity of the perfect man, an idea which likewise appears in *Me'irat ʿEnayim.* The expression *iš elohi* similarly appears in *Even Sappir,* MS. Paris BN 728, fol. 154; cf. Idel, "*Hitbodedut* as Concentration," *Studies,* essay VII.

292. See above, *Ôr ha-Sek̲el,* MS. Vatican 233, fol. 120b.

293. See Idel, "Mundus Imaginalis," *Studies,* essay V; MS. Vatican 233, fol. 7b; and see also the concluding poem, fol. 128b.

294. *Ibid.,* fol. 8a.

295. MS. Rome - Angelica 38, fol. 2b.

296. See the description of *Sefer ha-Maftеḥot* in Idel, *Abraham Abulafia,* p. 20.

297. See Scholem's remarks, *Abulafia*, p. 131 ff, as well as the important article of Mircea Eliade, "The God who Binds," *Images and Symbols* (New York, 1969), pp. 92–124.

298. On the use of this expression in magic, see R. C. Thompson, *Semitic Magic* (New York, 1971), p. 166, p. 169, n. 3; S. J. Shah, *Oriental Magic* (London, 1956), p. 82. The expression, "the binding of the bridegroom" (*asirat he-ḥatan),* which appears during the Geonic period, also bears a magical significance: see L. Ginzberg, *Geonica* (New York, 1909), II, p. 152; S. Lieberman, *Greek in Jewish Palestine* (New York, 1942), p. 110. On the subject of magic and the knot, see Vajda's above-mentioned study, p. 110–112.

299. This Platonic idea appears in several places in Abulafia; see, for example, *Sitre Torah,* MS. Paris BN 774, fol. 160a: "to open blind eyes, to remove the prisoners from bondage, from prison those who dwell in darkness," etc.; *Ôr ha-Seḵel,* MS. Vatican 233, fol. 117a ff.

300. The motif of nature seducing the soul in order to sink within it is an old one; see *Mussare ha-Filosofim,* I, 18, 8.

301. *Ôẓar ᶜEden Ganuz,* MS. Oxford 1580, fol. 23b.

302. Joel 3:5.

303. P. 144.

304. *Ôẓar ᶜEden Ganuz,* MS. Oxford 1580, fols. 133b-134a.

305. *Ibid.,* 56a; teli=440=*mekasef* (witch). This *gemaṭria* is widely used by Abulafia. The knots which sustain the human body are already alluded to in R. Judah Barceloni's *Peruš Sefer Yeẓirah,* (Berlin, 1885) p. 17: "the creature will be separated and the knots will be undone, and he will die."

306. *Ibid.,* fol. 131b.

307. On the expression, "his law and his portion," see Steinschneider, *Al-Farabi,* p. 103, n. 37, and p. 247.

308. *Ôẓar ᶜEden Ganuz,* MS. Oxford 1580, fol. 131b.

309. On the "creational" fettering of man, see Hans Jonas, *The Gnostic Religion* (Boston, 1963), p. 204.

310. *Ôr ha Seḵel,* MS. Vatican 233, fol. 117a. The matter of the "fettering" and the putting on of the spiritual form also appears in *Sefer ha-Qanah* (Koryscz, 1784), fol. 106d; "And the intention is that Enoch cast off the bodily element and put on the spiritual element, and was fettered by a spiritual knot."

311. Ibid., *fol. 115b; haqqešer* (the knot)=605=*hitir* (united). See Idel, "Mundus Imaginalis," *Studies,* essay V.

312. *Ôẓarᶜ Eden Ganuz,* MS. Oxford 1580, fol. 132a, based on *Guide of the*

Perplexed II:2 and Samuel ibn Tibbon, *Peruš Millim Zarot* (ed. J. Even-Shmuel), p. 82.

313. *Ḥayye ha-Nefeš,* MS. München 408, fol. 63a.

314. "Myth and Mysticism: A Study of Objectification and Interiorization in Religious Thought," *Journal of Religion* 49 (1969), pp. 328–239.

315. See Binyamin Uffenheimer, *Ḥazon Zeḳareyah; min ha-Nevuʾah la-Apoqaliptiqah* (Jerusalem, 1961), pp. 135 ff, and the bibliography cited in the notes.

316. *Ibid.*, fol. 127b–128a.

317. *Ḥayye ha-ʿOlam ha-Ba,* MS. Oxford 1582, fol. 50a.

318. *Ôr ha-Seḵel,* MS. Vatican 233, fol. 125b.

319. *Ibid.*, fols. 127b–128a.

320. *Guide for the Perplexed* II:37. On the prophet-messenger in Avicenna, see F. Rahman, *Prophecy in Islam* (London, 1958), pp. 52ff., pp. 86ff., and compare *We-zot li-Yihudah,* pp. 18–19.

321. *Sitre Torah,* MS. Paris BN 774, fol. 154b.

322. Isa. 50:6.

323. *Ibid.*, v. 9.

324. *Ḥayye ha-Nefeš,* MS. München 408, fol. 47a.

325. MS. Jerusalem 8° 1303, fol. 73b. The passage is based entirely upon fragments of verses connected with various different prophets.

326. Further on, Abulafia quotes a series of verses expressing the bitter lot of the prophets.

327. MS. Rome - Angelica 38, fol. 34a.

328. See Idel, *Abraham Abulafia,* pp. 402–408, esp. n. 71. In addition to the passages cited there, see *Sefer ha-Ôt,* p. 68 and *Sefer ha-ʿEdut,* MS. Rome - Angelica 38, fol. 13b.

329. See Idel, "Abraham Abulafia on the Jewish Messiah and Jesus," *Studies,* essay III.

330. See Idel, *Abraham Abulafia,* p. 412.

331. MS. Rome - Angelica 38, fol. 12a; MS. München 285, fol. 37b. The definition of the supernal revelation as predicated upon knowledge of the Ineffable Name is reminiscent of R. Abraham Bar Hiyya's description of the climax of prophecy as the revelation to Moses of the significance of the Ineffable Name is reminiscent of R. Abraham Bar Hiyya's description of the the supreme order of them all (in the types of prophecy) is that he will tell

him the meaning of the name, as he told it to Moses, etc."

332. *Sefer ha-Hafṭarah,* MS. Rome - Angelica 38, fol. 37a.

333. On the Torah as the Name, or sequence of Names, of God, see Idel, "The Concept of the Torah," pp. 45–84.

334. *Ôẓar Ḥayyim,* MS. Moscow-Günzburg 775, fol. 160a. It is appropriate to cite here the interpretation given there to the passage from *Ḥayye ha-ʿOlam ha-Ba,* MS. Montefiore 332, fol. 8b, "and the Messiah is the High Priest." This idea is interpreted in terms of the theosophic approach:

> The secret of the deed is from Israelite to Levite, and from Levite to Priest. . . . For it is known that [the Sefirah] *Yesod* is called Israel, and it is the place of physicality, and *Tiferet* is called Levite, and it is the place of spirituality; and *Keter ʿElyon* (the Supreme Crown) is called the Priest, and it is the place of the intellect, and it is the priest. Therefore, it was said to the High Priest Joshua, "Behold, I bring my servant Zemah" [Zech. 3:8], meaning that by means of the upper Messiah he will bring the lower Messiah.

The term, "upper Messiah," also appears in *Sefer ha-Temunah,* fol. 29b, while the lofty status of the Messiah is mentioned in *Peruš Šem ben M"B Otiyot* by R. Moses of Burgos, in a fragment published by G. Scholem, Tarbiẓ 5 (1934), p. 55 and n. 6. As in the passage from R. Isaac of Acre, in the note from MS. Montefiore as well the Messiah is identified with the Sefirah of *Keter.* Generally speaking, the Messiah enjoys a relatively low status, and is identified with the Sefirah of *Malkut;* see, for example, R. Moses de Leon's *Šeqel ha-Qodeš,* pp. 90–91. On the definition of the Messiah as "a Divine power," see R. Azriel of Gerona, *Derek ha-Emunah we-Derek ha-Kefirah,* published by Scholem, "New Remnants of the Writings of R. Azriel of Gerona" (Heb.), *Sefer Gulak we-Klein* (Jerusalem, 1942), p. 211. The Messiah's "divinity" becomes a central element in Sabbatian Kabbalah, but the approach *per se* is rooted in earlier Kabbalah--a point which I cannot discuss in depth here. Compare the remarks of Reuchlin, *De Arte Cabalistica* (Basel, 1557), p. 862; "est enim Messiha (sic) Virtus Dei."

335. Meṭaṭron, the Prince of the Presence.

336. *Ôẓar ʿEden Ganuz,* Ms. Oxford 1580, fol. 174a. Compare R. Abraham ibn Ezra's short commentary on Ex. 23:20 (ed. Fleischer, p. 202). On fol. 134a of the same work, Abulafia again describes reality in bleak terms: "for everything that is with us is all earthly, and we have no control over it, nor complete power over it, except in a very few cases and occasions; and all is imagination and mockery, like a dream which passes by in the night which, when the sleeper awakes from it, thus shall he find it. And even when he looks at the day past, he will see that all his days are like a passing shadow."

337. Compare Isa. 28:8.

338. *Sitre Torah,* MS. Paris BN 774, fol 155. The motif of Satan or the imagination perpetually lying in wait for the mystic, who for this reason is

required to conduct an unending war against his thoughts, is a common one in hesychasm. See G.A. Maloney, *Russian Hesychasm* (Morton, 1973), pp. 73–79.

339. *Sitre Torah,* MS. Paris BN 774, fols. 155–156a.

340. *Ôẓar ʿEden Ganuz,* MS. Oxford 1580, fol. 32b.

341. *Ibid.,* fol. 27b. In *Sitre Torah,* MS. Paris BN 774, fol. 120a, it stated that the intelligibilium "will be eternal and exist like the stars forever and ever."

342. *Mafteaḥ ha Hokmot, MS. Moscow 133, fol. 6b.*

343. *Ôẓar ʿEden Ganuz, MS. Oxford 1580, fol. 101b.*

344. On this idea, see A. Altmann-Stern, *Isaac Israeli* (Oxford, 1958), pp. 201–202: I. Jadaane, *L'Influence du stoïcisme sur la pensée musulmane* (Beyrouth, 1968), pp. 232ff.

345. MS. München 58, fols. 317a–b; and compare *Sefer ha-Meliẓ,* MS. München 285, fol. 15a: "He who wishes to die in the coming [world] shall live in this one, and he who wishes to die in this, will live in the next. And the principle of it is, that in killing his Evil Impulse he will make his Good Impulse to live, and if he kills his Good Impulse he makes his Evil Urge to live."

346. *tamut* (will die) = 846 = *tiḥyeh* (shall live 423) *tiḥyeh* (423). See above, p. 98.

347. *Tamid* 32a. The author of *Sefer ha Malmad* (MS. Oxford 1649, fol. 207a), similarly stresses the concept of willed death, as in the example of his teacher:

> . . . for in truth, if a man lives it, that man will live; as the philosphers say: "If you wish to live by nature, die voluntarily and live by nature; and if you wish to die by nature, live voluntarily and die by nature." And this is clear to a man who has been granted by God knowledge and understanding and intellect; blessed is He who has graced us knowledge. And our sages said likewise, in their saying: "What shall man do to live? He shall die. And what shall man do and die? He shall live."

348. Num. 19:14.

349. See Maimonides, *Hilkot Yesode ha-Torah* 3:12; a discussion of the sources connected with this idea appears in I. Twersky, "Aspects of the Mishneh Torah," *Jewish Mediaeval and Renaissance Studies* (Cambridge, Mass., 1967), p. 99, nn. 14–19.

350. Compare the words of R. Levi b. Abraham in *Liwyat Ḥen (Yešurun,* ed., Pollack, vol. 8, p. 131): "He shall subdue his matter and force it down

and place it in the service of the Divine power, and he shall afflict his body and hit it with wounding blows, for truthful are the blows of a friend, as [our rabbis] of blessed memory said, 'With what shall a man give life to his soul? He shall kill his body, until he return from the children of On High and attain everything, from the earth to the firmament, and from one end of the heavens to the other, and he shall live for eternity.'"

351. The opinion of H. Graetz, *History of the Jews* (Philadelphia, 1956), IV:5, concerning the need for intense preparations, afflictions and isolation, have no basis in the writings of Abulafia.

352. *Ôẓar ʿEden Ganuz,* MS. Oxford 1580, fol. 162a.

353. *Ôr ha-Seḵel,* MS. Vatican 233, fol. 125b.

354. *Gan Naʿul,* MS. Munchen 58, fol. 328a.

355. *Kiddušin* fol. 71a.

356. See particularly the list of conditions Abulafia required of those disciples who would be worthy of receiving the secrets of Kabbalah, in which any extreme ascetic element is conspicuously absent; *Ḥayye ha-ʿOlam ha-Ba,* MS. Oxford 1582, fol. 34a.

357. *Ôẓar Ḥayyim,* MS. Moscow - Günzburg 775, fol. 170b.

358. Compare also the appearance of "equanimity" *(hištawwut)*—lacking in the writings of Abraham Abulafia—in R. Isaac of Acre, again apparently under Sufic influence; see Idel, "*Hitbodedut* as Concentration," *Studies,* essay VII.

359. *Ôẓar ʿEden Ganuz,* MS. Oxford 1580, fols. 165b-166a.

Chapter Four

Erotic Images for the Ecstatic Experience

In their attempts to portray the connection between the human soul and the Active Intellect or the Divine, medieval Jewish mystics made use of erotic images. While these images are part of the stock in trade of mystical literature generally,[1] they are particularly common among those mystics belonging to theistic religions, and in those religions in which love enjoys a high place on the scale of values. These images may be classified into two principal groups:

1. Images portraying the spiritual connection between the lover and his beloved, i.e., descriptions of such emotions as longing, submission, etc. Such imagery is extremely common, and by its means one may portray spiritual stances continuing over a period of time; these images appear alike in mystical literature and among philosophers, religious poets, and exegetes of the Song of Songs. A wide variety of such images appear in Hebrew literature, and these have been discussed by a number of scholars.[2] In this respect, one finds no radical innovations in Abulafia, who follows Maimonides in seeing the love of God as the apex of intellectual worship.[3]

2. Images portraying the physical connection between the lover and his beloved. These images are rarer, and are most often used to depict events which by their nature are limited in time. These tend to be restricted to mystical literature, and only rarely appear among non-mystic authors. In this respect, one finds in Abulafia daring use of physical acts as images for the connection between the Active

Intellect and the human mind.

Generally speaking, these two kinds of images relate to different aspects or directions of the connection. While those in the former group describe the relationship of the soul to God or to the Active Intellect, the latter illustrate the feelings of the mystic during those moments at which God reveals Himself with greatest intensity. In the attempt to convey the nature of this revelation, use is made of bodily imagery in a manner which at times seems to border on the profane. Analysis of Abulafia's writings suggests that the images belonging to this latter category may be divided into five groups, to be discussed here according to their natural, chronological order: the kiss, sexual union, seed, impregnation, and birth. It is superfluous to add that there is no comprehensive or systematic discussion of any one of these groups in Abulafia; the material discussed here has been gathered from statements found in various places throughout his writings, organized here systematically for purposes of comparison and reconstruction.

1. The Image of the Kiss

The term, "death by a kiss,"appears a number of times in Talmudic and Midrashic literature,[4] where it is used in connection with the deaths of Moses, Aaron, and Miriam to express death without suffering, referring to a concrete act of God, whereby He removes the soul of the righteous by means of a kiss on his mouth. For this reason, the kiss is not thought of as an image for the relationship between man and God.[5] The transformation of the expression of "death by a kiss" into a figurative image already occurs in Maimonides, who writes in *Guide* III:51 (pp. 627-28):

> When this perfect man is stricken in age and is near death, his knowledge mightily increases, his joy in that knowledge grows greater, and his love for the object of his knowledge more intense, and it is in this great delight that the soul separates from the body. To this state our Sages referred, when in reference to the death of Moses, Aaron, and Miriam they said that death was in these three cases nothing but a kiss. . . . The meaning of this saying is that these three died in the midst of the pleasure derived from the knowledge of God and their great love for him. When our Sages figuratively call the knowledge of God united with intense love for Him a kiss, they follow the well-known poetical diction, "Let him kiss me with the kisses of his mouth."[6] This kind of death, which is in truth deliverance from death, has been ascribed by our Sages to none but

to Moses, Aaron, and Miriam. The other prophets and pious men are beneath that degree; but their knowledge of God is strengthened when death approaches.[7]

Maimonides' interpretation of the verse from Song of Songs, and of the expression, "death by the kiss," requires some explanation. In his view, death by the kiss took place as a consequence of the natural process of aging, which in the cases of Moses, Aaron and Miriam intensified their intellectual powers;[8] this intensification was accompanied by the love associated with the process of enlightenment, whereby the soul separated itself from the body. This understanding is based upon the Biblical and Talmudic sources, describing the deaths of Moses, Aaron and Miriam as natural ones, occurring in advanced old age. An additional point must be stressed here: that that these three figures did not die a voluntary death. To the contrary, Moses did not wish to depart from this world, as we are told at length in the many legends surrounding his death.[9]

The *Guide of the Perplexed* was doubtless the source of inspiration for Abulafia when he wrote in his *Ḥayye ha-ʿOlam ha-Ba,*[10] "but one whose soul is separated from him at the time of pronouncing [the Divine Names] has died by the [Divine] kiss: of this they said,[11]: 'R. Akiba's soul departed with [the recitation of the word] "One."' While Maimonides interprets death by the kiss as the result of a natural process, in Abulafia it is the result of a deliberate process, whereby the mystic enters a state of ecstasy; if death occurs while reciting God's Name, this is a sign that he has attained a very high level. The reference to age as a factor making it easier to reach ecstasy is totally absent in Abulafia's writings; death by the kiss is conditional exclusively upon the use of a certain technique. For this reason, Abulafia substituted Rabbi Akiba for Moses, Aaron, and Miriam, all of whom died natural deaths, despite the fact that it is not stated that Akiba died by the kiss, and he died an unnatural death. One might say that Abulafia so to speak reversed the order of things: whereas Maimonides holds that the process of aging strengthens spiritual insight while weakening the powers of the body, Abulafia believes that intense spiritual apprehension may itself attenuate the connection between body and soul and bring about death. Elsewhere in Abulafia, we read: "For he will kiss him of the kisses of his mouth: immediately he will awaken from his slumber and know the day of his death and understand the great difference between his soul and his body."[12] The voluntaristic aspect of the process here is striking: when the Active Intellect pours its "kisses" upon the soul, the soul understands that it must acquire its eternity by means of study, thereby obliterating death. While in Maimonides the word "death" is intended literally, Abulafia uses it in the metaphorical sense. In *Ôr ha-Sekel*, he writes as follows about the moment of mystical experience: "think in that hour that your soul shall be separated from your body and you shall die from this world and live in the next world."[13] It seems clear that Abulafia is not referring here to actual bodily death, but to the mystic's transformation into a participant in eternal life. According to Abulafia's approach, one does not require bodily death in order to attain this level.[14] Death is here a mystical process: man leaves this world so long as he succeeds in adhering to the Active Intellect, and thereby inherits the World to Come.

Abulafia's disciples generally speaking accepted his system, but seem to be unaware of the subtle but important distinction between literal and mystical death. Thus, even while basing themselves upon Abulafia, they repeated Maimonides' formulations regarding the separation between the body and the soul. For example, in *Sullam ha-ʿAliyah*[15] R. Judah Albotini writes as follows concerning the moment of pronouncing the Divine Name:

> Without doubt, at that moment he has departed the realm of the human and entered into the realm of the Divine, his soul becomes separated [i.e., from matter] and refined, cleaving to the root of the source from which it was hewn. And it has happened that one's soul became entirely separated at that moment of separation, and he remained dead. Such a death is the most elevated one, as it is close to death by the Divine kiss, and it was in this manner that the soul of Ben Azzai, who "gazed and died", left this world, for his soul rejoiced when it saw the source whence it was hewn, and it wished to cling to it and to remain there and not to return to the body. Of his death it is said, "Precious in the eyes of the Lord is the death of his pious ones."[16] Some of the masters of Wisdom and those who have engaged in such acts have said that one who does not wish his soul to separate itself from him during that vision ought to make his soul swear an oath, by a curse or by the Great and Awesome Name, prior to the act but while still in his own domain and in his human condition, that at the time of the vision and the appearance, when he shall no longer be under his own volition, his soul shall not separate itself and cling to its source, but return to its container.

This double aspect of ecstasy—the fullness of human experience, on the one hand, and death, on the other[17]—reappears elsewhere in the writings of Abulafia's disciples. In a passage reserved in two manuscripts containing material from his circle, we read:

> And he explained [the verse] "by the mouth of God" [Num. 33:38; Deut. 34:5] as follows: this is compared to the kiss, and it [refers to] the cleaving of the intellect to the object of its intellection so closely and intensely that there is no longer any possibility for the soul [to remain in] matter, and that intense love called the kiss is a rebuke to the body, and it remains alone, and this is the truth. And on the literal level, [it means that] there was none of the weakness of the elements or any element of chance but the edict of God, may He be blessed.[18]

One of Abulafia's disciples, the author of *Sefer ha-Malmad,* designates those who receive the true Torah as "the seekers of the kiss" *(mevaqqše ha-nešiqah):*

> Indeed Moses received the Torah at Sinai and gave it over to those who sought the kiss, and this is a great secret; there is no place in the entire Torah which arouses the soul to its initial thought like this. And this is the secret of the seekers of the kiss—that they may be cleansed of the punishment of Mount Sinai and receive the known cause on Mt. Gerizim, upon which dwells the created light, which is holy to God; and the entire law hangs upon it, and also all deeds and the Tabernacle, and upon it revolve the heavens, which the entire people accepted and [nevertheless] did not accept upon themselves—that place which is the sanctuary of the soul with the intellect.[19]

It seems to me that the expression "seekers of the kiss" ought to be interpreted here as an allusion to the ecstatic mystics who receive the genuine Torah; the mountain evidently alludes to the soul, while the Torah refers to the intellect.[20] Hints of the nature of this ecstasy likewise appear in the continuation of the passage quoted above: "Indeed, Gerizim is ten names, but they are only known to those who have heard Torah, in which its truth is hinted, and he is one that the Divine Presence dwells with him and in his heart."[21]

It is interesting to compare the opinion of the author of *Sefer ha-Ẓeruf,* which has been attributed to Abulafia, with that of Abulafia himself. In *Sefer ha-Ẓeruf,* we read:

> When the soul is separated from the body she has already apprehended the purpose of [all] purposes, and cleaved to the light beyond which there is no other light, and takes part in the life which is the bundle of all life and the source of all life, and he is like one who kisses something which he loves utterly, and he is unable to cleave to it until this time. And this is the secret of the kiss spoken

> of regarding the patriarchs, of whom it is said that they died with the kiss: that is, that at the moment that they departed they attained the essence of all apprehensions and above all degrees [*ma'alah*], because the interruptions and all the obstacles which are in the world left them, and the intellect returned to cleave to that light which is the Intellect. And when he cleaves in truth, that is the true kiss, which is the purpose of all degrees.[22]

I have cited here the view of those authors close to Abulafia, examination of whose writings indicates that they departed from his path. It is interesting that it was particularly the Neoplatonic tradition within Jewish thought which fostered the viewpoint close to that of Abulafia concerning the subject of death by the kiss—but we cannot discuss this matter in depth in the present context.[23]

2. The Image of Intercourse

While the image of the kiss is a very common one, expressing the connection between the human soul and the Active Intellect,[24] that of sexual intercourse, in the sense in which this is used by Abulafia, is far rarer.[25] The emotional power suggested by this image is thoroughly appropriate to the intense experience designated by Abulafia by the term *prophecy* or *ecstasy*. R. C. Zaehner's comments on this point are significant:

> This is absolutely appropriate, for just as the human body knows no sensation comparable in sheer joyful intensity to that which the sexual act procures for a man and woman in love, so must the mystical experience of soul in the embrace of God be utterly beyond all other spiritual joys.[26]

In those sources related to the ecstatic Kabbalah, the image of intercourse already appears in the writings of Abulafia's teacher, R. Barukh Togarmi. In his *Commentary to Sefer Yeẓirah*, he writes[27]:

> And [behold] the jealousy of the male and the female, its cycle is full tint, and in truth it is the beginning of the counting or the Prince of the World. And it is said: twenty-two letters are the foundation, that is, the foundation of the entire world, and this is the secret of, "Mouth to mouth I will speak to him,"[28] that is, in the union of the king and the queen, that is, in the kiss.

This passage is based upon a series of plays upon the *gemaṭria* of the words used: immediately prior to the sentences quoted appear, we read, "a thousand men in the heavens," whose numerical value in Hebrew is 651, equal to the subsequent expressions, *ha-qinah ʿal zakar u-neqevah* (the jealousy of the male over the female); *maḥzor diyo šalem* (its cycle is full tint); *roš ha-minyan* (the beginning of the count); and *sar ha-ʿolam* (the Prince of the World). This last phrase undoubtedly refers to the Active Intellect, which is frequently known in medieval literature by the term "Prince of the world." The numerical value of the expression "twenty-two letters" *(ʿesrim u-šetayim ʾotiyot)* is 2199 which, if the thousands are changed into units, becomes 201 (i.e., 2+119), whose value in *gematria* in turn equals *kol ha-ʿolam* (the entire world); *peh el peh* (mouth to mouth); and *ha-melek weha-malkah* (the king and the queen). It is clear that all this refers to a particular kind of revelation, alluded to by the verse, "mouth to mouth I will speak with him"—an image for the union of the king and queen, in which the king corresponds to the Active Intellect and the queen to the human soul. Further on in this passage, R. Barukh writes: "'In you is the tint'—that is, in you is the foundation of God, which is the intellect which flows into the soul . . . for the soul or the intellect both appear in the holy language, and when they are united together—that is, the soul and the intellect—they receive pleasure." Again, *ha-nefeš weha-sekel* (the soul and the intellect) = 796 = *lešon ha-qodeš* (the Holy Tongue) = *šaʿašuʿim* (pleasure).

The erotic allusions found in R. Barukh Togarmi were extensively developed by Abulafia, who frequently speaks of the union between the intellect and the soul in terms of the secrets of language. Abulafia uses the image of intercourse more extensively than that of the kiss, which may be an indication that he considered his own experiences to transcend the first level of connection with the active intellect. The primary sources of this image are naturally found in the Song of Songs: the lover is the Active Intellect, while his beloved is the human intellect:

> And by this secret was the Song of Songs composed, that is, in the meaning of the desire of those whose desire is towards their beloved, following the imaging of the love of their loved ones. And this is the image of groom and bride.[29]

However, the most interesting use of the image of intercourse appears in *Sefer Mafteaḥ ha-Sefirot*:[30]

> Apprehension of the nature of prophecy [i.e., ecstasy]: there is nothing more difficult for man to apprehend in all human

> apprehensions [than this], and the human mind has not the power to apprehend this until it is attached to the divine intellect, in a connection similar to that of the body and the soul, or the connection of form and matter, similar to the union of male and female, the best and sweetest of which is the first [union]—that is, a virgin groom with a virgin bride—for the longing between the two of them has continued a long time before their uniting. [Thus,] at the time of their union they attain the pinnacle of their desire, and the movement of the first desire . . . And their hearts receive a great peace, and the movement of their desire is from then on a calm one, in a moderate manner, neither excessively rapid nor excessively slow, but as is fitting: and after the two minds settle on one matter, they begin to move in the form of the desire of their giving birth, and they will attempt to guide their actions with the intention of impregnation, for they have already moved from one desire of a certain aim to another desire, and it is also doubtless a purposive one, and thus the thing continues from purpose to purpose, and all things follow one purpose or another. . . . But I must inform you here of the matter of those who seek out 'prophecy', which is similar to what I have said concerning the simile of the groom and the bride, and of this it is said,[31] "If all the songs (sic) are holy, Song of Songs is Holy of Holies." For the entire intention of that poet was to tell us by means of parables and secrets and images the form of true 'prophecy' and its nature and how to reach it. And the essence of 'prophecy' is that the intellective soul, which is the mover within the body, is first united with all the ways of the Torah and with the secrets of the *miẓwot* and knowledge of their reasons in general, and after it has ascended the rungs of apprehension included in knowledge of the truth and removal of the illusions according to Kabbalah . . . and the last is the purpose of the general prophecy.

The interpretation given here to the Song of Songs is strikingly different from that generally found in Jewish philosophy and in theosophic Kabbalah; in this approach, Song of Songs is seen as a love song which describes the erotic contacts between bride and groom, on the literal level, and the character of prophecy or mystical experience, on the esoteric level. As in the relationship between a man and a woman, so in the mystical experience there is a progression in the character of experience and its goals. It is worthy of note that the soul is understood as a woman, a very widespread image in mysticism:[32] just as the ultimate sexual contact is the outcome of a long-continued quest, the soul likewise attains 'prophecy' only after great intellectual effort, the main elements of which are, first, study of the secrets of Torah and, second, knowledge of reality as it is.[33] Having seen that the image of sexual union is intended to portray the relationship of the Active Intellect to the soul, we may now proceed to another passage. In *Gan Naᶜul,*[34] Abulafia writes:

> . . . the Song of Songs is a parable of the community of Israel with the Holy One, blessed be He,[35] who is like a bridegroom, is perfect in every respect, and she is to him like a bride perfect in every respect, He in His Divinity and she in her humanity.[36] And the *devequt* and love between them is shared via ascents and descents: she ascends and He descends.[37] "Who is it that ascends from the desert"[38]; "to the garden of nuts I descended."[39] This is an allusion to a virgin, over whose virginal blood one recites the benediction, "Who placed a nut in the Garden of Eden."[40] And the partnership of the two of them is like that of male and female, man and woman.[41] . . . And human love cannot share in the divine save after much study of Torah and much attainment of wisdom, and after having received prophecy, and this is the secret of *Ḥatan* (bridegroom): Torah, [the letter] *tav,* between *Ḥet*—Wisdom *(Ḥok-mah)* on its right and "Prophecy" *(Nevuʾah)* on its left.

As in the quotation from *Mafteaḥ ha-Sefirot,* here too prophecy is preceded by two stages: the study of Torah and of wisdom. Abulafia expresses the idea that within the bridegroom *(Ḥatan),* namely within the Active Intellect, there exist Prophecy, Wisdom and Torah-knowledge, by interpreting the word *Ḥatan* as an acronym *(notariqon): Ḥ—Ḥokmah* on the right; *T—Talmud Torah* in the middle; *N—Nevuʾah* on the left. The sexual connection is alluded to here, among other things, by the words *ascent* and *descent* borrowed from Song of Songs. On the mystical level, this refers to the influx of the Active Intellect, alluded to in the term *descent,* and the elevation of the soul, alluded to in the term *ascent.* Here, too, Abulafia follows Maimonides, who sees these terms as homonyms.[42] He returns to the concept of ascent and descent in *Ôr ha-Sek̲el:*

> This is the [great] power of man: he can link the lower [part] with the higher one, and the lower [part] will ascend and cleave to the higher, and the higher will descend and kiss the entity ascending towards it, like a bridegroom actually kisses his bride, out of his great and real desire characteristic to the delight of both, from the power of the Name [of God].[43]

In *Ḥayye ha-Nefeš,*[44] we read:

> . . . the cleaving of all knowledge to the Name in its activities, in the secret of the pleasure of bridegroom and bride.[45] And it is known that this wondrous way is one accepted to all the "prophetic"

> disciples, who write what they write according to the Holy Spirit, and they are those who know the ways of prophecy.

A leitmotif of these passages is that of the delight accompanying mystical experience. One might argue that this is merely a theoretical inference from the pleasure which accompanies sexual union, but in several passages Abulafia makes it quite clear that this pleasure is in fact the aim of mystical experience. In *Ôr ha-Sekel,* he says:

> The letter is like matter, and the vocalization is like spirit, which moves the matter, and the apprehension of the intention of the one moved and of the mover is like the intellect; and it is that which acts in spirit and matter, while the pleasure received by the one who apprehends is the purpose.[46]

As is well known, in the hierarchy customary in the Middle Ages, the ultimate purpose [*telos*] of a thing is seen as the most important.[47] For that reason, this passage of Abulafia may be understood as an indication of the primacy of pleasure above apprehension. However, there are also places in which the distinction between apprehension and pleasure is not so sharp, although there too pleasure may be seen as the final goal. Thus, he writes in *Mafteaḥ ha-Tokaḥot:*

> The purpose of marriage of man and woman is none other than their union, and the purpose of union is impregnation, and the purpose of impregnation is [bearing] offspring, and the purpose of [offspring] is study [i.e., of Torah by the child born], and the purpose of that is apprehension [of the Divine], whose purpose is the continuing maintaining of the one apprehending with pleasure gained from his apprehension.[48]

In addition to these theoretical expressions, there are descriptions of the mystical experience and of the sensation of pleasure accompanying it. In *Ôẓar ʿEden Ganuz,*[49] for example, we read:

> And you shall feel in yourself an additional spirit arousing you and and passing over your entire body and causing you pleasure, and it shall seem to you as if balm has been placed upon you, from your head to your feet, one or more times, and you shall rejoice and enjoy it very much, with gladness and trembling; gladness to your soul and trembling of your body, like one who rides rapidly on a horse, who is happy and joyful, while the horse trembles beneath him.[50]

Abulafia is ready to see physical pleasure as an appropriate means of expressing the feelings which accompany the mystical experience, unlike other authors who, while using the metaphor of intercourse in order to describe their love of God, were more hesitant to do so to express God's love for them.[51] Abulafia does not suggest anywhere that this image is an inappropriate one to its subject: on this point, Abulafia departs radically from Maimonides' teaching. Following Aristotle,[52] Maimonides sees the apprehension of the Divine as the highest goal of human activity; the joy which accompanies it is only a side effect of this activity.[53] Abandoning his path in this respect, Abulafia crystallized an approach, apparently based upon personal experience,—that there is an additional stage to the acquisition of intellectual perfection—namely, that of the pleasure deriving from the mystical experience.[54] In following this path, Abulafia is close to the Moslem mystics, who were accused by Ibn Bajja of limiting the expression of union with God to conceptions of pleasure.[55] Under the influence of Plotinus, a number of Italian Renaissance thinkers thought of pleasure as a value preferable to apprehension; it would seem worthwhile to examine whether the translation of Abulafia's books into Latin might not have also contributed to this tendency.[56]

The image of sexual union is used as well in other books from Abulafia's circle. The anonymous author of *Šaʿare Ẓedeq* describes the relationship between the soul and the body as that between the mistress of the house and her servant, while that between the soul and the intellect is like that between a woman and her husband. He writes as follows of the connection between the intellect and the soul: "'For thy maker is thy husband.' This is her true husband, in terms of the maintenance [of her]."[57] In *Ôẓar Ḥayyim*,[58] R. Isaac of Acre writes:

> Likewise, the saying of the Sages:[59] "A wife is acquired in three manners: by money [in Hebrew: also "silver"], by a document, and by intercourse." "See life with a woman whom you love";[60] "He who finds a wife finds goodness";[61] "Who shall find a woman of valour"[62]—all these allude to Torah, to wisdom and to intellect, which a man acquires by three principles, if he is enlightened in the secrets of three worlds: the lowly world, from which one mines silver—which is a mineral, neither seeing nor hearing nor feeling: this is alluded to [by silver]; the intermediate world, from which there comes light to the sages who read books written upon documents of parchment, paper alluding to the document—"For the commandment is a candle and the Torah is light";[63] and the upper world, the world which the intellect desires, and will rejoice and be glad to come and dwell within the pure reflective soul, as a bridegroom rejoices over his bride, for more than the calf wishes to

suck the cow wishes to give suck[64]—this is symbolized by intercourse.

Elsewhere in the same work,[65] R. Isaac of Acre interprets another rabbinic saying:[66] "'A woman speaking [i.e., engaged in intercourse] with her husband'—this alludes to the rational soul and the upper world, which is the world of intellect." We see that in both passages, the relationship between the intellective soul and the upper world, the world of the Intellect, is indicated by explicitly erotic images. We learn here of the cleaving between the soul and its supernal source, whether by its own ascent or by the "descent" of the upper world to dwell in the speaking soul. A similar approach appears in a brief discussion in which R. Isaac compares the words of prophecy, received during the course of a mystical experience, to the role of the matchmaker, who acts as a go-between for purposes of marriage:[67]

> Moreover, the word [68] used in the Arabic language to refer to one who speaks of a match between a man and a woman, to make matches and weddings, is *qatib.* And the words of prophecy[69] of God to the prophet are [also] called *qatib.*

Finally, I wish to mention the words of R. Nathan, who was seemingly an avenue by which R. Isaac of Acre learned of Abulafia's teachings, who provides the following reading in a collection gathered by R. Isaac:[70]

> That we ought not to remove our thoughts from God, and that our intellective souls shall always long for supernal knowledge, which alludes to the supernal influx[71] and which sweetens[72] it, just as it is sweet to a woman to receive the influx from her husband who loves her with a strong love; and if she does so, then they shall always be attached in a true union.

The frequent use of the image of intercourse in order to portray the mystical experience, or at times even the experience of *unio mystica,* is one of the signs of the existence of a Kabbalistic circle for whom mystical experiences was an ideal, and who gave expression to their attainment of these experiences by means of a unique set of images.

3. The Image of Seed

Already in ancient times the motif of spiritual union was linked with that of spiritual seed.[73] Iraeneus quotes a sentence from the Gnostic Marcos associating the two motifs: "Prepare yourself as a bride prepares herself, waiting for her bridegroom, so that you may be that which I am, and I will be that which you are; receive in your bridal chamber the seed of light."[74] The idea of intellective seed, which is widespread in Stoic literature,[75] found its way to Abulafia via channels that are unclear to me. In *Ôẓar ʿEden Ganuz,*[76] he writes:

> The seed is a matter of that which exists through the existence of the Active Intellect, which is the influx by which the soul receives it, and it is like the image of the seed born from the man and woman. Of this it is likewise said by way of parable, "and choose life, that you may live, you and your seed,"[77] which is the life of the world to come. . . . "Who is wise? He who sees the future [lit.: 'That which is to be born']"[78] He sees the seed which we have mentioned, which is the son that is born.

It follows from this that the seed is an image for the influx which reaches the intellective soul, transforming it into intellect in actuality. In *Ḥayye ha-ʿOlam ha-Ba,* Abulafia briefly returns to the point that "every man is the fruit of God, may He be blessed, and His seed, by way of allegory, and he is His son in truth."[79] This idea likewise appears in *Šaʿare Ẓedeq,* where the anonymous author writes that "'and she bears seed' [Num. 5:28] which is the Holy Spirit, and it is a lasting son."[80] His contemporary, R. Nathan, states in an extant collection from his writing that the Sefirah of *Malḳut:*

> . . . is the male among the separate intelligibilia and among the souls of human beings, for the influx which comes from it to the intellective soul is like the seed, which comes from the man to the womb of the woman. And just as a man matures in years, so does his intellect, which is the influx, grow with him.[81]

The use of the image of seed is a logical sequel to the use of the image of intercourse, in addition to the fact that according to the medieval world view, the connection between the brain and the seed is an organic one: the source of the seed, like the intellect, is in the brain.[82] This outlook is clearly expressed in *Sefer ha-Bahir*[83]; it was accepted by the earliest Kabbalists,[84] and became the dominant view within the Kabbalah. Abulafia himself associates the two subjects, and writes of the brain and the heart that "both of them know their Creator . . . and from both together is issued the power of birth."[85]

4. The Secret of Impregnation

As we have seen, the pleasure which accompanies sexual union rendered it an appropriate image for the mystical experience. But there is an additional aspect which was exploited by Abulafia in order to draw a connection between sexual union and ecstasy: the aim of fruitfulness.[86] We have seen above how, in the quotation from *Mafteaḥ ha-Sefirot,* one of the purposes of sexual union is seen as impregnation. The meaning of this term in the context of mystical experience is the flow of the intellective influx into the intellective soul and its absorption by the soul. Abulafia was not the first to interpret the term in this manner; already in the earliest phase of Kabbalah, "impregnation" was a symbol for the reception of influx. Thus, in one of the manuscripts containing material from the Kabbalistic school of Gerona we find the following statement:

> I received from R. A[braham] that when the influx descends from the attribute [i.e., sefirah] via the paths, a holy intercourse takes place, and this is the secret of impregnation explained to the pious ones; that when they receive a merciful [sic—should read "spiritual"] flow, this is a form of impregnation.[87]

But whereas in Geronese Kabbalah, this term is generally connected with the doctrine of transmigration of the soul,[88] in Abulafia it acquires an entirely different meaning. In *Sefer ha-Geʾulah,* he writes:

> The secret of impregnation depends upon the movements and the Zodiac; for behold, when your soul becomes wise it is impregnated with knowledge and gives birth to insights and wisdom in its thoughts, and the active intellect is her husband, and his name is *išim* (i.e., "people"), and he is her husband. And the vessels prepared for her are the letters, which are the material, and they fulfill the place of the womb of the woman [in relation to] the soul.[89]

Abulafia attempts to relate the original Talmudic meaning of the term *sod ha-ʿibbur* (here translated as "the secret of impregnation") —that is, the calculations necessary in order to determine the additional amount of time to be added to a leap year—to the meaning which he gives to the same term. The intercalation of the year is dependent upon calculations pertaining to the movements of the constellations, for which reason *sod ha-ʿibbur* in its literal sense pertains to the realms of time and space. Abulafia adds the soul to these two dimensions, so that we arrive at the well-known triad of

Sefer Yeẓirah,[90] "soul [i.e., man], world and year" *(nefeš, ʿolam, šanah).*" The connection between the impregnation of the soul and the intercalation of the year and the world lies in the fact that both are connected with calculations: The soul becomes impregnated when it calculates *gematriot* and combinations, so that it becomes wise and gives birth to "understandings" under the influence of the Active Intellect. It is worth noting that, like the calculations of *gematriot,* the calendrical calculations are performed in Hebrew with the help of letters. The triad mentioned in connection with intercalation also appears in *Ner Elohim:*[91]

> He who knows the secret of intercalation, which is the secret of the year, will [also] know the secret of the impregnation [*ʿibbur*] of the world and of the impregnation of the soul. For this reason all the letters are twenty-two [in number], and there is the divine Name there: on one side the name *YHWH* and on the other side the name *Ehyeh.* The names *YHWH* and *Ehyeh* add up in *gematria* to 47, which is the sum of the number of years in the "great cycle" of the sun, 28, and in the lunar cycle, 19.[92]

Let us now go on to another distinction between two different kinds of impregnation. In *Sefer Imrê Šefer,* Abulafia writes:[93]

> There are two kinds of impregnation *(ʿibbur),* that is, two forms which alternate with little difficulty and are similar in most respects and in their common use, and which differ in their offspring, to bear fruit similar to themselves. And if the upper one passes on the seed prior to the lower one, which is impregnated, the offspring will be similar to the lower one, possessing the opening *(neqev),* which is called female *(neqevah)* or woman *(ʾišah);* and she is Eve *(Ḥawah),* because she desired mystical experience, and obliged herself to be the material to the upper one, [who] conquers and inscribes himself in his place below, and is rooted and becomes a model to what comes after him, and it sealed in his form and image to protrude out. And when the lower matter comes to him and is connected with him, and embraces and kisses him and is attached and united with him, warp and woof, like the image of the torch within a torch or of thunder within thunder or of lightning within lightning, and they become connected to one another, then the latter becomes a concave seal, and her opening is opened. And this is the secret, "when this is opened that is shut, and when that is open this is shut." And in the hands of the two is a magical key, which portrays all its forms, warp and woof, and if the action is reversed between the two who are giving seed, and the lower matter conquers the upper, then the names formed are four: *Adam* (Adam), *Zak̲ar*

> (Male), *Iš* (Man), *Ḥayah* (Living Creature); "and no man remembered that unfortunate man."[94] And as is the offspring between the two of them, so is the offspring of [mystical] "prophecy" in the two substances: the lower and upper matter.

This passage is based upon a Rabbinic saying in *Niddah* 31b: "R. Isaac said in the name of R. Ammi: If the woman discharges seed first, then she shall bear a malechild; if the man discharges seed first, then she shall bear a female child." The meaning of this Talmudic saying is that the seed which is discharged last determines the sex of the child. It follows that there are two kinds of impregnation: the former, that brought about when the upper or male partner discharges seed first, and the latter, which takes place when the lower or female partner discharges seed first. On the metaphoric level, the upper or male is the Active Intellect, which "passes" the seed, while the lower is the human soul, which becomes impregnated. The result of the former type of impregnation, in which the Active Intellect "emits seed" first, is negative, i.e., female; as the soul is not yet prepared to receive the intellective influx, her offspring is similar to herself: that is, she gives birth not to a male, i.e., intellect, but to a female force, i.e., the soul.[95] The sequence of terms: *defus* (imprint), *ḥotam* (seal), *ẓelem* (image), and *boleṭ* (protruding) allude to the Active Intellect and its activities.[96] In this case, one speaks of a seal, that which it is intended to "seal" coming by itself and being "underneath." The sense of the verbs *pataḥ* (open) and *satam* (seal) is not altogether clear; it may be that the expression, "when this opens that shuts" refers to a situation in which the lower matter is prepared to receive the influx, while the upper is still "shut." The negative implication of such a match follows from this; this type of impregnation is also portrayed in the negative images of "warp and woof,"[97] "key" and "magical."

The meaning of the second kind of impregnation is generally clearer; the "reversed activity" seems to refer to a situation in which the one who emits seed first is the lower matter, in which case the result will be positive, i.e., intellective. This is the context of the verse from Ecclesiastes, which refers to the first image as wisdom, "and they found there a wise but unfortunate man, and he fled the city in his wisdom." However, it is difficult to understand the significance of the expression "the lower matter shall conquer the upper."

The two passages analyzed above prove that Abulafia saw the image of impregnation as an appropriate one for the receiving of the influx from the active intellect.[98]

Several of the elements discussed above are combined together in a discussion found in *Še'erit Yosef*[99] by R. Joseph ibn Ẓayyaḥ, a sixteenth-century Jerusalem Kabbalist, who on some points follows Abulafia's path:

> For the secret of his right [hand] is the circle of man, and the secret of his left hand is the circle of fire, and the secret of both of them is "the activity in the woman," which is [tantamount to] "he acts in the man," from which there comes "love to the influx," which is "influx to love," [symbolized by] the "roof" of the [letter] *Heh,* with the aspect of God portrayed, like the letter *Dalet,* whose number is four, the secret of impregnation, which is squared, and the number of *Heh* is five, which is the secret of impregnation.

Despite the fact that this passage is rather obscure, it may well be that it refers to the connection between the intellective aspect symbolized by the expression, "the circle of man," "his right hand," and the material aspect, symbolized here by the words "his left hand" and "the circle of fire." These phrases are evidently understood in terms of the connection of male and female, who correspond to the intellective and material parts. This is also suggested by the use of the term *šefaʿ* (influx), whose results are evidently the impregnation or the "secret of impregnation." This would indicate that Abulafia's type of thought penetrated into the latter Kabbalistic school of mid- sixteenth-century Jerusalem. It is also quite plausible that the above-quoted section is in fact a fragment from one of Abulafia's lost writings, or one of his circle. In any event, we shall now go on to the results of the process of "impregnation."

5. The Son and the New Birth

As we have seen above, the desired outcome of the pregnancy is a male child: the birth of a son symbolizes the appearance of the Intellect within the human soul;[100] in several places, Abulafia designates the Intellect by the term son. Thus, in *Ḥayye haʿOlam ha-Ba,* he writes: "the human intellect is the fruit of God, may He be praised, and by way of simile is His seed, and he is in truth His son."[101] In *Ôẓar ʿEden Ganuz,*[102] he states: "We require redemption in any event from the one who destroys, and this is the secret of the redemption of the son, as is said, 'All first-born of my sons I will redeem,' and this is a hint of the commandment of redeeming the first born of the powers within man, which is the intellect."[103] At the end of the above-mentioned work, we read: "I said at the beginning of this book, in the introduction, that it is a worthy act to redeem the son, who is in the image of the *A[leph]*, that is, one and unique from the perfect one, which is the intellect in truth."[104] In *Sefer ha-Meliẓ*, we read, "that when this intellect is born, which is his son *(ben)*, from the root "understanding" *(binah)*, he will be assisted by God, because the way [of man] is the way of the turning fiery sword, and he cannot give birth except by study of the intelligibilia."[105] The alleged semantic connection between *ben* (son) and *binah* (understanding) reappears in *Ôẓar ʿEden Ganuz:* "For there is his intellect, called 'son,' from [the word] 'understanding.'"[106] Likewise in *Sefer ha-Geʾulah* we read:[107] "For the disciples of the prophets are called their sons [i.e., *bene ha-neviʾim*], and likewise birth itself, as is said, 'And he begate in his image and likeness,' and we shall explain this matter of image and likeness, which also refers to understanding."[108] Further on in this same passage, we encounter another "etymology":

> [A son *(ben)*], which means *Šem* [i.e., the name of Noah's son; in Hebrew: "name"], which causes man to understand and to gain understanding from it, and to exist in it, just as the son is the cause of the existence [or continuation] of the species. And it is known that the material [i.e., human] intellect is son to the Divine intellect.

With some minor changes, Abulafia reiterates the interconnections among *ben* (son)—*boneh* (builds)—*binyan* (building) in *Sitrê Torah:* "For *šem* (name) comes from the word desolation *(šemamah)* and destruction, while *ben* comes from the term 'understanding' *(binah)* and 'construction' *(binyan)*."[109] The significance of these etymological exegeses seems clear—the son who is born is the builder, that is, the Intellect which is the true building of man, which attains eternal life for him.[110] In the sequel to the above-mentioned passage from *Sitrê Torah*, we read that "man is composed of a desolate and wasted desert *(midbar)*, like his body, and a rational being *(medabber)*, which is prepared and built for perfect and eternal existence." Abulafia's words cited here are reflected in another passage in *Sitrê Torah:*

> "The donkey *(ḥamor)* brays." The pure bodily matter, "your soul" "the magician" (*kašfan;* an anagram of *nafšeḳa*, "your soul"), and it is the appetitive soul. "Dogs barking"—this refers to the material powers, that is, the power of imagination and excitation, and the other powers, which are partly spiritual and partly material. "A woman speaking [i.e., coupling with] her husband"—matter and form. "And a baby"—intellective power—"suckling from its mothers breast"—the Active Intellect.[111]

In the writings of R. Judah Romano, a younger contemporary of Abulafia's, the image of the potential intellect is compared with a child, while the active intellect is portrayed as a king.[112] It is worth noting here the parallel in R. Isaiah b. Joseph of Greece between the influx of the active intellect and the power of birth:[113]

> For because the effect of the influx, which is our Active Intellect,[114] is to give birth and to constantly take its spiritual influx, and through this [it] shall constantly be renewed for those who receive apprehension after apprehension, continuously. Likewise, Jacob our Father, peace upon him, was to begat many sons . . . in the essence of strengthening, and in the supreme crown, which is the Active Intellect of the separate intelligibilia, which is called the Throne of Glory, there is likewise the power of giving birth to the influx. Therefore, the power of Jacob our father, peace upon him, is similar to the power of birth from the influx of the supreme crown.

Finally, it is worth noting that the derivation of the word *binah* from *ben* has an interesting history in the Christian Kabbalah. The apostate Abner of Burgos, known as Alfonso de Valledolid, writes as follows: "The Christians relate to the understanding of the Holy One, blessed be He, to the name 'son,' because he was born out of Wisdom, for *ben* and *binah* and *tevunah* are all from one root."[115] The exegesis found in *Sefer ha-Zohar,* in which the name of the Sefirah *Binah* is divided into *Ben* and *yah* ("son" and "God"), influenced R. Reuben Ẓarfati, a fourteenth-century Italian Kabbalist,[116] and through the Latin translation of his work reached Pico della Mirandolla.[117]

The emergence of the intellect within the human soul is also discussed by Abulafia from another point of view: that the son born is the true man or the new man. The idea is an extremely widespread one in mystical literature: Hermes Trismegistus taught Tat that man becomes a son of God by means of the new birth,[118] while Christian mysticism speaks of the birth of the son of God within the soul of the mystic.[119] Islamic mysticism knows of the "spiritual child," who is a symbol of renewal,[120] while Buddhism speaks about the man who has received enlightenment as the son of Buddha.[121] In all of the cases mentioned above, and apparently also in Abulafia, the appearance of the intellective element is seen as a new birth, which transforms the mystic into a son of the divine.[122]

In his commentary to *Sefer ha-Hafṭarah,* Abulafia writes:[123]

> In truth, when a man is forty years of age, he is ready by his nature to be redeemed[124] from the physical forces, and he will understand

> one thing from another; and they have already alluded to this in saying, "When he was forty years old Abraham came to know his Creator."[125] And the Torah likewise alluded to this concerning Isaac, "And Isaac was forty years old when he took Rebecca."[126] And this is the secret of the forty years that the Israelites wandered in the desert, and the form of the fetus in the womb is completed after forty days, to require the one pregnant for a male and twice that for a female,[127] and this is [likewise] the secret of the [Hebrew letter] *mem*, which gives birth.[128] . . . Therefore it is said [of Moses], [129] "forty days and forty nights he did not eat bread and did not drink water."

The phrase, "to be redeemed from the power of the physical forces" is reminiscent of the above passage from *Ôẓar ʿEden Ganuz*, dealing with the redemption of the first-born "from the powers within man, which is the intellect."[130] The spiritual birth is alluded to here by the parallel to physical birth, forty years as against forty days; there is likewise an association here with saying in Avot 5:23, "one who is forty years old—for understanding." In *Ḥayyê ha-ʿOlam ha-Ba*,[131] Abulafia again discusses the above- mentioned idea:

> *Yafefiyah* [the Prince of the Torah] . . . taught Torah, that is, the entire Torah, to Moses our teacher for forty days and forty nights, corresponding to the formation of the fetus in its mother's womb,[132] [the time necessary] to distinguish between male and female. Therefore it is possible for a person to enjoy the radiance of the Shekhinah in this world without food for forty days and forty nights, like Moses and Elijah.[133] And the secret of the names of both of them is known to you, and he combines one with the other: first Moses, and then Elijah, and their combination emerges as a Divine Name (*šem ha-elohi;* an anagram of *Moše, Eliyahu*), and it is in its secret [meaning] the name of the son, and he is the son of God [pun on *šem* and *Ha-Šem]*.

Prima facie, the above-cited passages from Abulafia's works are no more than theoretical discussions of the spiritual development of Moses and Elijah: Abulafia relies upon literary sources that were known long before him, and upon the number forty years, which is a formulary number. One may ask whether his discussion is merely an intellectual exercise, or whether there are indications of Abulafia's personal experience underlying these arguments; i.e., was the intellect which transformed Abulafia into a son of God born within his soul?[134] The only two books in which I have found a connection drawn between the appearance of the intellect and the number forty were written in 1280, that is, the Hebrew year 5040, which was the fortieth year of Abulafia's life.[135] It seems to me that behind these "objective" comments there is a personal confession, his fortieth year also having been the year at the end of which Abulafia went to the pope, a journey entailing explicit messianic characteristics. In the commentary to *Sefer ha*ᶜ*Edut,* also written in his fortieth year, we read:[136]

> He said that he was in Rome at that time, and they told him what was to be done and what was to be said in his name, and that he tell everyone that "God is king, and shall stir up the nations,"[137] and the retribution(!) of those who rule instead of Him. And he informed him that he was king and he changed [himself] from day to day, and his degree was above that of all degrees, for in truth he was deserving such. But he returned and again made him take an oath when he was staying in Rome on the river Tiber . . . and said, anoint him as king by the power of all the Name, for I have anointed him as king over Israel [138] over the congregations of Israel, that is, over the commandments, and you have called his saying and name *Šadday,* like My own Name, whose secret is "my breasts" *(šadday)* in the corporeal sense. Understand all the intention, and likewise his saying, "that he is I and I am he" . . . But the secret of the corporeal Name is "Messiah of God" *(mašiah ha-Šem)* and also "Moses will rejoice" [*yismaḥ Moše,* the anagram of the previous phrase].

These allusions, which indicate a vision of both a messianic and an intellective type, strengthen the claim that the fortieth year was an important one in Abulafia's spiritual life, one in which he saw the beginning of his spiritual renewal as Messiah, anointed to rule over the people of Israel. In several other places in the same book, we read of experiences which constitute progress in his mystical life: "And at the end of the fortieth year another sublime opening in vision was opened."[139] There are detailed testimonies of his unusual experiences during this year, and this is not coincidental, for it was during this period that he began to write his prophetic books, which are indicative of personal experience.

It is illuminating to trace the influence of the idea of spiritual renewal during the fortieth year in two books from Abulafia's circle. In *Ša*ᶜ*are Ẓedeq,* the anonymous author writes:

> And behold Moses changed his nature according to the letters of the name, and he begat a male child before he descended from the mountain, for he stood there forty days and forty nights, as does natural offspring of man. . . . And when his formation was

> completed after forty days, the skin of his face shone, and therefore he extended [the stay of] in the desert of those who left Egypt for forty years, because of their great poverty, and he, peace upon him, only needed one day for each year.[140]

R. Isaac of Acre writes in a similar vein in his book *Ôẓar Ḥayyim:*[141]

> The enlightened one who goes to separate himself and to concentrate, to draw [down] upon his soul [142] the divine spirit, in wondrous and awesome deeds which are too terrible to relate; from the day he came from God, strong desire and intense love in the heart of his father and mother gave birth to him, and he who gave birth to him, to connect with [him] and to labor in him until he is today forty years old, which is the time of completion of the building of his intellect and its sanctuary, to adjure evil and to choose good. "For until forty years [man wishes] fine food"[143]—these allude to the sensory and corporeal realms. "From then on, [he wishes] fine beverage"—this is the Divine spirit, to apprehend the intelligibilia, and this is what is said in he verse,[144] "God has [not] given you a heart to know and eyes to see and ears to hear, until this day'—which is the fortieth year—"and has led you forty years in the wilderness"[145]—an allusion to the house of seclusion.

The understanding of the age of forty as a turning point in the spiritual development of man also appears in another work written under the direct influence of Abulafia. In *Toldot Adam,* written in the fifteenth century, we read:

> If you wish to learn before a great master, who is the angel of prophecy, whose name is Raziel, and if you understand all that I have hinted of his power and his teaching, then you will know the secret of his name. And if you wish to be one of his disciples and to learn in his book, which is that of the completely righteous, and you wish to be inscribed with them immediately for eternity, then take care to study continually from [the age of] thirteen years until [the age of] forty years in the book of the intermediate ones before the good angel Gallizur, who is the intellective master; and from forty years onwards let your principal study be before Raziel, and then secrets of wisdom shall be revealed to you, for you shall already be a great man among the giants.[146]

Comparison with the following passage from the introduction to Abulafia's prophetic books[147] indicates a certain resemblance between the two books: "I, Abubrahim the young, studied before Raziel my master for thirteen years, and while I was yet thirteen years old I was unable to understand a thing from his books." Despite the differences between the passages, it seems to me that they complement one another: both speak about Raziel as a master, while the periods of study complement one another: *Toldot Adam* speaks of two later periods of study—from 13 to 40 and from age 40 on—while the introduction speaks of the earliest stage, until the age of thirteen.[148] It is worth mentioning that the anonymous author of *Toldot Adam* often copied from the works of other authors without mentioning them by name, and therefore the above passage may be a reworking of an idea of Abulafia's without its source being mentioned.[149]

Finally, I would like to cite the view of several Jewish authors on the subject of spiritual rebirth. First, I would like to quote the author of the Zohar:[150]

> Come and see: whoever reaches the age of thirteen years and on is called a son of the congregation of Israel,[151] and whoever reaches the age of twenty years and onwards is called a son of the Holy One, blessed be He.[152], for certainly "You are sons of the Lord your God."[153] When David reached thirteen years and was meritorious, on that day that he entered his fourteenth year, it is written,[154] "God said to me, you are my son, this day I have begotten you." What is the meaning? That before that day he was not His son and the supernal soul did not dwell upon him, for he was in his years of uncircumcision. For that reason—"this day I have begotten you." "Today" certainly "I have begotten you" and not the Other Side *(siṭra aḥra)*, as it had been until now.

It is clear from this passage that the author of the *Zohar* also interprets the appearance of the soul, which is the supernal component within the personality, as a new birth, transforming man into a son of God. The statement at the end that man is under the domination of the Other Side until the age that one is required to perform the commandments reminds one of Abulafia's statement that prior to the appearance of the intellect the bodily powers of man are predominant. The perception of the appearance of the intellective soul or the intellect as a symbol of renewal appears in two later authors. In book *Yesodot ha-Maskil*, R. David Yom Tov ibn Bilia, a fourteenth century Portuguese philosopher with mystical leanings, writes as follows:[155]

> For were the intellective soul itself present within man at the time of his birth, this would require that we immediately apprehend the supernal knowledge and wisdom, and we do not see this: for if one

> does not engage in study one knows nothing, and if one does so one becomes something else by oneself,[156] and this is the proof that the soul which comes into being with the person is no more than a preparation. And we learn this principle from the saying of the Psalmist, of blessed memory, who says to his soul, "He who does good on behalf of me, renew as an eagle my youth."[157] There is no doubt that the Psalmist was only speaking to his intellective soul, which is renewed after man is born, and this renewal is like that of the eagle, which is renewed by itself (sic) after a [certain] known period.

A combination of the motifs of the self-renewing eagle (probably an allusion to the phoenix)[158] and the man of intellect appear in R. Abraham Bibago, a fifteenth-century Spanish philosopher, who gives striking expression to the way in which the intellect flows into man from the upper world as a son:

> However, the human intellect is like the son which flows down from the world of intellect, and afterwards,just as there is a relation between the son and his father, so is it possible that there may be cleaving between us and the world of the intellect; thus, when God said to me "you are my son" i.e., I will give you understanding brought down into the world, "this day I have begotten you," and that day that you cling to Me, you will be born in a renewed and eternal birth. And this is meant by his saying, "renew as an eagle my youth."[159]

One should also note the words of R. Menahem ʿAzariah de Fano, a sixteenth-century Italian Kabbalist, in *Maʾamar ha-Nefes:* "And then God said to me, 'You are my son,' and in this saying he emanated upon him a spark of the spirit. 'This day I have begotten you'—this refers to the spark of the soul, for both of which [the two sparks] he will shine into him, 'today,' in their images."[160]

Finally, I wish to comment upon the great similarity between several elements in Abulafia's approach concerning man's true birth, i.e., that of the intellect and the remarks of the Renaissance thinker, Lodovico Lazarelli, in his work, *Crater Hermetis,*[161] Basing himself upon a version of *Peʿulat ha-Yeẓirah,*[162] Lazarelli interprets the appearance of the *golem,* referred to in that work, as a spiritual process of the appearance of renewed man. As in Abulafia, this appearance is defined as the birth of the disciple's intellect under the tutelage of the master's intellect,[163] Using the image of seed,[164] the act of true birth of man is described by Lazarelli in terms of the teacher's resemblance to the creative power of God.[165] Evidently Abulafia's doctrines became known to Lazarelli, by one channel or another, and he used them in practice, as is illustrated by the details of the spiritual renewal Lazarelli has caused to the King Ferdinand of Aragon.

6. Intercourse as Metaphor and as Symbol

Having discussed the use of erotic images for mystical experience, it is worthwhile noting the specific character of these images in Abulafia, drawing a comparison between Abulafia's use of the image of sexual union and that of the theosophical Kabbalah.

Scholars of Kabbalah have already remarked upon several unique characteristics of Kabbalistic symbolism.[166] I would like to begin by discussing the use of sexual union as a symbol; as scholars have noted, in Sefirotic Kabbalah "the symbolic relationship is imbedded in the very nature of the symbol." Human sexual union was chosen to serve as a symbol of unification within the Sefirotic realm because, while it is understood as an act whose components are likely to be lowly, but when this act occurs a new element is added to it, incomprehensible and holy, by which it is transformed into a sacral act; from this perspective sexual union becomes, on the one hand, a symbol of and, on the other hand, a factor in the divine life. In order to exemplify the approach of the theosophical Kabbalists, I would like to cite here a story told by R. Isaac of Acre in *Me᾽irat ῾Enayim:*

> A certain sage asked his colleague about the subject of the [Temple] sacrifices, and said: How is it possible that a matter as disgusting as the burning of fat and the sprinkling of blood, with the smell of the skin and hair of the burnt-offering which is completely consumed, should be a matter by which the world is sustained, that it be a cause for unification above and for blessing and for the sustaining of all that exists? He answered: I will tell you a parable, as to what this resembles. A child is born and is left alone when he is little, and he sustains himself by herbs and water, and he grows up and it happens that he comes within the habitation of human beings, and one day he saw a man coupling with his wife. He began to mock them and say: what is this foolish person doing? They said to him: you see this act; it is that which sustains the world, or without this the world would not exist. He said to them: how is it possible that from such filth and dirt there should be the cause for this good and beautiful and praiseworthy world? And it is nevertheless true—and understand this.[167]

The aim of this parable is to demonstrate that there is a certain mystery in the sexual act, and that this mystery, which cannot be given clear expression, enables it to serve as a symbol for the sublime mysteries,[168] and even to influence the divinity despite its "gross" components.

Abulafia, under the influence of the philosophical approach,[169] perceives the sexual act as a lowly one. In *Ôẓar ʿEden Ganuz,* [170] he writes: "Intercourse is called the Tree of knowledge of good and evil,[171] and it is a matter of disgust and one ought to be ashamed at the time of the act [and be away] from every seeing eye and hearing ear." Abulafia emphasizes the lowliness of the sexual act: the aura of mystery which accompanies it in the Sefirotic Kabbalah is here completely absent. If, nevertheless, Abulafia chose it as an image for mystical experience, he did so because in his approach there is no necessary connection between the image and the process or thing to which that image refers. While the theosophical Kabbalists emphasized the mysterious aspect of the sexual act, Abulafia stresses more its "didactic" element; that is, the sexual act is one that is parallel to mystical experience because of the similar set of components and the interrelationships among them. We do not find any assumption in Abulafia of a substantive connection between the processes; he seeks a schema which is appropriate and well-known for describing mystical experience, so that he can exemplify its occurrence in a simple way. Another distinction is to be added to what we have said thus far: intercourse is an act whose nature is known to us, and it is used to describe an event which may also be apprehended and defined in intellectual terms. Not so in Sefirotic Kabbalah: the supernal union is a hidden process, which is reflected in human sexual union without our being able to understand its exact nature.[172]

Let us now turn to another distinction between the sexual act as symbol and as image. Generally speaking, the human sexual act is used in Sefirotic Kabbalah to allude to processes within the Godhead. Abulafia's use of the sexual act as an image for the connection of the intellective soul with the Active Intellect and its cleaving to it do not appear in earlier Kabbalah. According to Scholem erotic symbolism was interpreted as a symbolism dealing with Godhead, while the connection between man and God was not explained by the use of such symbols except in the later period, of Safedian Kabbalah.[173] It follows from this that the process alluded to in Abulafia is entirely different from that referred to by theosophical Kabbalists. These Kabbalists refer to an act whose actual performance acquires a certain theosophic meaning, provided that it is done accompanied by knowledge and mystical intention towards its true goal. There is no hint of this demand in Abulafia: there is in principle no need for actual sexual contact in order for this contact to serve as an image, while intercourse itself is of no importance whatsoever in the mystical technique of Abulafia.

An additional and significant difference between the understanding of the sexual act in the two systems is the identity of the components of this union. In Abulafia, the male or the bridegroom is the Active Intellect, while the female is the human soul. As the mystics were men, there was a certain difficulty involved in this reversal; but precisely on this point, Abulafia is close to other widespread non-Jewish mystical systems, which consistently portray the soul of the mystic as a female.[174] On the other hand, the theosophical Kabbalists preserve the "proper" psychological relationship in describing, in those rare sources were one can find the connection between Man and the Shekhinah, the mystic as the male and the Shekhinah as the female.[175] However, as surmised by R. J. Z. Werblowsky,[176] it is difficult to assume that the descriptions of this subject in *Sefer ha-Zohar* and in the other mystics stem from personal experience. On the other hand, there is ground for assuming that Abulafia underwent mystical experiences, which are alluded to in his writings with the help of erotic imagery.

The great gap between Abulafia and the Sefirotic Kabbalah is likewise revealed in the results alluded to by means of the erotic imagery. While in Kabbalah human sexual union may cause harmony in the Divine world by strengthening the connection between the sefirot of *Tiferet* and *Malkut*,[177] the mystic only indirectly benefitting from this harmony;[178] in Abulafia mystical experience has no influence upon the Active Intellect or upon God. The human soul is the only element which benefits from the connection with the Active Intellect: the meaning of mystical experience is psychological, private, in certain circumstances social, but always without the cosmic and theosophical meaning which stems from the theurgic nature of sexual union in Sefirotic Kabbalah.[179]

Notes to Chapter Four

1. James H. Leuba, *The Psychology of Religious Mysticism* (London, 1925), pp. 137–155; G. C. Anawati - L. Gardet, *Mystique Musulmane* (Paris, 1961), pp. 161–174; M. Idel, "Metaphores et pratiques sexuelles dans la Cabbale," in *Lettre sur la Sainteté,* ed. Ch. Mopsick (Paris, 1986), pp. 329–358.

2. See Tishby, *The Wisdom of the Zohar* II, pp. 280–306, and the notes there; R. J. Z. Werblowsky, *Tarbiz* 34 (1965), pp. 204–205; *idem, Joseph Karo,*

pp. 57–58.

3. On love as intellectual worship, see Tishby, *ibid,*, pp. 283–284. Abulafia's view on this subject appears in the section entitled "the worship of God via love," *Sod* 2. 10, *Sitre Torah* and *Ḥayye ha-Nefeš*. There are brief discussions of this subject in several other sources: see *Mafteaḥ ha-Sefirot*, MS. Milano - Ambrosiana 53, fol. 176a. Vajda, *L'amour de Dieu dans la theologie juive du Moyen Age* (Paris, 1957), pp. 203–204, describes Abulafia's approach to this subject, based upon *Ḥayye ha-Nefeš* alone. On pp. 197–198 he gives a translation of a passage from *Imre Šefer* discussing intellectual love, without mentioning either the source of the section or its author, See also Idel, *Abraham Abulafia*, p. 27.

4. *Bava Batra* fol.17a; *Sifrei Devarim*, sec. 357; *Moᶜed Qatan* fol. 28a; etc.

5. See the midrash, *Peṭirat Moše Rabbenu*, in Eisenstein, *Ôẓar ha-Midrašim*, II ,pp. 370, 383.

6. Song of Songs 1:2.

7. It would appear to me that this passage from the *Guide of the Perplexed* influenced, not only Abulafia and his disciples, but also those Kabbalists belonging to the theosophic school. Its impression may already be noticed in R. Azriel, *Peruš ha-Aggadot*, p. 5 and p. 59:

> And the sages said [*Sifra Wa-yikra*, 32: 12), "'no man shall see me and live' [Ex. 33:20]—in their lifetime they can not see but at the time of their deaths [they may]," and they are like the candle whose light waxes just as it is about to be extinguished. And this is what is written, "you gather [lit.: "add"] their spirits and they die" [Ps. 104:29]—in that addition their spirit departs.

This passage was influenced by the sentence proceeding the above passage in the *Guide:* "Yet in the measure in which the faculties of the body are weakened and the fire of desires is quenched, the intellect is strengthened, its lights achieve a wider extension." R. Moses de Leon borrowed this idea of R. Azriel's in his *Sefer ha-Rimmon*, MS. Cambridge 151b, fol. 54a and in *Miškan ha-ᶜEdut*, MS. Cambridge 1500, fol. 14a, as well as in *Sefer ha-Zohar* I, 218b–219a.

8. On this topic, see Idel, "On the History," pp. 3–6.

9. See L. Ginzberg, *Legends of the Jews* (New York, 1946), vol. 6, p. 161, n. 948. Unlike Maimonides, who saw death by the kiss as the result of the weakening of man's physical powers, Moses is depicted here as being at the height of his powers at the time of his death: "and his eye was not dim" [Deut. 34:7].

10. MS. Oxford 1582, fol. 146. In *Berit Menuḥah* (Jerusalem, 1950), p. 16a. we read, "and when the same in his wisdom reaches this place, he dies by

the kiss, because of his great longing."

11. *Berakot* fol. 61b.

12. *Ôẓar ʿEden Ganuz,* MS. Oxford 1580, fol. 48b.

13. MS. Vatican 233, fol. 109a.

14. See above, Chapter 3, sub-section: *devequt.*

15. Published by Scholem in *Kabbalistic Manuscripts,* p, 228. Another disciple of Abulafia, the author of *Ner Elohim* (MS. München 10, f. 167b), writes that:

> He ordered us to hold our tongues against excessive speech concerning them [i.e., the sefirot] and to place a rein to our thoughts and balances to our desire for the love of God, lest the soul become separated from the body in its great desire, and seek the kisses of the lips of He who pours wisdom and love.

The substitution of Ben Azzai for R. Akiva as the one who died by the kiss likewise appears in a passage in MS. Vatican 41, fol. 34b, in the margins: "and Ben Azzai likewise desired the secret and went beyond the bounds to seek it, and he died with the kiss." It is possible that R. Judah al-Botini grafted the idea found in *Ḥayye ha-ʿÔlam ha-Ba* onto a description of the death of Ben Azzai, MS. Vatican 283, fol. 71b:

> "Ben Azzai looked and died." He gazed at the radiance of the Shekhinah, like a man with weak eyes who gazes into the full light of the sun, and his eyes are dimmed, and at times he becomes blinded, because of the intensity of the light which overwhelms him. Thus it happened to Ben Azzai: the light overwhelmed him, and he gazed at it because of his great desire to cleave to it and to enjoy it without interruption, and after he cleaved to it he did not wish to be separated from that sweet radiance, and he remained immersed and hidden within it. And his soul was crowned and adorned, and that very radiance and brightness to which no man may cling and afterwards live, as is said, "for no man shall see Me and live"[Ex. 33:20]. But Ben Azzai only gazed at it a little while, and then his soul departed and remained [there], and was hidden away in the place of its cleaving, which is a most precious light. And this death was the death of the pious, whose souls are separated from all the ways of the supernal world.

This passage was evidently written during the first half of the thirteenth century; cf. R. Azriel's *Peruš ha-Aggadot,* ed. Tishby, p.19. For other descriptions of Ben Azzai's ecstatic death, see R. Isaac of Acre, *Ôẓar Ḥayyim,* MS. Moscow - Gunzburg 775, fol. 138a; R. Menahem Recanati, *Peruš la-Torah,* fol. 37d; etc.

16. Psalms 116:15.

17. This duality also appears in Gnosticism; see Hans Jonas, *The Gnostic Religion* (Boston, 1963), p. 285. Sufism also contains testimonies to the death of the mystic in a state of ecstasy. See above, Chap. 2, n. 50.

18. MS. Jerusalem 8° 1303, fol. 53b; MS. Vatican 295 fol. 6b. In his book, *Ẓeror ha-Mor*, Ch. 6 [in Jellinek, *Kerem Ḥemed* 9 (1956), p. 157], R. Isaac ibn Latif writes: "When the human intellect actually cleaves to the intelligibilia, which are the Active Intellect, in the form of the kiss." Ibn Latif's approach influenced R. Yohanan Alemanno, *Šaʿar ha-Ḥeseq* (Livorno, 1790), fol. 35a-b; *Collectanaea*, MS. Oxford 2234, fol. 187a. In his *Collectanaea*, fol. 30a, Alemanno cites a passage from Narboni's commentary to Averroës' *On the Possibility of Conjunction* which speaks of the "preparation" of the Active Intellect: "Let Him kiss him with the kisses of His mouth, and let him receive the Active Intellect in the light of his soul which rises upon her." See Kalman P. Bland, *The Epistle on the the Possibility of Conjunction with the Active Intellect by Ibn Rushd with the Commentary of Moses Narboni* (New York, 1982), p. 96.

19. MS. Oxford 1649, fol. 204a.

20. See above, Chap. 3, par. 6.

21. The author of this work may be alluding to the *gematria* 10 x 26 [i.e., the name *YHWH*]=260 [the *gematria* of *Gerizim*, in the deficient spelling used in Scripture].

22. MS, München 22, fol. 187a; MS. New York JTS 839, fols. 105b–106a. The vision of light while in the ecstatic state at the time of death, described in *Sefer ha-Ẓeruf*, is similar to what is already found in a text from the circle of *Sefer ha-ʿIyyun*. Several manuscripts contain a passage belonging to this circle (MS. Vatican-Urbino 31, fol. 164a; MS. New York JTS 839, fol. 5b; etc.), which reads:

> From the time that the righteous person departs to his eternal home, he sees the light of the sphere of the intellect, and immediately he departs. As if the Holy One, blessed be He, has created it and made it known to the eye. And Moses saw the light of the Zebul, and immediately died. And why all this? Because the body has no strength to stand it.

Here, there is no direct connection stated to death by the kiss, but the author of *Sefer ha-Peliʾah* did draw a connection between the passage from the circle of *Sefer ha-ʿIyyun* and the image of the kiss (Koretz, 1788, fol. 106b):

> Know that at the time that the righteous person departs to his eternal abode, he sees the light of the sphere of the intellect, and his soul immediately departs and leaves the body. And know that he is shown it in accordance with the level of that righteous person and his cleaving to that light, and he immediately cleaves [to it], for there is no strength in the body to withstand

the soul's longing when it sees that light; and Moses, as soon as he saw the light of the dwelling of the supernal Zebul, immediately cleaves there. And the vision of the light which is visible to the righteous whose soul is there is called the kiss.

Here, as in *Sefer ha-Ẓeruf*, death is the cause of ecstasy, and not *vice versa*. The vision of and cleaving to the light are a Neoplatonic motif, which appears frequently in Bahya Ibn Pakuda.

One ought to point out that in a text from the circle of *Sefer haʿIyyun*, the meaning of the sphere of the intellect is similar to that of *empyreum*. On the relationship between the two concepts, see Colette Sirat, *Marʾot Elohim le-Rabbi Ḥanok̲ ben Šelomo al-Qonstantini* (Jerusalem, 1976), pp. 16–17, and see also the Talmudic discussion of the light concealed for the righteous in *Ḥagiggah l2a*.

23. I refer to the passages in Recanati, *Peruš la-Torah*, fol. 38b and 77c. These statements have an explicitly Neoplatonic cast, based upon the ideas found in R. Ezra, *Peruš la-Aggadot*, printed in *Liqquṭê Sik̲eḥah u-Feʾah*, fols. 7b–8a, and in R. Azriel's *Peruš ha-Aggadot*, p. 40. While R. Ezra and R. Azriel do not draw any connection between the cleaving of the individual soul to the supernal soul and death by the kiss, such an association does appear in Recanati. Recanati's *Peruš la-Torah* influenced, on the one hand, R. Judah Hayyat's *Maʿarek̲et ha-Elohut* (Mantua, 1558), fol. 95a–96b, and Christian Kabbalah, on the other. See Ch. Wirszubski, *Three Chapters in the History of Christian Kabbalah* [Heb.] (Jerusalem, 1975), pp. 11–20; Edgar Wind, *Pagan Mysteries in the Renaissance* (Darmondsworth: Penguin, 1967), pp. 155–156; F. Secret, *Les Kabbalistes Chretiens de la Renaissance* (Paris, 1964), pp. 39–40; B. C. Novak, "Giovanni Pico della Mirandola and Johanan Alemanno," *JWCI* vol. 45 (1982), pp. 140–144.

24. See Moses ibn Tibbon, *Peruš Šir ha-Širim* (Lyck, 174), p. 14; R. Ezra, *Peruš Šir ha-Širim* (in *Kitve ha-Ramban*, ed. Chavel p. 485), which was directly influenced by Maimonides and by R. Joseph ibn Aknin, *Hitgalut ha-Sodot ve-Hofaʿat ha-Meʾorot* (Jerusalem, 1964), p. 24; and A. S. Halkin, "Ibn Aknin's Commentary of the Song of Songs," *Alexander Marx Jubilee Volume* (New York, 1950), pp. 396ff.

25. On the difference between Abulafia and the Kabbalists in their use of the image of sexual union, see the end of Chap. 4.

26. R. Zaehner, *Mysticism, Sacred and Profane* (Oxford: Oxford University Press, 1961), p. 151. There is a similarity between Abulafia's understanding of sexual union and that appearing in Ibn *ʿArabi, La Sagese des Prophetes* (Paris, 1955), pp. 186–187. On prophecy seen as intercourse between the human intellect and the *logos*, see R. A. Baer, *Philo's Use of the Categories Male and Female* (Leiden, 1970), pp. 55ff., p. 57. The pair of concepts, Active Intellect and Passive Intellect, were identified as male and female by Postel: see *De Etruriae regionis* (Florence, 1551), p. 144. This treatise is cited in the

introduction to the English edition of *Colloquium* of J. Bodin - M. L. D. Kuntz, ed. (Princeton, 1975), pp. lviii–lix, n. 112.

27. Published by Scholem, *Abulafia*, p. 232; and compare the end of *Sefer ha-Ẓeruf*, MS. Paris BN 774, fol. 33b, and above, Chap. 3, n. 223.

28. Numbers 12:8.

29. *Ôẓar ʿEden Ganuz*, MS. Oxford 1580, fol. 131b–132a; compare also Idel, *Kabbalah - New Perspectives*, pp. 206–207.

30. MS. Milano Ambrosiana 53, fols. 170b–171a.

31. On the sources for this evaluation of Song of Songs, see S. Lieberman's comments in Scholem's book, *Jewish Gnosticism*, p. 119, and n. 1.

32. On the comparison of the soul to a woman, see Hans Jonas, *The Gnostic Religion*, pp. 283–284. and Plotinus' remarks in *Ennead* VI, 9.9 (ed. MacKenna, p. 629): "The soul is always an Aphrodite. . . . The soul in its nature loves God and longs to be at one with Him, in the noble love of a daughter for a noble father." See also Werblowsky's comment in *Tarbiz* 34 (1965), p. 204, and Meister Eckhart's, "Woman—that is the most noble term with which we may designate the soul: it is a more noble word than virgin." See R. Schurmann, *Maitre Eckhart ou la joie errante* (Paris, 1972), p. 46, 181; A. E. Waite, *The Way of Divine Union* (London, 1915), p. 203.

33. The two stages in progress towards prophecy correspond to knowledge of conventional truth, i.e., the secrets of Torah and the reasons for the commandments, and knowledge of the intelligibilia. This evaluation places the commandments on a lower level than most Jewish philosophers would he prepared to acknowledge, Abulafia's distinction here between conventional truth and the intelligibilia is similar to that of his Provencal contemporary, R. Levi b. Abraham, who writes in *Liwyat Ḥen*, MS. München 58, fol. 84b:

> The Torah said, "Behold, I have placed before you today life and goodness, and death and evil." [Deut. 30:15] [This refers to] the practical commandments, of which it is said, "good and evil," that is, "life"—knowledge and intellectual commandments—and foolishness—that is, death. And the good in his eyes and the evil in his eyes [refers to] the practical commandments, of which it is said good and evil.

This division of the commandments, based upon R. Saʿadya Gaon, radically alters his schema. It should be noted that a similar division to that of R. Levi is found in a work written in the Orient, strikingly reflecting Sufic influence; see fol. Rosenthal, "Judaeo-Arabic Work under Sufic influence," *HUCA* vol. 15 (1940), pp. 448–449.

34. MS. München 58 fol. 323a, printed with some variations in *Sefer*

ha-Peliʾah, fols. 52b–c. I have made some minor corrections to the version in MS. München, hased upon the text in *Sefer ha-Peliʾah.* In an epistle known as *Maẓref la-kesef,* MS. Sasson 56, fol. 33b, Abulafia writes:

> And by his concentration, he prepares the bride to receive the influx from the power of the bridegroom. The Divine elements [i.e., the divine letters and the intelligibilia] should move the intelligibilia, and by persisting in his concentration and intensifying and strengthening it, and by his great desire and the strength of his longing and the persistence of his yearning to attain the cleaving and the kiss, the strength of the bride and her name and her power will be mentioned favorably and preserved for ever, for this is their law, and the separated things will be joined and the conjoined things separated, and reality will be turned about.

Here, too, the image of bride and groom alludes to the human soul and the Active Intellect, which are united by the special technique of Abulafia. On "Torah, wisdom and prophecy," See also above, Chap. 1, in a quotation from *Ôẓar ʿEden Ganuz* (n. 21).

35. See *Canticles Rabba* 1:11.

36. The meaning of the idiom *Kenesset Yisraʾel* [the collectivity of Israel] is explained as follows in *Imre Šefer,* MS. Paris 777, p. 57: "The secret of Kenesset Yisrael, whose secret is *Kenesset Yod Šar el* [i.e., the collectivity of *Yod,* the prince of God], for the whole person is one who gathers all and is called the congregation of Jacob." Further on, Abulafia speaks of Kenesset Yisrael in the sense of the Shekhinah or the tenth sefirah but, as we have seen in our discussion of the concept of Shekhinah, this is also liable to be part of the human soul. See *Liqquṭê R. Nathan,* MS. New York - JTS 1777, fol. 34a:

> Maharan [said], *Kenesset Yisraʾel* alludes to the gathering of the souls of the righteous of Israel, which brings down mercy and favor upon the poor one, but not upon all the souls within the body, for it alludes only to the Intellective soul.

In *Ôr ha-Menorah,* a work written in an Abulafian vein, MS. Jerusalem 8° 1303, fol. 28b, we read:

> And the power of speech, called the Rational Soul, which received the Divine influx, called *Kenesset Yisraʾel* whose secret is the Active Intellect, which is also the general influx, and which is the mother of the intellect of the world.

See R. Moses Krispin, *Peruš Šemaʿ Yisraʾel,* MS. Parma 105 fol. 45b. It may be that this represents a metamorphosis of the Kabbalistic interpretation of Kenesset Yisrael, as was already known to the school of Naḥmanides, who writes of *Kenesset Yisra'el* that "she is the gathering of all." See Scholem, *Pirqê Yesod,* p. 284.

37. Compare the acrostic of the poem appearing in the epistle, *Ševa' Netivot ha-Torah,* p. 5: "Abraham Abraham descended, Abraham Abraham ascended," In light of what has been stated in *Gan Na'ul,* it may be that we ought to interpret the verbs *yarad* and *'alah* (descended; ascended) as referring to the mystical ascents and descents of Abulafia himself.

38. Song of Songs 3:6.

39. *Ibid.,* 1:11.

40. See *Siddur Rav 'Amram Gaon,* ed. Frumkin (Jerusalem, 1912), vol. 2, pp. 406–407. The text of the blessing recited by the bridegroom is, "Blessed art thou, o Lord God, King of the universe, who placed a nut in the Garden of Eden, a lily of the valleys, that no stranger may rule the closed well, therefore have you placed the beloved fawn in purity." It is clear that this refers to the virginal blood, and the fact that this blessing was recited over a cup of wine—"he is required to recite it if there is a cup"—strengthens its' sexual connotation. While the editor argues that, in his opinion, "there is a textual error here, and in bless of *egoz* [nut] one should read *zug* [couple]," this argument in fact has no basis in either the manuscripts or in the subject itself. The version as cited by Abulafia, as well as the interpretation that he gives, completely rules out any possibility of the reading, *zug.*

41. The comparison of the woman and the soul to a nut and a garden likewise appear in *Peruš Šir ha Širim* of R. Moses ibn Tibbon (Lyck, 1874), fol. 20b: "And it may be that they compared the woman to the nut because of her meanness and her attachment to matter, and she is called a garden *(ginnat)* in the feminine form, because of her meanness . . . and the soul of man is compared to the nut."

42. *Guide* I:l0, without referring or relating to the verbs in Song of Songs.

43. MS. Vatican 233, fol. 115a, and see note 180 in the previous chapter.

44. MS. München 408, fol. 65b; see Idel, *Abraham Abulafia,* p. 193. Compare also fols. 72a–b there with the passage printed here.

45. The following *gematria* appears in the passage at the end of *Sefer ha-Ẓeruf,* MS. Paris BN 774, fol. 35a: *ta'anug (pleasure)*=529=*he-ḥatan veha-kalah* (the groom and the bride)=*ha-ḥokmah ha-Elohit* (the Divine wisdom), which concisely expresses the main features of Abulafia s view of the subject.

46. MS. Vatican 233, fol. 106b–107a.

47. See, e.g., *Guide* III:13, "its object or its final end, which is the most

important of the four causes," Further on, in the passage from *Sefer Ôr ha-Sekel*, Abulafia writes, "and the purpose is the most elevated of the reasons."

48. MS. Oxford 1605, fol. 7b; cf. *Ôr ha-Sekel*, MS. Vatican 233, fol. 128a, "and according to the prophet who derives pleasure in attaining the form of prophecy [i.e., a mystical experience]."

49. MS. Oxford 1580, fol. 163b–164a.

50. The comparison of the soul and the body to a horse and its rider is a common one. See the material gathered by H. Malter, "Personifications of Soul and Body," *JQR* vol. 2 [N. S.] (1911), pp. 466–467.

51. See *Sefer Raziel*: "More than a young man, who has gone many days without going to a woman, and he desires her and his heart burns, etc.—all this is as nought in comparison with [his wish] to do the will of the Creator." In R. Eleazar of Worms' *Sefer ha-Malakim*; "And at the time that a young man engages in intercourse and shoots like an arrow [i.e., ejaculates], that selfsame pleasure is as nought compared with the slightest pleasure of the World to Come." *Sefer Ḥasidim*: "And that joy [in the love of God] is so strong and so overwhelms his heart, that even a young man, who has not gone to a woman for many days, and has great desire, and whom his seed shoots like an arrow he has pleasure—this is as naught compared with the strengthening of the power of the joy of the love of God." These sources are gathered by M. Guedemann, *Ha-Torah weha-Hayyim be-yeme ha-Benayim* (Tel-Aviv, 1953), I, p. 124, n. 2 In ᶜ*Eẓ Ḥayyim* by R. Isaiah b. Joseph, a Byzantine Kabbalist, written in the first half of the fourteenth century (MS. New York - Columbia 161.S.1, p. 60), we read:

> Know that the pleasure of the indwelling of prophecy, which is the influx of the Active Intellect, known in Arabic as *kif ᶜaqal faᶜal*, is similar to the pleasure derived from intercourse, with the following difference between them: namely, that when a man completes the evil act of intercourse he despises it, but the influence of the intellect is the opposite.

See note 113 below.

52. *Metaphysics* XII, 7, fol. 1072b; *Ethics*, end of Chap. 7, fol. 1174a–1176a.

53. *Hilkhot Tešuvah* 8:2; *Haqdamah le-Pereq Ḥeleq*, (*Sefer ha Ma'or*, Tel-Aviv, 1948, pp. 121–122): *Guide* III:51. Maimonides took care to emphasize that the pleasure which accompanies apprehension "does not belong to the genus of bodily pleasures."

54. Compare his statement, appearing in his earlier work, *Mafteaḥ ha-Raᶜayon*, MS. Vatican 291, fol. 21a: "And I see that until Him [i.e., God], the quintessence of all experience arrives as there comes from in all the wisdom of logic [and] to every intellective soul [comes] the pleasure of

vision." Compare also the comments of R. Isaac b. Jacob ha-Cohen in his work, *ha-Aẓilut ha-Semalit*, in Scholem, *Maddaʿe ha-Yahadut* II, p. 85: "And the force of this great influx is that it is the pleasure of the inner souls, and the joy of the spiritual bodies."

55. Sami S. Hawi, *Islamic Naturalism and Mysticism* (Leiden, 1974), pp. 72–73.

56. See Edgar Wind, *Pagan Mysteries* (*op cit.*, n. 23), pp. 60ff.

57. MS. Jerusalem 8° 148, fols. 29b-30a. The author makes use of the verse, "for your maker is your husband, the Lord of Hosts is his name" (Isa. 54:5), in order to emphasize that only by the soul's connection with the intellect has it eternal existence.

58. MS. Moscow-Günzburg 775 fol. 179b; see above, note 43.

59. *Qiddušin* fol. 2a.

60. Eccles. 9:9.

61. Prov. 18:22.

62. Prov. 31:10.

63. Prov. 6:23.

64. *Pesaḥim* fol. 112a.

65. MS. Moscow-Günzburg 775, fol. 181a.

66. *Berak̲ot* fol. 3a.

67. MS. Moscow-Günzburg 775, fol. 160a.

68. On this phenomenon, see Werblowsky, *Joseph Karo*, pp. 50–54.

69. Is there a connection between the use of the Arabic word and its connection to prophecy, and the statement in *Berak̲ot* fol. 55b: "R. Joḥanan said, 'If he woke up and there was a verse on his lips, this is a minor [form of] prophecy'"?

70. MS. New York - JTS 1777, fol. 33b.

71. In *Liqqute R. Nathan*, the crown *(atarah)* sometimes refers to the world of intellect; see Idel, "Mundus Imaginalis, *Studies* essay V.

72. The word *matoq* (sweet), used to refer to a sensation of pleasure, also comes to refer to spiritual pleasure. See MS. Jerusalem 8° 148, fol. 67a. See also Geo Widengren, *Literary and Psychological Aspects of the Hebrew Prophets* (Uppsala - Leipzig, 1948), pp. 101–102.

73. On the spiritual seed, see J. G. Liebes, "Illumination of the Soul and Vision of the Idea in Plato" (Heb.), *Studies in Mysticism amd Religion Presented to Gershom G. Scholem* (Jerusalem, 1967), pp. 152–161.

74. See Leisegang, *La Gnose,* pp. 28–29; Philo, *De Somniis,* I, 199–200.

75. See Walter Wili, "Die Geschichte des Geistes in der Antike," *Eranosjahrbuch* vol. 13 (1945), pp. 79–87.

76. MS. Oxford 1580, fol. 75a.

77. Deut. 30:19.

78. *Tamid* fol. 32a.

79. MS. Oxford 1582, fol. 78b.

80. MS. Jerusalem 8° 148, fol. 31a. See also Seneca, *Epistulae ad Lucilium* 73, sec. 14: "There is no wisdom without the help of God; in the bodies of people are scattered Divine seeds." See also Nicolas Cusanus, in *Idiota* III, de mente, c. 5, "Mens est divinum semen."

81. MS. New York JTS 1777, fol. 33a: see also R. Judah Loeb of Prague, *Deruš ʿal ha-Torah* (Warsaw, 1871), p. 72:

> There is a complete similarity between man and the earth; for just as the earth has sown in it wheat and all kinds of seed, clean and good, which take root in it within the dust, and which it then causes to spring forth; so does God, may He be blessed, place the pure and clean soul within man, a Divine portion from above, within the human body.

The planting of the soul with the body also appears in *Sefer ha- Neʿelam,* written at the beginning of the fourteenth century; MS, Paris BN 817, fol. 73b.

82. It is worthy of note that the connection between seed and light, which appears in Tantra, is alluded to in *Sefer ha-Zohar* II, fol. 167a:

> Similar is the foundation of man at his birth. First he is the "seed" which is light, because it carries light to all the organs of the body, and that "seed" which is light sheds itself abroad, and becomes "water."

Cf. *Iggeret ha-Qodeš,* Chap. 3 (Chavel, p. 326): "for man's seed is the vital substance of his body and the light of his radiance." See also Mopsik, *Lettre sur la Sainteté* (n. 1 above), p. 289, n. 86.

83. See section 155 in ed. Margalioth, and Scholem's remarks, *Das Buch Bahir* (Darmstadt, 1970), pp. 111–112, and p. 169.

84. See, for example, R. Ezra, *Peruš ha-Aggadot,* MS. Vatican 441 f. 53b; *Liqqute Šikeḥah u-Fe'ah* (on *Maseket Qiddushin*), fol. 14a; R. David b. Judah he-Ḥasid, ed. Matt, *Mar'ot ha-Zov'ot,* p. 135.

85. *Sefer Ḥayye ha-ʿÔlam ha-Ba,* MS. Oxford 1582, fol. 27a–b.

86. On the image of impregnation in Gnosis, see Leisegang, *La Gnose,* pp. 28–29.

87. See G. Scholem, "On the Doctrine of Transmigration in Thirteenth Century Kabbalah" (Heb.), *Tarbiz* 16 (1945), p. 136, n.5. The source of the quotation is MS. Parma, de Rossi 68, fol. 16a; cf. Scholem, *Les Origines,* pp. 481–485; E. Gottlieb, Introduction to *Mešiv Devarim Nekoḥim* (Jerusalem, 1969), p. 20, sec. 4; and G. Vajda, *Recherches sur la Philosophie,* p. 81, n. 1. See also MS. New York - JTS 1889, f. 32a, "and to those singular elders who are worthy of entering into the secret of the *ʿibbur,* to them was the secret of the Shekhinah revealed."

88. *Les Origines,* pp. 481–482, n. 205.

89. MS. Leipzig 39, fol. 8b.

90. On a possible connection between *sod ha-ʿibbur* and *Sefer Yeẓirah,* see Vajda's note, cited aove, n. 87.

91. MS. München 10, fol. 163a.

92. See Idel, *Abraham Abulafia,* pp. 133–136.

93. MS. Paris BN 777, pp. 46–47; MS. Muñchen 40, f. 247a–b. The passage is based upon several *gematriot: neqevah* (female; 157) = *išah* (woman; 306) = *ḥawah* (Eve; 19) = *ḥašqah ha-nevuʾah* (she desired prophecy) = 482; *šeti wa ʿerev* (warp and woof) = 988 = *pitеḥo patuaḥ* ([his] opening is opened) = *pataḥ* (opened) = *satam* (closed) = *Mafteaḥ kašfani* (magical key).

94. Eccles. 9:15.

95. In *Sitre Torah* (*Sod* ha-Šem Ben, MS. Paris BN 774, fol. 121a), Abulafia defines the difference between male and female as follows:

> And know that every thing which is a cause or an influx or the like is called son, and if it is a lowly power, it is called daughter or female or woman or some similar name, and among these is *Bat Qol* ("heavenly voice"; literally "a daughter of a voice"), and if it is a strong power, it is called a male son or a man.

96. On the term *ḥotam* (seal) as a designation for the Active Intellect, see *Ginnat Egoz,* fol. 58c (the second folio), "For he, may He be blessed, places form in all shapeless matter, and by means of this the Tenth Intellect, called *išim,* whose basis is the name *YHW (išim=361=šem YHW)* which is given over to him by the natural seal, and therefore he is able to portray and to give form to shapeless matter." On the seal and the impression as an image for the Active Intellect, see R. Isaac ibn Latif, *Ginze ha-Melek,* Chapter 5 (*Kokve Yiẓḥaq* vol. 28, p. 14): "And on the upper impress found in the intellect, the seal, the forms without purpose and without time"; see there also Ch. 8, p.

7, Likewise, in *Rav Peʿalim (Kokve Yizhaq* 25, p. 9), sec. 14:

> The secret of the supernal imprint and the lower one is also through that which the mouth cannot utter nor the ear hear, which is alluded to somewhat in a closed manner, "in our form and image," "in his image and form." And what is like this is not this, and the sages said [see Rashi on Gen. 1:27], "in the image made to him."

See also Ibn Latif's *Ẓurat ha-ʿOlam*, p. 17; *Liwyat Ḥen* of Levi b. Abraham (MS. München 58, fol. 84b); and M. Steinschneider, *Al-Farabi* (St. Petersburg, 1869), p. 253, n. 2.

97. The expression "warp and woof" *(šeti wa-ʿerev)* also carries a sexual connotation. In *Ôzar ʿEden Ganuz*, MS. Oxford 1580, f. 4b–5a, Abulafia writes:

> *peraš milah berit ʿEsav* (half, circumcision, covenant, Esau › 988), which is warp and woof *(šeti wa-ʿerev* › 988), to make it known that thusly do we this covenant: We cut the flesh of desire to the honor of the Name, and we reveal the crown and cut the permitted flesh, warp and woof, and we make a covenant of peace *(berit šalom* › 988). In circumcision [*milah*] we cut along the warp, and in *periʿah* [i.e., the secondary stage of circumcision] we cut along the woof.

See also *ibid*,, fols.51a, 65a and 169b–170a.

98. Abulafia speaks of impregnation elsewhere, again with extreme brevity: *We-Zot li-Yihudah*, p. 14; *Ševaʿ Netivot ha-Torah*, p. 1; *Imre Šefer*, MS. München 40, fol. 277b, but his discussions there are obscure.

99. MS. Warsaw 229, fol. 9a. This passage is based upon the following *gematriot*: *yemino* (his right hand) 116 *galgal ha-adam* (the sphere of man); *semolo* (his left hand) 377 *galgal ha-išah* (the sphere of the woman). The sum of the two, plus the conjunctive letter *vav* (6) is 499=*peʿulah be-išah* (act in the woman)=*poʿel ba-iš* (act in the man). The sum 493 [that is, the same sun without waw)=*šefa ʿle-ahavah* (influx to love)=*ahavah la-šefaʿ* (love to influx). *Arbaʿah* (four)=278=*ʿibbur* (impregnation); *ḥamišah* (five)=353=*sod ha-ʿibbur* (the secret of impregnation or intercalation). For further details concerning this Kabbalist and his works, see Eliav Shochetman, "Additional Information on the Life of R. Abraham Castro" (Heb.), *Zion* 48 (1983), pp. 387–405. The phrase "the sphere of man," occurs already in Abulafia's works; see Chap. 3, n. 170.

100. The metaphor of the father, mother and son also appears in R. Abraham Kohen Herrera, *Šaʿar Ha-Šamayim* (Warsaw, 1864), who writes in Part 8, Chapter 14 (fol. 73b–74a):

> For just as from the father and the mother, who are two distinct subjects, with different personae, there takes place the complete, whole beginning of the becoming of the son, so from the intelligibilia and the power of the intellect, like male and female who between them also change, there comes about the beginning of the intellection or of the intellect which is completely in actu. . . . And know that, just as the father may not sire the son without an intermediary, but by means of the seed sown in the belly of the mother . . . so it is with the intelligibilia which is not connected.

See his comments concerning Aristotle and Galen further on in this same chapter.

101. MS. Oxford 1582, fol. 78b. It is worth mentioning that the redemption of the son already has eschatological significance in the Talmud, *Bava Kamma* fol. 80a; it is referred to there as *yešuʿat ha-ben;* the remarks of the Tosaphistic authors on this passage allude to an eschatological aspect.

102. MS. Oxford 1580, fol. 3a.

103. Ex. 13:15.

104. MS. Oxford 1580, fol. 155b. On fol. 122a in the same work, it is stated "and the meaning of the [commandment of] the first-born is known, namely, that it is the human intellect."

105. MS. Rome - Angelica 38, fol. 12a; MS. München 285, fol. 14a.

106. MS. Oxford 1580, fol. 163a.

107. MS. Leipzig 39, fol. 1a.

108. Gen. 5:3.

109. MS. Paris BN 774, fol. 121a; MS. New York - JTS 2367, fol. 19b.

110. In the Adab literature, we find the saying "Wisdom is the eternal child of man." See Franz Rosenthal, *Knowledge Triumphant* (Leiden, 1970), p. 321. Muslim mysticism also recognizes the idea of destroying the body in order to rebuild the new man with the aid of wisdom: see L. Massignon, *Eranosjahrbuch* vol. 16 (1947) p. 403 and Meyerovitch, *Mystique et poesie,* pp. 261–262, and n. 7. The connection among *ben - binah - binyan* appears in the fifteenth century writings of R. Moses ha-Kohen Ashkenazi. In his polemic with R. Michael ha-Kohen, which took place in Candia, Crete, he writes (MS. Vatican 254, fol. 7a):

> "In his form and image"—physical offspring and spiritual offspring. Then he established for him from them an eternal building, which shall never die, for it is an established *halakah* that one must beget a male and a female. And this alludes in the male to begetting spiritual sons, that is, who are on the level of a male, and the female alludes to physical children, for the preservation of the species, and these are on the level of female.

Building, as a symbol of acquiring a perfection which is not destroyed, is alluded to in R. Judah Moscato's *Nefuẓot Yehudah, Deruš* 9 (fol. 27a):

> These three attainments—wisdom, strength and wealth—include all the goods of the soul, the body and possessions, and the three are incorporated in the verse, "Let not the wise man rejoice in his wisdom, etc." [Jer. 9:22]. Finally, our eyes have seen that the world—that is to say, man, who is called a microcosm, as is known—is constructed like Adam before his sin, and was destroyed after his rebellion, and was rebuilt in Abraham and his seed, in their receiving of the Torah, and was destroyed when they corrupted their ways in making the golden calf, and it is to be rebuilt permanently when they return to their former level, and then destruction will cease forever. And corresponding to these are the three temples, for the first was built and destroyed, and the second was built and destroyed, and the third shall be built and will be established, it will not be moved but will forever be settled.

See also *Berakot* 33a: "Whoever possesses understanding, it is as if the Temple was built in his lifetime." R. Shalem Shabazi, in his *Ḥemdat Yamim* (Jerusalem, 1956), f. 3a, writes "The Temple alludes to the rational soul of the righteous man."

111. MS. New York JTS 2367, f. 61a. The passage is based upon a saying in *Berakot* 3a. This Talmudic dictum was interpreted in a similar fashion by R. Joshua ben Moshe ha-Levi in his answer to R. Joseph Gikatilla, MS. New York—JTS 1589 (ENA 1674), fols. 86b–87a:

> "And the third watch is when an infant cries in the bosom of its' mother, and a woman speaks [i.e. couples with] her husband." Now, my brother, know and understand that the infant refers to the Intellective Soul, which is pure and clean, from underneath the throne of glory and, like the infant, who does not know either to abominate evil or to choose good, so is the Intellective soul unable to receive and to understand the wisdoms from the intelligibilia, because it is sunken in refuse and filth. And the animal soul, together with it, suck from the breasts of their mother, and those breasts from which she sucks are the two Torahs, the Written Torah and the Oral Torah, and her mother is the Divine wisdom, as is said, "Yea, if thou call for understanding" [Prov. 2:3]—do not read im [if], rather em [mother; i,e., the verse should be read, "call understanding your mother"]. And the woman coupling with her husband is the intellective soul, which unites with her husband, who is the Holy One, blessed be He, as is said, [Isa. 54:5], "for your Maker is your husband, the Lord of Hosts is his Name."

112. See Guiseppe Sermonetta, "Judah and Emmanuel of Rome—From Rationalism to Mystical Faith" (Heb.), *Hitgalut, Emunah, Tevunah* (Ramat-Gan: Bar-Ilan University Press, 1976), p. 58ff.

113. *Ôẓar ha-Ḥokmah,* MS. Mussaioff 55, fols. 104a–105a, with omissions. On another similarity between R. Isaiah and Abulafia—the metaphor comparing the mystical process with sexual intercourse—see note 51 above and Ch. 2, p. 58.

114. The reference here is to the Active Intellect, which flows "into the world and not upon a portion of the human soul." The term *šelanu* (our) is intended to distinguish it from "the Active Intellect of the separate intelligibilia," a term appearing further on in the passage, and referring to the first separate intelligibilium, identified with *Keter*.

115. See Yitzhak Baer, "Kabbalistic Teaching in the Christological Doctrine of Abner of Burgos" (Heb.), *Tarbiz* 27 (1958), p. 281, and nn. 7–8 [reprinted in his *Meḥqarim u-Masot be-Toldot ʿAm Yisrael* (Jerusalem, 1986), vol. 2, p. 372].

116. *Zohar* III, 290b. On the souls as sons of God, that is, as the outcome of the union between *Tiferet and Malkut*, see *Zohar* I, 82b, and see also *Sefer ha-Nefeš ha-Ḥakamah,* fol. 3, col. 2b: "All the higher soul is an example of her Creator, like the image of the son from the father, for he is its building, literally; thus, the higher soul is the building of her Creator."

117. See Ch. Wirszubski, *Three Chapters in the History of Christian Kabbalah* (Jerusalem, 1975), p. 54 and n. 4, and p. 56, n. 4. It is worth mentioning that this identification between God and Wisdom appears again in Abulafia in *Sefer ha-Geʾulah,* MS. Chigi, I, 190.6, fol. 292a, "and they called Wisdom son and related it to the son" (in the Hebrew source). See also note 122 below.

118. *Hermetica,* ed., Walter Scott (London, 1968), I, pp. 240–241; R. Reitzenstein, *Hellenistische Mysterienreligion* (Leipzig, 1970), pp. 75ff.

119. Underhill, *Mysticism,* pp. 122–123.

120. Meyerovitch, *Mystique et poesie,* p. 264.

121. I refer to the concept *sakya putto*—i.e., the son of the Buddha. See also Mircea Eliade, "Rites and Symbols of Initiation," *The Mysteries of Birth and Rebirth* (New York, 1965), pp. 53 ff; *The Secret of the Golden Flower,* ed., R. Wilhelm (New York, 1962), p. 9.

122. Giles Quispel, "The Birth of the Child," *Eranosjahrbuch* vol. 40 (1971), pp. 235-288; Erich Neumann, *The Origin and History of Consciousness* (New York, 1962), p. 253; H. Corbin, *Creative Imagination in the Sufism of Ibn 'Arabi,* (Princeton, 1969) p. 172, pp. 346–348, nn. 70–71; *idem,* "Divine Epiphany and Spiritual Birth," *Man and Transformation, Eranosjahrbuch,* vol. 23, (1959), p. 109, and n. 94. While *al-walad al-tamm,* the birth of the complete child, takes place in the pleroma, there, too, the sense is the actualization of "the spiritual man." It is worth mentioning here the words of Pico della Mirandola, in his work *On the Glory of Man,* dealing with the transformation of man into an angel and a son of God by means of his intellective powers. Perhaps in this context one ought to interpret the term *intellectus* as referring to the human

intellect: in *Chaldean Thesis,* No. 13, we read, "Per puerum apud interpretes, nihil aliud intelligibiler quam intellectum." Ch. Wirszubski, *Three Chapters in the History of Christian Kabbalah,* p. 34, explains the word *puer* ("youth") here as alluding to Metatron, i.e., the Active Intellect. However, it may be that Pico is referring here specifically to the human intellect; see p. 66, n. 23 in that work, and note 117 above.

123. MS. Rome-Angelica 38, fol. 36a. On the subject of intellective and mystical development at the age of forty, see Idel, "On the History," where we discuss the quotations cited below.

124. The concept of man's spiritual redemption is discussed by Idel, "Types of Redemptive Activity," pp. 259–263. I have cited there additional material from the writings of Abulafia and his circle on this subject.

125. See Idel, "On the History," pp. 2-3.

126. Genesis 25:20.

127. For the sources of this view, see the material gathered by Urbach, *The Sages,* p. 790, n. 60- 61.

128. *molad* (the birth) 80 (i.e, the Hebrew letter) *Mem.* It is worth noting that the parallel *molad* 80 *me"m* *limud* (study) appears in *Ševaʿ Netivot ha-Torah,* p. 17, which discusses the spiritual creation of study and the physical creation of birth. Compare also the remarks cited by R. Ḥayyim Vital, *Šaʿare Qedušah,* Sec. 4 (MS. British Library 749, fol. 21a– b):

> I have found that the matter of the nature of prophecy is that it is an influx poured out by the Name, may He be blessed, upon the intellectual faculty by means of the Active Intellect, and afterwards upon the imaginative faculty, [so that] he forms parables and images. But Moses, our teacher, did not [prophesy] via the imaginative faculty at all, but [the flow was] from the Active Intellect to the separate human intellect. Therefore Moses fasted . . . for forty days, corresponding to the formation of matter [i.e., of the human fetus] during forty days, to weaken all powers of matter, in order to attain prophecy with wholeness.

As R. Ḥayyim Vital knew at least two of Abulafia's works, it seems probable that he read the above passage in one of his books or those of one of his circle.

129. Exodus 34:28.

130. See above, note 102.

131. MS. Oxford 1582, fols. 22b–23a.

132. See the *Derašot* of R. Joshua ibn Shuaib (Cracow, 1573), f. 86d: "'Forty times he may hit him, he may not add' (Deut. 25:3). Our sages

explained that this number corresponds to the fetus, which is formed on the fortieth day, and to the Torah which was given at the end of forty days." See also R. Judah Moscato, *Nefuẓot Yehudah, Deruš* 9, fol. 25b.

133. Based upon Exodus 24:18; I Kings 19:8.

134. It is worth mentioning here the words of Meister Eckhart:

> We are celebrating the feast of the Eternal birth which God the Father has borne *and never ceases to bear* in all Eternity: whilst this birth also comes to pass in Time and in human nature. Saint Augustine says this birth is ever taking place. . . . But if it takes place not in me, what avails it? Everything lies in this, that it should take place in me.

Quoted from Underhill, *Mysticism*, p. 122. See also the comment of Angelus Silesius in his book, *The Cherubic Voyager*, I, 61; "But if Jesus were to be born a thousand times in Bethlehem, but not inside you, you would be lost for eternity."

135. I have found this idea alluded to only in *Imre Šefer*, MS. München 40, fol. 247b, where Abulafia writes, with extreme brevity, "the power of imagination *(koaḥ ha-ẓiyyur)*, which is mingled with the creative power *(koaḥ ha-yoẓer)* and the creaturely power *(koah ha-yeẓẓur)* until the fortieth year, which are in the image of the forty days.

136. MS. Rome-Angelica 38, fol. 14b–15a: MS. München 285, fol. 39b: München 43, fol. 208a. For a detailed analysis of this quotation see above, Chap. 3, the section on *devequt*.

137. Psalms 99:1.

138. Based upon II Kings 9:12; 3; 6.

139. MS. Rome-Angelica 38, f. 18b, and see also fol. 10a, "But he practiced *hitbodedut* (i.e., concentration) and saw visions and wrote them down and thus came about this book, and call it a book of testimony, because it is a witness between us and God that he risked his soul on the day he went before the Pope (Hebrew: *apifiyuta* [sic]), therefore there were born to him two mouths *(šetey piyot)*."

140. MS. Jerusalem 8° 148, fol. 33b. The expression, "natural change" *(šinnuy ṭivʿi)* regarding the change involved in the appearance of the intellect is also mentioned in another book connected with Abulafia's circle, namely, *Sefer ha-Ẓeruf* (MS. New York JTS 1887, fol. 105b):

> Now when the sphere of the intellect is moved by the Active Intellect and the person begins to enter it and to ascend the sphere which returns, like the image of a ladder, and at the time of the ascent his thoughts shall be really

> transformed and all the visions shall be changed before him, and there will be nothing left to him of what he had earlier. Therefore, apart from changing his nature and his formation, as one who was uprooted from the power of feeling [and was translated to] the power of the intellect.

The idea of a change occurring at the moment of cleaving to the Active Intellect also appears in Maimonides; in *Yesode ha-Torah* 7:1, he writes:

> And when the spirit rests upon him, his soul shall be intermingled with the grade of angels who are called *Išim* [i.e., the Active Intellect] and he becomes another person, and he shall *understand* by himself that he is not as he was, but that he has ascended above the grade of other sages, as it is said regarding Saul [I Sam. 10;6], "and you shall prophesy and become another person."

141. MS. Sasson 919, p. 215. It is interesting that, further on, R. Isaac of Acre refers to the letter-combinations that one is to perform in the house of seclusion, all according to Abulafia's system. In *Ôẓar Ḥayyim*, MS. Moscow-Günzburg 775, fol. 148a, we read: "for the perfection of matter [comes a out] in forty days, and the perfection of intellect in forty years, and the [number of] letters in this section is forty."

142. On the significance of *hamšakah* ("drawing"), see Idel, "*Hitbodedut* as Concentration," p. 52, n. 95; *idem*, "The Perceptions of Kabbalah."

143. *Šabbat* fol. 152a.

144. Deut. 29:3.

145. *Ibid.*, v. 4.

146. MS. Oxford 836, fol. 162b. The name of the author there is unknown, but it may be that the book was written in 1444.

147. MS. Rome- Angelica 38, fol. 2a.

148. The reference to the first thirteen years of study must not necessarily be interpreted literally. It seems to me that this refers to the period from the beginning of one's studies, and not from birth. To demonstrate the feasibility of this interpretation, let me cite a story which was widespread at the time of Abulafia:

> The sages of philosophy told that a certain king once asked an honorable sage, whom he saw bent in stature and with white hair and many wrinkles, and asked him, "How old are you?" He replied: "Twelve years old." In amazement, he [the king] said to him: "Explain this riddle of yours!" He answered him: "For twelve years I have engaged in wisdom and in the service of God, and whatever I have lived apart from this is not [counted] by me as days and years. [Menahem ha-Meiri, *Peruš le-Mišle* (Fürth, 1844), f. 5b.]

149. One is already struck by this in the introduction to the book, where the anonymous author copied from three different works of Ibn Latif without mentioning the source:

> [from *Toldot Adam,* MS. Oxford 836, fol. 143a:
> 1. This gate will be closed and not opened, and no unclean man will enter therein, but the God of Israel will come by it, and it will remain closed.
> 2. The speech of the man, who writes in his hand to God, for I have dared to speak and I am dust and ashes, and do not know any book.
> 3. And because I have chosen eternal life, my soul has longed and yearned, and goes from a temporary dwelling to a permanent dwelling, which is Hebron, Kiryat Arba, and ascends to the city of heros, which is the city of the great king.
>
> [from the works of Ibn Latif]
> 1. This gate will be closed and not opened, and no unclean man will enter therein, but the God of Israel will come by it, and it will remain closed.
> 2. The speech of the man, who writes in his hand to God, for I have dared to speak and I am dust and ashes, and do not know any book.
> 3. And by reason of my choosing eternal, true life, my soul has longed and yearned . . . to leave its temporary dwelling, which is Kiryat Arba, and to ascend to the city of heros, the city of the great king, which is its permanent abode.

Section 1 is taken from Ibn Latif's introduction to *Šaʿar* 3 of *Ša'ar ha-Šamayim;* Section 2, from Chapter 5 of *Ẓurat ha-ʿOlam,* which is formulated as an introduction; Section 3 from the introduction to *Ginze ha-Meleḵ.* The title may also have been influenced by a lost work of the same title by Ibn Latif.

150. *Zohar* II, fol. 97b–93a *(Sabba de-Mišpatim).*

151. *Kenesset Yisrael,* i.e., the Sefirah of *Malḵut.*

152. Sefirat *Tiferet.*

153. Deuteronomy 14:1.

154. Psalm 2:7.

155. Printed is *Divre Ḥaḵamim* (Mainz, 1849), p. 58. Compare *Guide* I:70.

156. See above, note 140.

157. Psalm 103:5.

158. The verse from Psalms is associated in medieval commentaries with the renewed birth of the Phoenix, See R. *Saʿadya* Gaon, Ibn Ezra, and R. David Qimhi on this verse, and R. Bahya ben Asher on Genesis 2:19 (p. 73–74 in Chavel ed.); cf. Dan Pagis, "The Eternal Bird; The Motif of the Phoenix in

Midrashic and Aggadic Literature" (Heb.), *Sefer ha-Yovel šel ha-Gimnasia ha-ʿIvrit bi-Yirušalayim* (Jerusalem, 1962), pp. 74–90.

159. *Dereḵ Emunah* (Constantinople, 1522), f. 37a. From there, this view was copied by R. Joseph of Rossheim, *Sefer ha-Meqanneh,* (Jerusalem, 1970), pp. 105–106, and also influenced R. Moses Almosnino's *Wi-Yidê Moše,* which likewise connects Ps. 2:7 with the birth of the intellect, whose cleaving to God is seen as a new birth. It is worth noting that, already in Qimhi's commentary to this verse, he speaks about the birth of the spiritual element within man—specifically, the birth of the holy spirit in David. But while Qimhi applies it to a past event, *Dereḵ Emunah* and *Wi-Yidê Moše* speak of a process which continually occurs in every enlightened person.

160. Pietrykow, 1893, f. 27 b.

161. P. O. Kristeller, "Marsilio Ficino e Lodovico Lazzarelli," *Studies in Renaissance Thought and Letters* (Roma, 1969), pp. 221–247; D. P. Walker, *Spiritual and Demonic Magic from Ficino to Campanella* (Notre Dame, Ind., 1975), pp. 64–72; cf. Moshe Idel, "Judaism and Hermeticism."

162. Lazzarelli quotes the text of R. Eleazar of Worms in Latin translation, as has been observed by Scholem, *Pirqê Yesod be-Havanat ha-Qabbalah u-Semaleha* (Jerusalem, 1976), p. 406, n. 62 (this subject only appears in the Hebrew version of his article on the *golem*). Scholem is puzzled by the way in which this text got to Lazarelli, and conjectures that "perhaps he saw it in Flavius Mithridates' translation from Kabbalistic literature?" However, it should be pointed out that this version appears in R. Yoḥanan Alemanno's *Collectanaea*, MS. Oxford 2234, fol. 95b, from whom Lazarelli may have taken it.

163. See Kristeller, p. 38, "mens mentem generet," and the expression, "syngenea mentis generato."

164. This sentence refers to Lazarelli's own "birth" by means of his bizarre teacher, Giovanni da Corregio. "Aethere tu me genuisti semine rursus atque terum nasci me sine fraude doces" (Kristeller, p. 239).

165. Kristeller, p. 233, summarizes the discussion, which is as yet in manuscript only, in these words: "Come Dio e fecondo, cosi all 'uomo, imagine di Dio, speta una sua fecondita la quale non riguorta soltano il corpi ma anche l'intelletto. . . . Come Dio crea gli angeli, cosi il vero uomo produce le anima divine." Compare Abulafia's statement in *Ḥayye ha-ʿOlam ha-Ba,* MS. Oxford 1582, fols 5a–b; MS. Oxford 1583, fol. 2a:

> And the greatest of all deeds is to make souls, as alluded to in [the verse], "and the souls they made in Haran." (Gen. 12:5) For as God created man directly, in the likeness of God making him, this deed is for us the most sublime of all good deeds. Therefore, the enlightened man is required to make souls more than he is required to make bodies, for the purpose is not

the making of bodies, but only in order to make souls. And thereby man comes to resemble his maker, as in the words of the prophet, "For a spirit shall enwrap itself before Me, and souls I have made" (Isa. 57:16).

Compare the words of Abulafia's student in *Ner Elohim*, MS. München 10, fol. 172b–173a, which opposes the literal understanding of the creation of the *golem*, arguing that it entails a mystery alluding to the creation of souls.

166. Scholem, *Major Trends*, pp. 26–28; Tishby, *The Wisdom of Zohar* I, 146–147; *idem,, Netive Emunah u-Minut*,(Ramat Gan, 1964) pp. 11–22; Idel, *Kabbalah: New Perspectives*, pp. 200-249.

167. Goldreich ed., p. 143. The section quoted here also appears in the collection entitled *Še'elot u-Tešuvot*, by R. Isaac of Acre, MS. Escorial G. 3.14, fol. 63a, and is based upon the words of the *Ḥaver* in *Kuzari* II:53.

168. See Werblowsky, *Joseph Karo*, pp. 133–134.

169. David Kaufmann, *Die Sinne* (Budapest, 1884), pp. 188–191.

170. MS. Oxford 1580, fol. 130b.

171. See David Qimhi on Gen. 2:17, in the version printed in the Kamlehr edition (Jerusalem, 1970), p. 30: "and the knowledge of good and evil was explained by the commentators as referring to knowledge of intercourse, because that tree of knowledge brought about sexual desire in man."

172. It is worth noting here the article by M. Harris, "Marriage as Metaphysics; A Study of the 'Iggereth hakodesh,'" *HUCA* vol. 33 (1962), pp. 197–220. The author, who has dealt with the question of erotic imagery in a number of other articles, argues that *Iggeret ha-Qodeš*, attributed to Nahmanides, is intended to teach Kabbalah—mistakenly identified by him with metaphysics—as a means of examining the union between man and woman (see p. 205). It seems to me that the exact opposite is the case: in the epistle under discussion, intercourse has no didactic purpose; its author's assumption is that, through knowledge of Kabbalah, one may understand the true value of sexual intercourse. Harris' perception of the epistle as opposed to the negation of sex in the Gnostic system is without basis; the author is rather polemicising against the negative evaluation of intercourse in philosophy.

173. *Major Trends*, p. 226; see also Tishby, *The Wisdom of the Zohar*, II, 298–300.

174. See Werblowsky, *Tarbiẓ* 34 (1965), p. 204

175. See Tishby, *The Wisdom of the Zohar*, II, pp. 298–300.

176. *Ibid.*, p. 204.

177. *Ibid.*, p. 609.

178. *Ibid.*, p. 299, n. 138.

179. There is no basis for the opinion expressed by S. Karppe, *Étude sur les origines et la nature du Zohar* (Paris, 1901), p. 304, who, relying upon an incorrect interpretation of the meaning of the *gemaṭria, zaḵar u-neqevah* (Male and female) *androgynos* (androgynous), argues that in Abulafia the polarity is transferred from male and female to the divine realm.

Bibliography

Monographs and Articles

Adler, *HWCM*———Israel Adler, *Hebrew Works concerning Music* (Munich, 1975)

Dan, *Studies*———Joseph Dan, *Studies in Ashkenazi-Hasidic Literature* [Heb.], (Givatayim - Ramat-Gan, 1975).

Dan, *The Esoteric Theology*———Joseph Dan, *The Esoteric Theology of Ashkenazi Hasidism* [Hebrew: *Torat ha-Sod shel Ḥasidut Ashkenaz*] (Jerusalem, 1968).

Goldreich, *Meᶜirat ᶜEinayin*——*Meᶜirat ᶜEinayin* by R. Isaac of Acre. Critical Edition by Amos Goldreich (Jerusalem, 1984).

Gottlieb, *Studies*———Ephraim Gottlieb, *Studies in the Kabbalah Literature* [Heb.], ed. J. Hacker (Tel Aviv, 1976).

Hallamish, *Kabbalistic Commentary*———*The Kabbalistic Commentary of R. Joseph ben Shalom Ashkenazi on Genesis Rabba*, Moshe Hallamish, ed. (Jerusalem, 1984).

Heschel, *Theology of Ancient Judaism*———A. J. Heschel, *Theology of Ancient Judaism* [Hebrew: *Torah min ha-Šamayim be-Aspaqlaryah shel ha-Dorot*], 2 vols. (London, New York, 1962–65).

Heḵalot Zuṭarti———*Heḵalot Zuṭarti*, ed. Rahel Elior, [Jerusalem Studies in Jewish Thought. Supplement. 1. (Jerusalem, 1982)].

Idel, *Abraham Abulafia*———Moshe Idel, *R. Abraham Abulafia's Works and Doctrine* [Heb.]. Doctoral Dissertation, Jerusalem: Hebrew University, 1976.

Idel, "Abulafia and the Pope"———Moshe Idel, "Abraham Abulafia and the Pope: An Account of an Abortive Mission" (Heb.), *AJSreview* vol. 7–8 (1982-83), [Hebrew Section] pp. 1–17.

Idel, "The Concept of Torah"———Moshe Idel, "The Concept of the Torah in Hekhalot Literature and Kabbalah" (Heb.), *Jerusalem Studies in Jewish Thought* I:1 (1981), pp. 23–84.

Idel, "On the History"———Moshe Idel, "On the History of the Interdiction Against the Study of Kabbalah before the Age of Forty" (Heb.), *AJSreview* 5 (1980), [Hebrew Section] pp. 1–20.

Idel, "*Hitbodedut* as Concentration"———Moshe Idel, "*Hitbodedut* as Concentration in Ecstatic Kabbalah" (Heb.), *Da'at* vol. 14 (1985), pp. 35–82; for a shorter English version of this paper, see *Jewish Spirituality*, ed. A. Green (New York, 1986) vol. 1, pp. 405–438, and *Studies*, essay VII.

Idel, "Infinities of Torah in Kabbalah"———Moshe Idel, "Infinities of Torah in Kabbalah," in *Midrash and Literature*, G. H. Hartman - S. Budick, eds. (New Haven and London, 1986), pp. 141–157.

Idel, "Inquiries"———Moshe Idel, "Inquiries into the Doctrine of *Sefer ha-Meshiv*" (Heb.), *Sefunot* 17 (1983), pp. 185–266.

Idel, *Kabbalah: New Perspectives*———Moshe Idel, *Kabbalah: New Perspectives* (New Haven, 1988) [forthcoming].

Idel, "Perceptions of Kabbalah"———Moshe Idel, "Perceptions of Kabbalah in the Second Half of the l8th Century" (forthcoming).

Idel, "Prophetic Kabbalah and the Land of Israel"———Moshe Idel, "Prophetic Kabbalah and the Land of Israel," in *Vision and Conflict in the Holy Land*, R. Cohen, ed. (Jerusalem - New York, 1985), pp. 102–110, and *Studies*, essay VI.

Idel, "The Worlds of Angels"———Moshe Idel, "The Worlds of Angels in Human Form" (Heb.), in *Studies in Jewish Mysticism Philosophy and Ethical Literature Presented to Isaiah Tishby*, J. Hacker, ed, [Jerusalem Studies in Jewish Thought, III:1–2, (Jerusalem, 1986)], pp. 1–66.

Idel, "The World of Imagination"———Moshe Idel, "The World of Imagination and the *Liqqutey ha-RaN*" (Heb), *Eshel Beᶜer Ševaᶜ* 2 (1980), pp. 165–176, and *Studies*, essay V, "Mundus Imaginalis."

Idel, "*Unio Mystica* and Abraham Abulafia"———Moshe Idel, "*Unio Mystica* and Abraham Abulafia," Studies, pp. 1-31.

Idel, "We Do Not Have"———Moshe Idel, "We Do Not Have a Kabbalistic Tradition on This," in *Rabbi Moses Nahmanides (Ramban): Explorations in His Religions and Literary Virtuosity*, I. Twersky, ed. (Cambridge, Mass., 1983), pp. 51–73.

Jellinek, *Beiträge*———Adolph Jellinek, *Beiträge zur Geschichte der Kabbala*, Erstes Heft (Leipzig, 1852).

Jellinek, *Bet ha-Midraš*——Adolph Jellinek, *Bet ha-Midrasch* (Jerusalem, (1967), 6 vols.

Leisegang, *La Gnose*———Hans Leisegang, *La Gnose* (Paris, 1971).

Maimonides, *Guide*———Moses Maimonides, *Guide of the Perplexed*, translated and with an introduction by S. Pines (Chicago, 1965).

Matt, *Marot Ha-Ẓoveot*———D. Ch. Matt, ed. *The Book of Mirrors: Sefer Mar'ot ha-Ẓove'ot by R. David ben Yehudah he-Ḥasid* (Scholars Press, 1982).

Meyerovitch, *Mystique et poesie*———Eva Meyerovitch, *Mystique et poesie en Islam* (Paris, 1972).

Peruš ha-Aggadot——*Peruš ha-Aggadot le-Rabbi Azriel mi-Geronah*, Isaiah Tishby, ed. (Jerusalem, 1984).

Schäfer, *Synopse*———Peter Schäfer, *Synopse zur Hekhalot-Literatur* (Tübingen, 1983).

Schatz, *Quietistic Elements*———Rivka Schatz Uffenheimer, *Quietistic Elements in 18th Century Hasidic Thought* [Hebrew: *Ḥassidut ke-Mistiqah*] (Jerusalem, 1968).

Schimmel, *Mystical Dimensions of Islam*———Annemarie Schimmel, *Mystical Dimensions of Islam* (Chapel Hill, N. C., 1975).

Scholem, *Abulafia*———Gerschom Scholem, *Ha-Qabbalah el Sefer ha-Temunah wešel Avraham Abulafia*, ed. J. ben Shelomo (Jerusalem, 1969).

Scholem, "The Concept of Kavvanah"———Gershom G. Scholem, "The Concept of Kavvanah in the Early Kabbalah," in *Studies in Jewish Thought*, A. Jospe, ed. (Detroit, 1981), pp. 162–180.

Scholem, "Devekut"———Gershom G. Scholem, "'Devekut' or Communion with God," in his *The Messianic Idea in Juadaism and Other Essays*, (New York, 1971), pp. 203–227 [reprinted from *Review of Religion* 14 (1949–50), pp. 115–139].

Scholem, *Jewish Gnosticism*———Gershom G. Scholem, *Jewish Gnosticism, Merkabah Mysticism and Talmudic Tradition* (New York, 1960).

Scholem, *Kabbalah*———Gershom G. Scholem, *Kabbalah* (Jerusalem, 1974).

Scholem, *Kabbalistic Manuscripts*———Gershom Scholem, *Kitvey-Yad be-Qabbalah* (Jerusalem, 1930).

Scholem, *Les origines*———Gershom G. Scholem, *Les origines de la Kabbale* (Paris, 1966).

Scholem, *Major Trends*———Gershom Scholem, *Major Trends in Jewish Mysticism* (New York, 1967).

Scholem, *The Messianic Idea in Judaism*———Gershom G. Scholem, *The Messianic Idea in Judaism, and other essays on Jewish Spirituality* (New York, 1971).

Scholem, "New Document"———Gershom G. Scholem, "A New Document for the History of the Beginning of Kabbalah" (Heb.), *Sefer Bialik* (Tel Aviv, 1934), pp. 141–162.

Scholem, *On the Kabbalah*——— Gershom G. Scholem, *On the Kabbalah and Its Symbolism* (New York, 1969).

Scholem, *Pirqe Yesod*———Gerschom Scholem, *Pirqê Yesod Be-havanat Ha-Qabbalah Usemalea* (Jerusalem, 1976).

Scholem, *Rešit ha-Kabbalah*——Gershom Scholem, *Rešit ha-Qabbalah (1150-1250)* [*The Origins of Kabbalah* (Heb.)] (Jerusalem - Tel Aviv, 1948).

Scholem, *Sabbatai Ṣevi*———Gershom Scholem, *Sabbatai Ṣevi: The Mystical Messiah* (1626–1676) (Princeton, 1973).

Sefer ha-Ôt———Abraham Abulafia's *Sefer ha-Ôt*, ed. A. Jellinek, in *Jubelschrift zum 70. Geburtstag des Prof. H. Graetz* (Breslau, 1887). pp. 65–85.

Ševa' Netivot ha-Torah——Abraham Abulafia's *Ševa' Netivot ha-Torah*, ed. A. Jellinek, *Philosophie und Kabbala* (Leipzig, 1854), Erstes Heft, pp. 1–24.

Tishby, *The Wisdom of the Zohar*———Isaiah Tishby, *The Wisdom of the Zohar* [Hebrew: *Mishnat ha-Zohar*] 2 vols. (Jerusalem, 1957–61).

Tocci, "Technique of Pronunciation"———P. M. Tocci, "Una Tecnica recitativa e respiratoria di tipo sufico nel libro *La Luce dell' Intelletto* di Abraham Abulafia," *Annali della Facolta' di Lingue e Letterature Straniere di Ca' Foscari* vol 14, 3 (1975), pp. 221–236.

Urbach, *The Sages*———Ephraim E. Urbach, *The Sages: Their Concepts and Beliefs*, translated into English by I. Abrahams (Jerusalem, 1979), 2 vols.

Werblowsky, *Joseph Karo*———R. J. Zwi Werblowsky, *Joseph Karo, Lawyer and Mystic* (Philadelphia, 1977).

Wertheimer, *Bate Midrašot*——Aharon Wertheimer, *Bate Midrašot* 2 vols. (Jerusalem, 1956).

We-Zot li Yihudah———Abraham Abulafia's *We-Zot li Yihudah*, ed. A. Jellinek, in *Auswahl Kabbalistischen Mystik* (Leipzig, 1853), Erstes Heft, pp. 13–28.

Index of Subjects and Proper Names

Note: Works by contemporary scholars mentioned in the footnotes are not listed in this index. However, references to these same scholars in the body of the text, as well as all references to classical works apart from biliographical references in notes, are listed here.

Index of Titles